Relearning from Las Vegas

Relearning

from Las Vegas

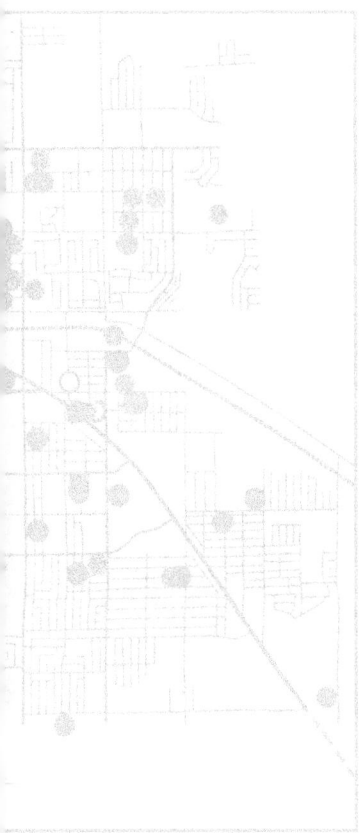

Aron Vinegar and Michael J. Golec, Editors

UNIVERSITY OF MINNESOTA PRESS   MINNEAPOLIS • LONDON

For information on previously published material in this book, see page 213.

Copyright 2009 by the Regents of the University of Minnesota

All rights reserved. No part of this publication may be reproduced, stored in a retrieval system, or transmitted, in any form or by any means, electronic, mechanical, photocopying, recording, or otherwise, without the prior written permission of the publisher.

Published by the University of Minnesota Press
111 Third Avenue South, Suite 290
Minneapolis, MN 55401-2520
http://www.upress.umn.edu

Library of Congress Cataloging-in-Publication Data
Relearning from Las Vegas / Aron Vinegar and Michael J. Golec, editors.
    p. cm.
  Includes bibliographical references and index.
  ISBN 978-0-8166-5060-6 (hc : alk. paper)—ISBN 978-0-8166-5061-3 (pbk. : alk. paper)
  1. Architecture, Modern—20th century—Philosophy. 2. Venturi, Robert. Learning from Las Vegas. I. Vinegar, Aron. II. Golec, Michael J.

NA680.R427 2009
720.973—dc22   2008025279

Printed in the United States of America on acid-free paper

The University of Minnesota is an equal-opportunity educator and employer.

15 14 13 12 11 10 09   10 9 8 7 6 5 4 3 2 1

Contents

Acknowledgments   vii

Introduction: Instruction as Provocation   1
ARON VINEGAR AND MICHAEL J. GOLEC

1   Aesthetic or Anaesthetic:
A Nelson Goodman Reading of the Las Vegas Strip   19
RITU BHATT

2   Format and Layout in *Learning from Las Vegas*   31
MICHAEL J. GOLEC

3   Photorealism, Kitsch, and Venturi   49
JEAN-CLAUDE LEBENSZTEJN

4   Theory as Ornament   79
KARSTEN HARRIES

5   Mobilizing Visions: Representing the American Landscape   97
KATHERINE SMITH

6   On Billboards and Other Signs around *(Learning from)* Las Vegas   129
JOHN McMORROUGH

7   Signs Taken for Wonders   147
DELL UPTON

8   The Melodrama of Expression and Inexpression
in the Duck and Decorated Shed   163
ARON VINEGAR

9   Learning from Las Vegas . . . and Los Angeles and Reyner Banham   195
NIGEL WHITELEY

Contributors   211
Publication History   213
Index   215

Acknowledgments

After organizing and publishing a special issue of the journal *Visible Language* 37.3 (Fall 2003) on the topic of *Learning from Las Vegas*, we were approached by the University of Minnesota Press to expand the issue into a book. We would like to thank the editor and publisher of *Visible Language*, Sharon Helmer Poggenpohl, for her support of the special issue and her willingness to allow us to reprint essays from it. Pieter Martin, our editor at the University of Minnesota Press, was enthusiastic about this project from the beginning and remained so throughout the publication process. We are grateful for his encouragement and support. A special thank you to Rosemi Mederos for her careful editing of the text and to Deb Gibson for producing the index.

Most of all, we are grateful to the contributors to this book. Ritu Bhatt, Dell Upton, and Nigel Whiteley kindly allowed us to reprint their essays from *Visible Language*. Three newly commissioned essays written by Karsten Harries, John McMorrough, and Katherine Smith join their contributions. Jean-Claude Lebensztejn graciously agreed to the inclusion of a new translation of his essay "Photorealism, Kitsch, and Venturi," which first appeared in his book *ZigZag* (Paris: Flammarion, 1982). This essay is still fresh and provocative more than twenty-five years after its first publication. We immediately thought of Vivian Rehberg for the retranslation and we are glad we did—she undertook the task with sensitivity and elegance.

On a personal note, we the editors would like to thank Amanda, Sibylle, and Bruno.

INTRODUCTION

Instruction as Provocation
ARON VINEGAR AND MICHAEL J. GOLEC

Since its initial publication in 1972, Robert Venturi, Denise Scott Brown, and Steven Izenour's *Learning from Las Vegas* has been recognized as a seminal statement in the history and theory of architecture and, for better or worse, hailed as one of the defining documents of postmodernism. As such it played an important role in early theorizations of the "postmodern condition" by such eminent figures as Fredric Jameson, Jean-François Lyotard, Charles Jencks, and Hal Foster. Its influence was felt both deep within the architectural scene and far beyond its particular institutional and professional boundaries. It was liberating to those in architecture, who were trying to find a way out of the strictures of the modernist legacy. Simply put, *Learning from Las Vegas*'s role in the identification and theorization of postmodernism shifted architecture to the center of cultural debates from which it has never departed. Most importantly, it is a book that makes a claim on us and how we might inherit it. This introduction, and the chapters that follow, are an acknowledgment of that claim.

Postmodernism and the Burlesque of Modernism

There would seem to be a difficulty, if not a tautology, in offering *Learning from Las Vegas* as "exemplary" of postmodernism when it was one of the texts that supposedly inaugurated the turn from modernism to postmodernism in the first place. As Judith Butler reminds us, "Once an 'example' of postmodernism is invoked, a problem has already occurred, for can postmodernism offer examples of itself, as a universal offers a set of instantiating particulars?"[1] Is that not the kind of "meta" reasoning that postmodernism characterized modernism *as*? Are we even clear what kind of gestures toward "totality" modernism was pointing to? As we are well aware, many straw modernisms have been constructed as postmodernism's other. In any case, we do not see *Learning from Las Vegas* as delivering an uncomplicated codification or ideology of postmodernism—whatever that might be. We take the essays in this book as attempts to capture the rich sense of ambivalence in *Learning from Las Vegas* that make such divisions between modernism and postmodernism possible in the first place.

The arrival of Venturi, Scott Brown, and Izenour's book in 1972, and then a revised edition in 1977, might have the structure of what Fredric Jameson has termed a "vanishing mediator": a sunken neutral term that operates as a catalyst that enables an exchange of energies between two terms to take place and then is removed once its function is over.[2] Thus, in an important sense, we have never come to terms with *Learning from Las Vegas*, because it is that very excess that has been foreclosed in the movement from the old (modernism) to the new (postmodernism). Instead of acknowledging its spectral qualities, we seem to opt toward repressing our anxieties toward it, converting it into what Richard Rorty has called a "neutral framework," a privileged terrain that legislates the appropriate terms of any debate.[3] One can therefore sympathize with Venturi and Scott Brown's rigorous opposition to any unproblematic categorization of their work as postmodern, including the drive to subsume them into the radically historicizing modes of speculation and production that their work has been accused of initiating. To hideously conflate style with ethical judgment, they were often characterized (or caricatured) as pursing a "pastiche-like affirmative postmodern architecture." If we approach *Learning from Las Vegas* with a more receptive ear—less eager to subsume it under any "givens" and more willing to listen to what it has to say—it shifts us into one of the *crucibles* that have produced the slightly out-of-synch stereo performance of discourses and practices that have occupied architecture and literary theory since the early 1960s.

We might take a hint about their attitude from the very title *Learning from Las Vegas*, that is, in the ambivalence marked by the destinal proposition "from," as in Learning *from* Las Vegas. We might expect that a book permeated by ambivalence would be marked by both a loosening and tightening of attachment to its "object-choice." Although it seems obvious enough, it is worth stating that *Learning from Las Vegas* is a departure from the actual city of Las Vegas. We need to take Venturi's question at the end of his first book *Complexity and Contradiction in Architecture* quite literally: what "slight twist of context" will make Main Street and Route 66 all right?[4] *Learning from Las Vegas* is that "slight twist of context"—its troping.

Learning is not only indebtedness "to" something but also a leave-taking, a form of departure and displacement. And we can take this as an allegory of their "abandonment" to the legacy of modernism, that is, a turning away that is still tethered to the position that is being turned away from.

Is the Las Vegas "Strip" allegorical of the stripping of the very criteria that would help us to identify any firm basis of saying that this is a "modernist" or "postmodernist" text in the first place? Or is postmodernism the burlesque of modernism? It might be better to live on in this in-between space of "both/and" rather than "either/or" as Venturi and Scott Brown might put it. In any case, it is best to dispense with postmodernism and modernism as strict temporal periods—a therapeutic particularly necessary in the field of architectural history, where dates like 1972 are supposed to mark an unusually sharp break between modernism and postmodernism, often down to the day and time of the dynamiting of the Pruitt-Igoe public housing project in St. Louis or the publication of *Learning from Las Vegas* that same year. After all, if one of the marks of "postmodernism" is a rethinking of temporality, then postmodernism cannot really come "after" a modernism that went "before." After all, if we are uncertain that Mies van der Rohe ever uttered or wrote the words "less is more," then one of the defining moments of modernism has been constituted "post" facto in a condition of "pure citationality."[5] Modernism as parasite.[6]

In thinking about all this, we have preferred to understand modernism and postmodernism as attitudes, "fundamental attunements," or an "ethos" rather than as stylistic or period terms. Is postmodernism, then, a shift in attitude and emphasis *within* modernism? Does such a shifting ever result in a twisting free that might result in some sort of "without," "out of," or "apart from" modernism? (It is very hard to come up with terminology to indicate a "break" or "separation" without including what has been separated from.) We are neither done with modernism—replaced by something we call postmodernism—nor can we think about modernism without a postmodern "turn." Is postmodernism another word for modernism's chance *now*? Or is modernism a chance for postmodernism *then*? One can still feel the strong winds of modernism blowing through the pages of *Learning from Las Vegas*.

Should we take Venturi at his word—assuming that his word is his bond: "I'm modern if modern (as opposed to Modern) is not an old style but a way of architecture."[7] We can certainly understand the urge to see the Las Vegas "Strip" as the urban, if not urbane, burlesque of modernism in all its forms. But is its skepticism a species of postmodern skepticism, as a critic like Thomas McEvilley might argue, or is it the kind of skepticism that Stanley Cavell has claimed is at the heart of modernism in all its forms?[8] Does *Learning from Las Vegas* mark "a tipping of the social balance from a previous regime of the word to a present regime of the image?"—a condition that T. J. Clark has seen as the litmus test for any full-blown postmodern condition?[9] Is this city with its "skyline of signs" the first glimmering of the full-scale imaging of the word that ushers in our postmodern era?[10] We have a hunch that *Learning from Las Vegas* is not there yet for all its supposed irony. Can we imagine its authors rolling the words "image," "simulacrum," and "hyperreal" off their tongues like so many tosses of the dice at a craps game? Their irony—if there is any—seems more akin to the radically skeptical account outlined by Paul de Man—irony as a "permanent parabasis": "the systematic undoing . . . of understanding"—rather than Manfredo Tafuri's insistence that all they were interested in were "superficial ironies."[11]

One or two things seem clear. First, *Learning from Las Vegas* is deeply concerned with aesthetic issues that are central to the modernist tradition. References in the text to "delays in judgment," an emphasis on the particular over the universal, and movement and agitation over stasis and calm are an ambitious attempt to work within, while *simultaneously* rethinking, some of the main lines of aesthetic modernism and the kinds of judgment it has produced.[12] And this interest in aesthetics and judgment has much less to do with "aesthetic populism," as Jameson claimed in *Postmodernism, or, the Cultural Logic of Late Capitalism*, or the complete eschewing of aesthetics in favor of issues of communication and representation, as some have argued. The subtitle of the 1977 revised edition suggests otherwise: *Learning from Las Vegas: The Forgotten Symbolism of Architectural Form*. Venturi and Scott Brown were dissatisfied with the current modes of "aesthetic comprehension"—primarily an aesthetic of the beautiful and its emphasis on the clear limits of form, the sharp demarcation between figure and ground propagated by gestalt-inflected theories of art and perception, and the bias against the ordinary and everyday in the available writings drawing on Kantian modes of criticism—that were unable to account for the kinds of sprawl, apparent disorder, agitated movement, ubiquitous signage, and general "noisiness" of a strip city like Las Vegas. (As we will see, the physicality of the book [actually books] is intrinsic to working out that aesthetic.) Far from espousing an "antiaesthetic" position, or an "aestheticizing" approach, it is rather a fully fleshed out, if not explicit, critique of aesthetic judgment of our urban condition. Any interest in "Aesthetics and Urbanism" relevant to our present condition will have to begin with *Learning from Las Vegas*.[13]

It would seem clear that one needs to rigorously eschew any knee-jerk temptation to subsume the text into an affirmative, conservative postmodern position that has led to the damning critique that *Learning from Las Vegas* is a full-scale embrace of the "society of the spectacle" and a brute apology for, and collusion with, the "culture industry." Not surprisingly, this position has been fuelled by Adornian-inspired critiques put forth by critics and theorists, such as Kenneth Frampton, Tomás Maldonado, Jurgen Habermas, Neil Leach, and Hal Foster.

From this perspective, *Learning from Las Vegas* is the locus and purveyor of the predigested "schema" offered up by the culture industry for easy consumption, in contrast to the active schematizing of any critical art practice. The title of Adorno's most important essay on the topic, "The Schema of Mass Culture," immediately sets up a Kantian tone to the argument in its very title that is also picked up by Clement Greenberg, who equates popular culture with kitsch and notes that it "operates by formulas."[14] The flavor of this Kantian critique is captured in Frampton's claim, in an early exchange with Scott Brown, that "Las Vegas is the manipulative city of Kitsch."[15] These Adornian positions often dovetail (all too easily) with Baudrillardian-inflected understandings of the "hyperreal" status of America and Guy Debord's analysis of the society of the spectacle.[16] We do not have time to delve deeper into the issue here, but it is *this* critical position that needs to be critiqued rather than assumed to be an adequate explanation of the relationship between the city of Las Vegas and the book *Learning from Las Vegas*. As Avital Ronell writes: "The seductive zones of popular culture—sports, music, mass media—need to be considered when exploring sites of contagion with regard to the anxious state of being made stupid, stupefied, or techno-ecstatic."[17] At the very least, the characterization (or caricature) of Venturi and Scott Brown as liberal ironists is superficial at best and completely misleading at worst.

A sophisticated Adornian approach to *Learning from Las Vegas* does not necessarily have to come to the aforementioned conclusions. But, alas, we have not had one yet. It would have to come to terms with what Cavell has called "the wild intelligence of American popular culture."[18] Listen again to Adorno: "The culture industry intentionally integrates its consumers from above. To the detriment of both it forces together the spheres of high and low art, separated by a thousand years."[19] This sounds more like the historical conditions of artistic production in Europe than America. Not only is there a different historical, political, and theoretical trajectory to the relationship between high and low culture in America, which critical theory tends to miss, but such scholarship also avoids a deeper question that Cavell raises: whether America ever inherited a distinction between high and low culture to begin with? The strict adherence to critical-theory-based interpretation might obscure the subtle aversive criticism that Venturi and Scott Brown are committed to and that can easily be misinterpreted as passive acceptance or uncritical collusion. And most importantly, as Cavell has noted in talking about a similar situation in the criticism of Henry James, "it reduces America's chance for sense."[20] We need to imagine a kind of criticism that can handle the following two passages in Lawrence Ferlinghetti's *A Coney Island of the Mind* and believe them to be utterly compatible: "On a concrete continent spaced with bland billboards illustrating imbecile illusions of happiness," and a few pages later, "I have ridden superhighways and believed the billboard's promises. . . . I have risked enchantment.'"[21]

By the Book

"Back to the book itself!" One of the endeavors of this collection of essays is to look at *Learning from Las Vegas as* a book. Several of our contributors approach the book as if it were an archaeological site and with an eye for the dispersions of words, images, tropes, and sentences, and the resulting patterns of meaning or nonmeaning that sediment out from this site. Other contributors focus on the transportability of the images in *Learning from Las Vegas* that can be reproduced and disseminated across a variety of platforms. This is what Elizabeth Eisenstein refers to as the "effect" of the printing press.[22] Since graphic representations are mobile, flat, reproducible, and can vary in scale, they can be remixed into new combinations, either in a single book or as they are reprinted in numerous volumes. The effects of reproduction and recombination can often lead to superimpositions of images from different sources and in different scales.[23] The results are a book marked by intensities and bold connections.

A reader always feels quite conspicuous carrying the 1972, first edition of *Learning from Las Vegas* from the library stacks to the closest available table. It is hard to imagine reading the book upright, relaxing in a chair. The first edition is far too large for informal reading in the studio, in the café, in the kitchen, or in the bedroom. It is easiest to handle opened flat on a large surface. The book's initial impact must have been even more jarring when the "chattering," noisy glassine dust jacket was still wrapped around it, with its series of chapter headings arranged in repetitive rows as if the reader were confronted by a wall of architectural one-liners. (Most readers will notice that the cover is ripped off or destroyed in most readily available copies in libraries; a pristine version with the dust jacket intact will set you back approximately $4,000 on eBay.) In a 2004 essay, Kurt Forster suggests that "facades are like the frontispiece of a book, asking to be deciphered"; a situation he contrasts with the present interest in membranes "that cannot be deciphered in the same way."[24] We are tempted to say that that shift occurs with *Learning from Las Vegas*: the cover was an indication that very divisions between inside and outside, text and context, and communication and chatter in and around architecture were being challenged. The cover of *Learning from Las Vegas* is a litany of monotonous "one-liners" divorced from any "thick" explanatory before and after; a parody of aphorism, all highlights and abbreviation in lieu of brevity and completeness. This erasure of context is not restricted to the mere cover of a much richer interior text; it is basic to the very conditions of the business of practicing architecture. As Venturi noted, "We architects can travel 3,000 miles for a three-quarter-hour interview where we have to be sloganeers and showmen rather than thinkers and doers."[25] The big book confronts the reader with "sources" *from* Las Vegas translated and transformed through conversation, writing, and imaging in and as a book.[26] We are not onlookers but rather active participants in a provocative conversation that undermines its very mission, *Learning from Las Vegas*, with "noise" and "contra-diction."

It is well known by now that the first edition of *Learning from Las Vegas* was "disavowed" (or is that "negated"?) by Venturi and Scott Brown for the smaller and more accessible revised edition published in 1977. We are interested in the mechanics of this disavowal, and we explore it rather than take it as a given.[27] The original format of the book was not to the authors' liking. In particular, Scott Brown felt that the MIT Press and its art director, Muriel Cooper, had forced a large-format, "Bauhaus"-like layout on the authors. The publication of the "revised edition" in 1977 corrected the mistakes made in the first edition. The improved book—its reduced size, serif typeface, tight margins, and edited illustrations—responded to the circumstances that originally produced the "compromised" text.

In the "Preface to the Revised Edition," Scott Brown writes, "This new edition of *Learning from Las Vegas* arose from the displeasure expressed by students and others at the price of the original version."[28] Rather than admit to even a modicum of indignation, Scott Brown transfers her disappointment to the reader. She soon admits, however, to the more nagging motivations behind her revisions to the original: "Changes in format further reduce costs, but we hope that they will serve too, to shift the book's emphasis from illustrations to texts, and to remove the conflict between our critique of Bauhaus design and the latter-day Bauhaus design of the book."[29] According to Scott Brown, the revised edition better suited the authors' critique of modernist orthodoxy, a set of principles that had dictated the design of the first edition. The revised edition of *Learning from Las Vegas* would appear to embody the delayed "intentions" of Venturi, Scott Brown, and Izenour. This may explain why the 1977 book—now in its eighteenth printing—has been so influential. Where the first edition is considered a collector's item, the revised or delayed edition has been circulated widely. We can also take this circulation literally: a reader who has the smaller second edition of *Learning from Las Vegas* in his or her possession is free to carry the book to any location. The book is more easily integrated into the reader's life and integrated into conversations in the seminar room, the studio, even the café. It would appear to circulate more widely across a range of private and public settings.

Scott Brown's redesign is an intervention in what Gérard Genette refers to as the "paratext"—the design devices and publishing conventions that constitute the mediation of the author's text in the form of a book to the reader.[30] Genette's definition encompasses all decisions that are made in the production of a book as an object: its mechanical reproduction, distribution, marketing, and sales. The paratextual elements of *Learning from Las Vegas* encompass every aspect of the book that comprises its delivery to, and reception by, an audience. It is the material thing on display in the bookstore, shelved in the library, and open in the reader's hands. In the case of the first edition, we can credit the paratext to the publisher and Cooper. In the case of the revised edition, the credit goes to the publisher and Scott Brown.

One of the benefits of attending to the book and the authors' disavowal is that we can understand Scott Brown's paratextual intervention as a "re-vision" of several issues and commitments made by the authors in the first edition of *Learning from Las Vegas*. First, the adjusted size—from 10 1/2 × 14 inches to 6 × 9 inches—makes the book more intimate in scale. The 1977 book's size and paperback format is closer to a "pocket edition" than it is to the epic size of the 1972 hardcover. It is less conspicuous, more comfortable to read, and less precious. Second, the addition of a subtitle would appear to place greater emphasis on the textual content of the book. As Brown states in the preface to the revised edition, the authors added "*The Forgotten Symbolism of Architectural Form*" to secure in the minds of the reader that the book is "a treatise on symbolism in architecture."[31] But the title's inclusion of the words "symbolism" and "form" would suggest an attempt to find a more continuous relationship between form and content rather than a sole emphasis on content. Third, the reformatting of the text required re-typesetting the entire book: the 1977 edition is set in serif type and the main text is composed of a single column of justified text.

In the first edition, the wide, triple "spacing" of the Univers typeface is striking. *Learning from Las Vegas* may argue for signs over space, but the original text was most definitely about "spacing." By now we are so used to associating the name Jacques Derrida with the word "spacing" that we are in danger of forgetting that spacing is an operation of typography: "that of extending to a required length by inserting additional space between words, also simply that of separating words, letters, or lines by inserting space or spaces."[32] These spacings would seem to invite interpretation "in" to fill in those spaces but at the same time suggest that they will not necessarily fit there comfortably. Interpretation tends to bump up against the materiality of a text that seems to be set adrift from argumentation, as words, even letters, are stranded in their material specificity, producing literal culverts and eddies where new paths might emerge unexpectedly.

The typography and layout of the revised edition, on the other hand, reflects the paratextual conventions of educational textbooks.[33] All titles, subtitles, and running heads are set in capitals. The change from Univers to Baskerville critically reflects what Scott Brown refers to as changes made "to 'de-sex' the text."[34] Finally, although the book itself is reduced in size, many of the illustrations from the first edition have been increased in scale relative to the reduced page dimension. Thus, wherever they appear, the maps, diagrams, charts, and photographs tend to dominate their respective pages. Whether or not Scott Brown's redesign constitutes a significant shift away from modernist abstraction exemplified in Cooper's "latter-day Bauhaus design of the book" is open to debate. We could say that Scott Brown's design decisions merely reflect a choice between competing paratextual conventions, both of which are equally abstract. And one could go even further and argue that the second edition is often at odds with their interest in complexity, the evocative force of subjective judgment, the imaging of density, and the emphasis on somatic pleasures and displeasures.

It might seem odd to say, "Pay attention to the book." But the fact that *Learning from Las Vegas* is a book and not the city nor a mimetic reflection of it is often ignored even in the most sophisticated writings on the topic. For example, it is common to come across the following claim: it is true that *Learning from Las Vegas* was the first to mark out many of the dimensions of our now contemporary urban life—architecture's ability to "mean" within postindustrial consumer-driven societies, the architect's function as an organizer of information, the disjunction between inside and outside that disrupts traditional notions of "transparency" and "organization," the emphasis on surface over depth, and so on—but now the book is dated because of the digital turn, shifts in globalization and global capitalism, our present-day network culture, and so on. These kinds of arguments fail to acknowledge the crucial "from" in the book's title: *Learning from Las Vegas*. The book was always already "preposterous" and, if anything, it is more relevant now than ever.

A Linguistic Turn in Architecture?

Vincent Scully forcefully claimed in his "Note to the Second Edition" of Venturi's *Complexity and Contradiction in Architecture* (1977) that despite the significance of Venturi's first book's introduction of "important modes of literary criticism into architecture," it was *Learning from Las Vegas* that was fundamentally linguistic in its approach. We assume that by "linguistic" Scully means to indicate ways in which we describe, represent, and construct our world through language. He says that *Learning from Las Vegas* is concerned with the "function of the sign in human art."[35] Here Scully, like many of his peers, takes "sign" to be exclusively linguistic, and perhaps implicit is that a semiotic approach to the text might be the most appropriate and revelatory. For most in the academy, the phrase "linguistic turn" brings to mind Rorty's turn away from "representational pictures of knowledge" in philosophy, best exemplified by his books *The Linguistic Turn* and *Philosophy and the Mirror of Nature*.[36] The extreme position in such a turn would result in what Ian Hacking called "linguistic idealism"; a belief that nothing has reality until it is spoke of, or written about.[37] But when push comes to shove, most of us are not willing to embrace such an extreme stance.

Of course, the contemporary characterization of *Learning from Las Vegas* as initiating a linguistic turn in architecture is not meant as a one-to-one equation with the linguistic turn in philosophy outlined by Rorty. It is meant in a much looser sense to suggest the general shift from the "material to the cerebral," to a period of high theory, and towards a general textual approach to architecture with an emphasis on "reading" (i.e., decoding).[38] And the claim for such a "linguistic turn" needs to be made on this level, as Venturi and Scott Brown worked very loosely with the semiotic theories and vocabularies available to them at the time, despite the occasional reference to "denotation" and "connotation" in *Learning from Las Vegas*.[39] Although this "linguistic turn" is embraced by a broad range of theorists with differing intellectual and political commitments (including some of the contributors to this book)—we, the editors, are not entirely comfortable conceding this "fact." In the increasingly fixed genealogy of postmodernism in the arts, architecture, and design, descriptions of architects, such as Venturi, Scott Brown, and Izenour, as participating in, if not inaugurating, a linguistic turn in architecture have led to the immediate assumption that they are ipso facto postmodernists.

Take, for instance, an analogous case, such as the pop artist Andy Warhol. Arthur Danto argues that descriptive language determines whether or not his famous *Brillo Boxes* (1964) are artworks or, as Danto says, "mere" things. Danto argues that the difference between Warhol's *Brillo Boxes* and the Brillo boxes found in the supermarket is a matter of interpretation—a matter of language—rather than perception. All our visual senses can tell us when we confront the pair is that the boxes are identical. Danto famously recommends, "To see something as art requires something the eye cannot decry [sic]—an atmosphere of artistic theory, a knowledge of the history of art: an artworld."[40] For a philosopher of Danto's stripe, modernism ended when pop art—specifically Warhol's *Brillo Boxes*, but also Claes Oldenberg and Robert Rauschenberg's beds; Jasper Johns's flags, targets, and maps; and Roy Lichtenstein's comic strips—begged the question: "can one have mistaken reality for reality?"[41] In other words, the way out of such a perceptual confusion is to bank on language or, better yet, to draw on the bank of language for adequate descriptions of objects that vex our perceptual capacities. Paraphrasing W. V. O. Quine, Danto observes that to refer to something as being "real" or to something as being "art" is simply to "satisfy a semantic function" and not a verifiably perceptual function.

This sounds somewhat like Venturi and Scott Brown's use of Ernst Gombrich's "physiognomic fallacy"—primarily read through Alan Colquhoun's famous article

"Typology and Design Method"—to argue against the modernist duck's expressionist attempt to exude meaning independent of convention in contrast to the "decorated shed" that avoids such conditions by separating the sign from the building as such (what that separation or connection "means" is up for debate).[42] Is this what Venturi and Scott Brown learned from pop art?[43] Perhaps. But it is also clear that they were equally interested in avoiding situations of "seeing as," as exemplified in Ludwig Wittgenstein's rabbit/duck example, and the interpretive turn or gestalt switch such a situation entails. We tend to forget that it was Wittgenstein himself who said that one could see the "duck-rabbit" simultaneously: "I *may* say 'It's a duck-rabbit.'"[44]

Scott Brown's "critique" of gestalt-inspired theories of urban perception and her embrace of modes of scanning and listening that avoided quick judgment and interpretation were pursued through an interest in a Freudian-inspired approach to receptive modes of engagement, such as techniques of "evenly suspended attention" put forth by perceptual theorists such as Anton Ehrenzweig and later taken up by urban theorists such as Amos Rapoport and Robert E. Kantor, who suggested, in the spirit of Ehrenzweig, that one should "disperse his attention over figure and ground at the same time, apprehending both equally."[45] This kind of approach would be more responsive to the entire field of urban phenomenon and would delay judgment until one listened to all that had been said.

Venturi and Scott Brown seem to be arguing that architecture, like philosophy, should avoid the kind of aggressive "grasping" for concepts, the precipitous kneading of experience into some definitive shape—a condition beautifully captured in the words of Ralph Waldo Emerson: "I take this evanescence and lubricity of all objects, which lets them slip through our fingers when we clutch hardest to be the most unhandsome part of our condition."[46] It is not the evanescence and lubricity of objects that is unhandsome but our grasping at them. Venturi and Scott Brown suggest that we forgo this clutching for receptivity and responsiveness; an exchange of the "unhandsome" condition of the "coercive" drives of modern architecture for the "handsome" condition of being responsive to the intricacy and wonder in given environments.

Some of the contributors to this volume on *Learning from Las Vegas* are also disposed to further complicate the so-called "linguistic turn" in *Learning from Las Vegas*. Some explore the interplay of linguistic and nonlinguistic symbol systems, and others suggest that language is just another element within the world and is not necessarily seen as a "veil" between us and the world. It is quite fashionable now in architectural circles to contrast linguistic-oriented approaches to architecture (read Peter Eisenman and Venturi), which involve "reading" buildings as "texts," with more prepredicative, noncognitive, and emotional responses to buildings. This is usually gathered under the terms of affect or mood. But this assumes a very limited understanding of "reading," solely in terms of semiotic decoding/tracking. Reading does not have to turn things—including building—into "texts" or treat them as such. Nor does everything have to "mean" for us in the way linguistic statements do. Perhaps words such as "responding" or "acknowledging" might be less textually biased and bring out some of the ethical, emotive, and bodily components of a "reading" that is not reducible to a "knowledge" or a "hermeneutic." In other words, do we really know what it means to read and be read? And what would it mean to have a voice in architecture and to respond to that voice and its pitch?

Issues of affect, mood, and atmosphere are clearly central to *Learning from Las Vegas* and intimately linked to a kind of "reading," but they are often overlooked and obscured by the manifest emphasis on communication, information, and legible signs. Issues of mood and attunement, the rhythmic qualities of the city that address issues of bodily response and unconscious and reflex levels of human perception, are clearly at issue throughout. For example, the density and palimpsesting of multiple modes of representation (aerial photographs, snapshots, filmstrips, signage, diagrams, maps, plans, elevations, sections, heraldry, graphs, sketches, charts, and lists) are clearly meant to take "a reading of"—in the sense of a thermometer—the perceptual intensity of the Las Vegas Strip.

Words are not everything and they are not nothing. But they are more than enough to provoke a decades-long *conversation* about architecture and the city. That is something!

Noises Off

Anyone scrutinizing the reception of Venturi and Scott Brown's academic and professional careers since their collaborative work with Izenour on *Learning from Las Vegas* would have to take note of the chatter within and in response to the writings and architectural work of Venturi and Scott Brown. To be fair, there is much in *Learning from Las Vegas* to suggest that Venturi and Scott Brown believe that we can carve out a space for unhindered communication from the din of Las Vegas without too much struggle. As they put it early on in the book, "How is it that in spite of 'noise' from competing signs we do in fact find what we want on the strip?"[47] But need we be reminded here of the title of Tom Wolfe's influential essay of 1966: "Las Vegas (What!) Las Vegas (Can't Hear You! Too Noisy) Las Vegas!!!"[48] Do we indeed find what we want? Can chatter be converted into meaningful communication so easily? The difficulties in parsing out chatter from "meaningful" communication—the fact that there are no strict criteria for differentiating them—is registered throughout *Learning from Las Vegas*, despite their claims to the contrary.[49]

In information theory this "chatter" is called noise. Noise is what is in the mix of information that constellates around any particular theme, idea, source, or articulation. For information theory, noise is not necessarily what interrupts the communication of information; rather, it is an inexorable outcome of generating ideas and of sending them off to populate our world. It is a sign of increase in complexity. It would then stand to reason that the more enticing and vital an idea (or set of ideas), the greater incidence of disruptive and creative noise that appears to obscure and illuminate it. Therefore, the state of knowledge on any topic is no worse for noise; it is only made richer and more complex.[50] But one would like to emphasize, as does Michel Serres, the "disruptive" element of this noise as well—its function as an interruption or eruption of the noise of the crowd. It is the empirical buzzing of the multiplicity of the world that is constantly disrupting smooth communication and community.[51] Noise is *Learning from Las Vegas*' lifeline to the empirical. In the "letter" of the actual book, in contrast to the "spirit" of Venturi and Scott Brown's explicit statements, *Learning from Las Vegas* is not "about" communication, but it is where the very issue of communication is put into question.

One can see that at times Venturi and Scott Brown have become victims of their own success—perhaps too ensconced in the "one-liners" and aphorisms that they wielded as sharp tools against stultified thinking in architecture but that now seem blunted through overuse and imprecision. At other times, they also have seemed too willing to embrace those "interpretations" of their work that really were not interpretations at all but echoes of their own positions. It is hardly surprising, then, that they claimed they were pushed aside for more "theoretically" inclined approaches to architectural building and thinking. Monitoring the noise level that has accompanied their collective output requires contending with both damning criticism and rampant hagiography in response to what Venturi and Scott Brown called their "little book."

How to proceed then? We eventually agreed that we did not want to write a summary introduction of each essay ("Ritu Bhatt's essay addresses . . . " or "In Dell Upton's contribution. . . . "), nor did we think it to our readers' advantage to engage in a thematic treatment of issues that the essays address ("Both Nigel Whitely and Katherine Smith discuss the difference between. . . . "). Neither of these standard approaches to the problem of the "Introduction" appealed to us. As coeditors, each of us holds opinions about the major lines of argumentation, intellectual commitments, and importance of *Learning from Las Vegas*, and thus we felt it would not strike the right tone for our introduction to feign impartiality as a "duty" of the supposedly neutral editorial function.

Within the spirit that noise is essentially disruptive and therefore productive of new constellations and formations, the issues we address are taken up, extrapolated upon, deviated from, and contradicted by each author, including us. That is all for the best. In keeping with the editorial philosophy of an earlier journal issue we coedited on *Learning from Las Vegas*, we have not tried to pave over the significant divergences between the essays nor tried to avoid their points of convergence.

Thus the purpose of this book is to produce not a consensus on *Learning from Las Vegas* but a series of interpretations of it that are at times bold, idiosyncratic, counterintuitive, and hopefully *provocative*. We took the title for this introduction from Ralph Waldo Emerson's address to the graduating divinity class at Harvard in 1838: "Truly speaking, it is not instruction, but provocation, that I can receive from another soul."[52] To our ears, the real strength of *Learning from Las Vegas* is that it exemplifies Emerson's line in every one of its lines. Venturi, Scott Brown, and Izenour's book poses the orthodox sense of "instruction"—outcomes and gains from messages sent and received—against the disruptive sense of Emerson's provocation—a call to arms, a means of arousing action. In other words, *Learning from Las Vegas* is a challenge. If provocation can suggest unfriendly behavior that causes anger and resentment, it also can provide needed encouragement. And who is to say in what pitch the voice of provocation may call forth? After all, in *Thus Spoke Zarathustra*, Friedrich Nietzsche philosophizes with a "kettle drum" to be heard but also warns his readers in *Ecce Homo* to be attentive to the "halcyon tone" of his writing. Whatever their tone, we believe the essays in this volume go a long way toward brushing away a lot of shopworn truisms about this text and, in doing so, recover a real sense of the challenges and possibilities it addressed to the architectural scene. We like to think of this book as both an instantiation and a prolegomenon to a further rethinking of this deservedly important text that merits critical responses equal to the ambitiousness of its claims.

Notes

1. Judith Butler, "A Skeptical Feminist Postscript," in *Postmodernism Across the Ages*, eds. Bill Readings and Bennet Schaber (Syracus, N.Y.: Syracuse University Press, 1993), 233. The passage goes on to note, "I want to raise the question whether 'postmodern' can operate as that which one is *for* or *against*, and as that which can enumerate and concretize itself in the form of examples."

2. Fredric Jameson, "The Vanishing Mediator; or, Max Weber as Storyteller," in *The Ideologies of Theory: Essays, 1971–1986*, vol. 2, *Syntax of History* (Minneapolis: University of Minnesota Press, 1988), 3–34.

3. Richard Rorty, *Philosophy and the Mirror of Nature* (Princeton, N.J.: Princeton University Press, 1979), 8.

4. Robert Venturi, *Complexity and Contradiction in Architecture* (New York: Museum of Modern Art, 1966), 102.

5. Rebecca Comay, "Almost Nothing: Heidegger and Mies," in *The Presence of Mies*, ed. Detlef Mertens (Princeton, N.J.: Princeton University Press, 1994), 184. And as Rosalind Krauss notes in her contribution to this volume on Mies, we now have a "postmodernist Mies" and a "poststructuralist Mies." See Rosalind Krauss, "The Grid, The /Cloud/, and the Detail," *The Presence of Mies*, 133–47.

6. See Michel Serres's book, *The Parasite* (Baltimore: John Hopkins University Press, 1982).

7. Robert Venturi, "Mal Mots: Aphorisms—Sweet and Sour—by an Anti-Hero Architect," in *Iconography and Electronics upon a Generic Architecture: A View from the Drafting Room* (Cambridge, Mass.: MIT Press, 1996), 311.

8. Thomas McEvilley, *Sculpture in the Age of Doubt* (New York: Allsworth Press, 1999); and Stanley Cavell, *Must We Mean What We Say?* (Cambridge: Cambridge University Press, 2002; 1969)

9. T. J. Clark, "Modernism, Postmodernism, and Steam," *October* 100 (Spring 2002), 161. Walter Benjamin's writings on the "script-image," "picture-writing," and "moving or mobile script" is highly relevant here in relation to the movement of writing from the book into the street and its intensified imagistic and mobile qualities enhanced by its contact with media and advertising.

10. Robert Venturi, Denise Scott Brown, and Steven Izenour, *Learning from Las Vegas: The Forgotten Symbolism of Architectural Form* (Cambridge, Mass.: MIT Press, 1977), 6.

11. Paul de Man, *Allegories of Reading* (New Haven, Conn.: Yale University Press, 1979), 301; Manfredo Tafuri, *The Sphere and the Labyrinth: Avant-Gardes and Architecture from Piranesi to the 1970s* (Cambridge, Mass.: MIT Press, 1990), 285. Tafuri's wording recalls Theodor Adorno's adage that "ironic toleration" is prevalent among those intellectuals who wish to reconcile themselves with the culture industry. See Theodor Adorno, "Culture Industry Reconsidered," in *The Culture Industry: Selected Essays on Mass Culture* (London: Routledge, 1991), 102.

12. It would appear that *Learning from Las Vegas* is primarily a reworking or rethinking of the sublime as it might relate to the modern urban condition.

13. See the section "Aesthetics and Urbanism" in *The State of Architecture at the Beginning of the 21st Century*, ed. Bernard Tschumi and Irene Cheng (New York: Monacelli Press, 2003), 11–24.

14. Theodor Adorno, "The Schema of Mass Culture," in *The Culture Industry*, 61–97; and Clement Greenberg, "Avant-Garde and Kitsch," in *Clement Greenberg: The Collected Essays and Criticism*, ed. John O'Brian (Chicago: Chicago University Press, 1986), 1–12.

15. Kenneth Frampton, "America 1960–1970: Notes on Urban Images and Theory," *Casabella* 36 (December 1971): 73.

16. See Jean Baudrillard's *America* (London: Verso, 1988), *Simulacra and Simulation* (Ann Arbor: University of Michigan Press, 1994), and *Seduction* (New York: St. Martin's Press, 1990); and Guy Debord, *The Society of the Spectacle* (New York: Zone Books, 1994). Without discounting the power of Debord's analysis, is it not about time to open the word "spectacle" up to speculation again? One could find no better place to start than with Jean-Luc Nancy's highly suggestive passages on the metaphysical biases underlying the situationist "spectacle" and how being in-common is a condition of society's exposure to itself. On all this and much more, see Jean-Luc Nancy, *Being Singular Plural* (Stanford, Calif.: Stanford University Press, 2000), 50–73; or John Sallis's deconstruction of the very divisions between the sensible and the intelligible, truth and appearance (the same could be said for Nancy), that underlie the very theorization of the image or simulacrum. See John Sallis, "Duplicity of the Image," *The Force of*

Imagination: The Sense of the Elemental (Bloomington: Indiana University Press, 2000), 77–97. Meghan Morris has clearly outlined the "organicist 'depth' nostalgia" in Baudrillard's theory of simulation. See Meghan Morris, "Great Moments in Social Climbing: King Kong and the Human Fly," in *Sexuality and Space*, ed. Beatriz Colomina (Princeton, N.J.: Princeton University Press, 1992), 120.

    17. Avital Ronnel, *Stupidity* (Urbana: University of Illinois Press, 2002), 56.

    18. Stanley Cavell, *Pursuits of Happiness: The Hollywood Comedy of Remarriage* (Cambridge, Mass.: Harvard University Press, 1981), 10, 14. A savvy Adornian reading would have to be written along the lines of J. M. Bernstein's attempts to think Adorno and Cavell together in some recent essays. See, for example, Bernstein's "Aesthetics, Modernism, Literature: Cavell's Transformations of Philosophy," in *Stanley Cavell*, ed. Richard Eldridge (Cambridge: Cambridge University Press, 2003), 107–42, and his excellent book *Adorno: Disenchantment and Ethics* (Cambridge: Cambridge University Press, 2001). Miriam Hansen's work on Adorno would also be an excellent place to start. See, for instance, "Mass Culture as Hieroglyphic Writing: Adorno, Derrida, Kracauer," in *The Actuality of Adorno: Critical Essays on Adorno and the Postmodern*, ed. and intro. Max Pensky (Albany: State University of New York Press, 1997), 83–111. As Hansen notes, an immediate dismissal of Adorno would be a repetition of the familiar cultural studies accusation of his "elitism" and "high-modernist stance" while deftly avoiding any significant encounter with his body of thought (83).

    19. Adorno, "Culture Industry Reconsidered," 85.

    20. Stanley Cavell, "Henry James Returns to America and to Shakespeare," in *Philosophy the Day After Tomorrow* (Cambridge, Mass.: Harvard University Press, 2005), 107.

    21. Lawrence Ferlinghetti, *A Coney Island of the Mind* (New York: New Directions Publishing, 1968), 9, 64–65.

    22. Elizabeth L. Eisenstein, *The Printing Revolution in Early Modern Europe* (New York: Cambridge University Press, 1993), 203.

    23. Bruno Latour, "Drawing Things Together," in *Representation in Scientific Practice*, ed. Michael Lynch and Steve Woolgar (Cambridge, Mass.: MIT Press, 1988), 45–46.

    24. Kurt Forster, "Thoughts on the Metamorphoses of Architecture," *Log* 3 (Fall 2004), 27.

    25. Robert Venturi, "Mal Mots: Aphorisms—Sweet and Sour—By an Anti-Hero Architect," *Iconography and Electronics upon A Generic Architecture: A View from the Drafting Table* (Cambridge, Mass.: MIT Press, 1996), 322.

    26. Stephen Mulhall, ed. *The Cavell Reader* (Cambridge, Mass.: Blackwell, 1996), 360.

    27. For a detailed account of the relationship between the first and revised editions of *Learning from Las Vegas* see Aron Vinegar, "Chp. 5: REDUCKS, 1972, 1977," *I AM A MONUMENT: On Learning from Las Vegas* (Cambridge, Mass: The MIT Press, 2008), 111–71.

    28. Robert Venturi, Denise Scott Brown, and Steven Izenour, *Learning from Las Vegas*, xv.

    29. Ibid., xv.

    30. Gérard Genette, *Paratexts: Thresholds of Interpretation*, trans. Jane E. Lewin (Cambridge: Cambridge University Press, 1997).

    31. Venturi, Scott Brown, and Izenour, *Learning from Las Vegas*, xv.

    32. John Sallis, *Spacings—of Reason and Imagination in Texts of Kante, Fichte, Hegel* (Chicago: University of Chicago Press, 1987), xiv–xv.

    33. Scott Brown explains that she used school textbooks as one model for her redesign. Denise Scott Brown, telephone interview with Michael J. Golec, January 26, 2003.

    34. Venturi, Scott Brown, and Izenour, *Learning from Las Vegas*, xv. What does "de-sexing" a text mean exactly? Is it "neutering" a text? Is it rendering it hermaphroditic? Can one desex a text? It does not prevent one from seeing the text as sexist as Neil Leach (*The Anaesthetics of Architecture*) claims in his analysis of the Tanya image that is found on the cover of both editions. See our discussion of critical theory in relation to interpretations of *Learning from Las Vegas* in the "Postmodern and the Burlesque of Modernism" section of this introduction.

35. Vincent Scully, "Note to th Second Edition," in *Complexity and Contradiction in Architecture* (New York: Museum of Modern Art, 1977), 12.

36. Richard Rorty, ed., *The Linguistic Turn; Recent Essays in Philosophical Method* (Chicago: Chicago University Press, 1967), and *Philosophy and the Mirror of Nature* (Princeton, N.J.: Princeton University Press, 1979).

37. Ian Hacking, *Why Does Language Matter to Philosophy* (Cambridge: Cambridge University Press, 1975): 182. See Richard Rorty's review of Hacking's book, "Ten Years After," included in the second edition of Rorty, ed., *The Linguistic Turn* (Chicago: Chicago University Press, 1977), 361–70.

38. Dell Upton, "Signs Taken for Wonders," *Visible Language* 38, no. 3, special issue edited by Michael Golec and Aron Vinegar, 332–50.

39. Much of their reading seems to have been derived by a few key articles by Charles Jencks, George Baird, and Alan Colquhoun in the influential book *Meaning in Architecture*, ed. George Baird and Charles Jencks (New York: Braziller, 1969).

40. Arthur C. Danto, "The Artworld," *Journal of Philosophy* 61, no. 19 (October 15, 1964): 580.

41. Ibid., 575.

42. Ernst Gombrich, *Meditations on a Hobby Horse* (New York: Phaidon, 1963); and Alan Colquhoun, "Typology and Design Method," *Arena* 83, no. 913 (June 1967), 14. Colquhoun makes direct reference to Gombrich's theories and links his critique of "expressionism" up with the ideology of certain strands of architectural functionalism's belief that "shapes have physiognomic or expressive content which communicates itself to us directly."

43. Denise Scott Brown and Robert Venturi, "A Significance for A&P Parking Lots, or *Learning from Las Vegas*," *Architectural Forum*, March 1968, 37; Denise Scott Brown, "On Pop Art, Permissiveness, and Planning," *Journal of the American Institute of Planners* 25, no. 3 (May 1969): 184–86; and Denise Scott Brown, "Learning from Pop," *Casabella*, December 1971, 15–23.

44. Ludwig Wittgenstein, *Philosophical Investigations*, trans. G. E. M. Anscombe (Oxford: Blackwell, 1953), §195.

45. Denise Scott Brown expressed her admiration for Freud's embracing of the nonjudgmental and nondirective attitude in her article "On Pop Art, Permissiveness, and Planning." This is a key article, and it needs to be read closely. See Amos Rapaport and Robert E. Kantor, "Complexity and Ambiguity in Environmental Design, *Journal of the American Institute of Planners* 23, no. 4 (July 1967): 210–20. It is obvious from the title and the content that they were inspired by Venturi's *Complexity and Contradiction*, which appeared the year before. What is fascinating about this article is its linking up of these insights with William Empson's work on ambiguity, Ehrenzweig's Freudian critique of "gestaltetes sehen," studies in environmental psychology/perception, and general works on urban theory.

46. Ralph Waldo Emerson, "Experience," *Ralph Waldo Emerson: Selected Essays, Lectures, and Poems* (New York: Bantam Books, 1990), 228.

47. Venturi, Scott Brown, and Izenour, *Learning from Las Vegas*.

48. Tom Wolfe, "Las Vegas (What!) Las Vegas (Can't Hear You! Too Noisy) Las Vegas!!!" *The Kandy-Kolored Tangerine-Flake Streamline Baby* (London: Jonathan Cape, 1966), 3–28.

49. On the issue of chatter, see Peter Fenves, *"Chatter": Language and History in Kierkegaard* (Stanford, Calif.: Stanford University Press, 1993).

50. On the generative nature of noise in theories of communication, see Mark C. Taylor, "Noise in Formation," in *The Moment of Complexity: Emerging Network Culture* (Chicago: University of Chicago Press, 2001).

51. The best introduction to noise is the fascinating writing of Michel Serres's books *Genesis* (Ann Arbor: University of Michigan Press, 1995), and *The Parasite* (Baltimore: Johns Hopkins University Press, 1982).

52. Ralph Waldo Emerson, "The Divinity School Address," *Ralph Waldo Emerson: Selected Essays, Lectures, and Poems* (New York: Bantam, 1990), 110.

1

Aesthetic or Anaesthetic: A Nelson Goodman Reading of the Las Vegas Strip

RITU BHATT

Learning from Las Vegas, first published in 1972, proposed that architecture should reposition itself from its modernist emphasis on space and structure to a postmodern reading of signs and symbols. This shift would allow architects to relearn to see and, as a consequence, make the practice of design socially less coercive and aesthetically more vital. The book introduced suspending judgment as a mechanism to free the imagination and make subsequent judgments more sensitive.[1] This process, it was hoped, would increase the architect's capacity to make discriminations and learn from the everyday. Such an approach to aesthetic cognition that involves learning has parallels with Nelson Goodman's arguments in his book *Languages of Art* (first published in 1968), in which he claimed that aesthetic experiences distinguish themselves as moments of disinterest, enlightenment, and transformation.

For Goodman, aesthetic experiences are not limited to works of art, but can happen any time. He stresses that the question to ask is not "What is art?" but "When is art?" And when art happens, it is the moment of nonjudgment and disinterest that allows the subject to expand the horizon of viewing and experience the deep transformative potential of aesthetics. Aesthetic experiences are dynamic rather than static. In fact, Goodman argues that pictures are symbols that refer to object and ideas much as words do. The difference lies in the semantic and syntactic structures that different arts employ. Experiencing aesthetics involves an elusive process of making delicate discriminations, discerning subtle relationships, identifying symbol systems, and analyzing what these symbolic systems denote and exemplify. Most of all, it involves interpreting works and reorganizing the world in terms of works and works in terms of the world.[2]

In *Learning from Las Vegas*, Robert Venturi, Denise Scott Brown, and Steven Izenour introduce the commercial strip as the new landscape of the automobile-driven environment. In this landscape of big signs, small buildings, and high speeds, architecture becomes a symbol or a series of symbolic systems in space competing with and often contradicting each other. The entire book—which is a collage of passages, short essays, maps, and diagrams initially conceived as a report of a design studio offered at Yale in 1967—aims to devise systems of thought that will allow architects to analyze the new emerging environment of the Las Vegas Strip. In this new landscape, buildings do not just denote the functions they house, but they function as signs conveying multiple meanings. For instance, Venturi, Scott Brown, and Izenour write,

> The big sign leaps to connect the driver to the store . . . and the graphic sign in space has become the architecture of landscape. . . . It is the highway signs, through their sculptural forms or pictorial silhouettes, their particular positions in space, their inflected shapes, and their graphic meanings, that identify and unify the mega texture. . . . Symbol dominates space. Architecture is not enough. Because the spatial relationships are made by symbols more than by forms, architecture in this landscape becomes symbols in space rather than forms in space. Architecture defines very little: The big sign and the little building is the rule of Route 66.[3]

In their book, Venturi, Scott Brown, and Izenour promote an "Ugly and Ordinary Architecture" (U&O), as an alternative to the heroic modern architecture of pure form. They point out that in U&O architecture, communication happens through denotative meanings derived from direct, literal references. For instance, the conspicuous sign that identifies the fire station just by the simple act of spelling it—FIRE STATION NO. 4—acts both as a symbol and an expressive architectural abstraction. Venturi, Scott Brown, and Izenour argue that such gestures of naming are not merely ordinary, but they represent ordinariness. Furthermore, they point out that other levels of meanings are evoked via association, past experience, conventions and other indirect references. For instance, the fire station's function and its civic character is evoked by particular aspects of the building—its decorated false façade, the banality of its standard aluminum sash and roll-up doors, the flagpole located in front, and so forth. This manner of identification points to the everyday ways in which aesthetic experiences can be discerned.

Goodman also emphasizes the day-to-day reasoning inherent in experiencing aesthetics and argues that the agent has the capacity to identify various particulars of an experience. In fact, aesthetic experiences in Goodman's work are understood as intentional states of mind in which we bear a responsibility for justification. For instance, judgments like "Louis Kahn's Salk Institute is, metaphorically, a monastic cloister" have the ability to change experience through arguments grounded in particulars. By the time we come to perceive the Salk Institute in this way, we have already deliberated about it. The serenity of the Salk Institute, the repetitive vocabulary of the building, the courtyard with a central channel of water, the concrete frame and teak cubicles, and even, perhaps, the idea of a religious experience in a monastic complex—all contribute to our "reading" of the institute. These particulars may or may not combine in particular ways for an aesthetic experience to happen. The more important point is this: the possibilities of permutation and combination are infinite, yet they are amenable to some form of articulation and analysis.[4]

What is interesting, however, is the shift in Goodman's thinking about architecture between the publication of his book *Languages of Art* and his essay "How Buildings Mean" in *Domus* (part of a special series commemorating the forty-fifth anniversary of the journal) in 1986. In *Languages of Art*, architecture poses problems for Goodman because he is unable to reconcile how notations such as plan drawings signify meanings and how that compares with the different ways in which buildings exemplify multiple meanings. In "How Buildings Mean," Goodman's analysis is singularly focused on indirect reference and exemplification. Goodman is invited, along with other thinkers and philosophers such as Hans Georg Gadamer, Jacques Derrida, and Kenneth Frampton, to respond to the predicament faced by architects in assimilating postmodernism and deconstruction.[5] In his introduction to Goodman's piece, editor Vittorio Magnano Lampugnani describes Goodman as an original and lively American thinker who stands for a return to a rationalistic discipline. More importantly, Goodman is described as a philosopher who insists that lies exist next to truths and that in this respect is a "constructivist" (or, as he defines himself, a "constructionalist"). Lampugnani ends his introduction by pointing out that "it goes without saying that as such he is the opposite of deconstructionalist Derrida."[6]

In this famous essay, Goodman cites Venturi's work and focuses his discussion entirely on exemplification and indirect reference. Goodman writes, "when Robert Venturi writes of 'contradiction' in architecture, he is not supposing that a building can actually assert a self-contradictory sentence, but is speaking of exemplification by a building of forms that give rise when juxtaposed, because they are also severally exemplified in architecture of contrasting kinds (for example, classical and baroque), to expectations that contravene each other. The contradiction thus arises from indirect reference."[7] In fact, Goodman argues, the expression of meaning in architecture is seldom denotational, or at the level of description or representation. In most cases, buildings express meanings through exemplification, that is, the building may not represent anything as such, but it may exemplify or express certain properties. Such reference, Goodman argues, runs not as denotation does, from the symbol to what it applies to as a label, but in the opposite direction, from the symbol to certain labels that apply to it or to properties possessed by it.[8] In fact, exemplification is one of the major ways in which architectural works express meaning; exemplified qualities are not qualities a building merely possesses but qualities that the building exemplifies. For instance, Goodman gives the example of the Verzehnheiligen pilgrimage church near Bamberg and shows that the qualities of syncopation and dynamism associated with the building depend not on how different formal properties relate to each other but on the properties the building exemplifies. The emphasis on exemplification is central to Venturi, Scott Brown, and Izenour's analysis, especially in how they demonstrate that, in the architecture of the highway strip, buildings do not inherently mean something. Instead the fronts of the buildings disengage themselves from the building mass and recombine themselves as a complex formation of false fronts standing perpendicular to the highway as big signs competing with and often contradicting each other.

In a similar vein, Goodman emphasizes that works of art are not inert, and they do not refer solely (if at all) to themselves. Works of art pick out, point to, and refer to some of their properties but not others. And most of these exemplified properties are also properties of other things, which are thus associated with, and may be indirectly referred to by, the work. Furthermore, Goodman emphasizes the normative dimensions of interpreting both the literal and metaphorical aspects of art. Understanding a work of art, Goodman writes, is not to appreciate it, enjoy it, or find it beautiful, but to interpret it correctly—and to recognize what and how it symbolizes and how what it symbolizes bears on other aspects of our world. Pointing out that metaphorical truth is as distinct as is literal truth from literal falsity, Goodman shows how metaphorical referencing in buildings can also be evaluated. For instance, a Gothic cathedral that soars and sings does not equally droop and grumble. Although both descriptions are literally false, the former, but not the latter, is metaphorically true.[9]

Goodman's most important contribution, however, is in the distinctions he draws between symbolic systems in general and those that can be argued to be functioning aesthetically. According to Goodman, the properties that distinguish aesthetic systems are syntactic and semantic density, repleteness, and exemplification. As symbol systems, these features are neither necessary nor sufficient for aesthetic functioning; they are indications that the item is functioning as a work of art:

Syntactic density: A work of art contains an undefined number of symbols. The symbol system that a work belongs to has an indefinite number of symbols, so that between any two there is a third. There is no claim that all of these symbols occur within a single work. Rather the point is that if there are infinitely fine differences between symbols of the system, it is not clear exactly which symbol belongs to the work.

Syntactic repleteness: Symbols function along relatively many dimensions. That is, relatively many of their features or aspects perform symbolic functions. We cannot say that only ten, or a thousand, symbols are significant in an artwork, and the rest are superfluous. There is no feasible way to quantify the number of aspects a symbol has.

Semantic density: The field of reference of a symbol system is such that between any two reference classes there is a third. All language is semantically dense and therefore paraphrase is impossible; the problem of paraphrase stems from repleteness.

In Venturi, Scott Brown, and Izenour's argument, the Las Vegas Strip emerges as a route of reference in which competing symbol systems—both literal and metaphorical—are open to analysis. They start with a basic analysis and identify that the Strip consists of two distinct visual systems: the obvious visual order of street elements and the difficult visual order of buildings and signs. They describe the two visual systems in the following passage:

> The zone *of* the highway is a shared order, and the zone *off* the highway is an individual order. The elements of the highway are civic; the buildings and the signs are private. In combination they embrace continuity *and* discontinuity, going *and* stopping, clarity *and* ambiguity, cooperation *and* competition, the community *and* rugged individualism. The system of the highway gives order to the sensitive functions of the exit and entrance, as well as to the image of the Strip as a sequential whole. It also generates places for individual enterprises to grow and controls the general direction of that growth. It allows variety and change along its sides and accommodates the contrapuntal, competitive order of the individual enterprises.[10]

Venturi, Scott Brown, and Izenour are searching for a vocabulary that will allow them to explain the ambiguity and apparent chaos that masks an order not obvious to the eye. The analysis of various building types, ranging from typical hotel-casino complexes, gasoline stations, motels, and service stations to wedding chapels, shows how building typologies connect to add syntactic density in the landscape and how it is possible to discern and recognize this process of accretion. For instance, they point out that the gasoline stations that one sees in Las Vegas are the typical buildings one sees in one's neighborhood, and their meaning connects at that level of everyday association. While not the brightest in town, "these less bright typologies" of the gasoline stations galvanize together to form yet another layer of meaning on the Strip.

What is of interest to them is to see how buildings sited for altogether different reasons eventually conform to some discernable conventions along the Strip. Some of these discernable conventions include perception of the moving eye, differing scales of movement along the highway, competition among the advertisers, and the photogenic qualities of the Strip as a whole. Most service stations, motels, and other simpler types of buildings conform to a general system of inflection toward the highway through position and the form of their elements. The scales of movement and the spaces of the highway relate to distances between buildings, which are sited so that they can be comprehended at high speeds. For instance, the side elevations are emphasized because they are seen by approaching traffic from a greater distance and for a longer time than the front façade. The parking spaces also function as signs. The front parking of a typical hotel-casino complex is meant to be a token. It reassures the customer of the prestige of the complex and negotiates its presence in a way so as not to obscure the building. The real parking spaces are located along the sides of the complex, allowing direct access while staying visible from the highway. Through all these gestures, it becomes evident that meaning in landscape is communicated through signs, and the actual distance between two points is immaterial.

It is important to note that each new element adds not only to the syntactic density of the visual system but also to its semantic density. Buildings on the Strip operate as signs referring to the world of the highway strip and constructively exemplifying its properties of transience, superficiality, illusion, glitter and so on. The obsolescence of signs depends less on factors such as physical disintegration and more on their location along the Strip, which is largely determined by the leasing system. The signs and casino façades are most changeable in the most unique and monumental parts of the Strip. Their rate of obsolescence depends more on how well they compete while being viewed from the moving automobile on the highway than on how they relate to the building of which they are a part. Furthermore, in Venturi, Scott Brown, and Izenour's reading, a billboard or neon sign acquires repleteness through its particulars—the particular style of fonts employed, use of neon lights, size, location, construction, and other innumerable qualities. All contribute to the glitter and transience and to its repleteness, which resists any form of paraphrase.

In their search for the various symbol systems, the particulars that Venturi, Scott Brown, and Izenour identify are so many and so indistinguishable that it is impossible to distinguish and delineate smaller symbol systems and how they combine in various ways to transform the Strip in itself into a symbol. In their analysis, such a predicament about paraphrasing is evident:

> On the Strip three message systems exist: the heraldic: which include all the signs that dominate the landscape; the physiognomic: the messages given by the faces of the buildings, for instance, the continuous balconies and regularly spaced picture windows of the Dunes saying "HOTEL" and the suburban bungalows converted to chapels by the addition of a steeple; and the locational—service stations are found on corner lots, the casino is in front of the hotel, and the ceremonial valet parking is in front of the casino. All three message systems are closely related on the strip, sometimes they are combined, as when the facade of a casino becomes one big sign or the shape of the building reflects its name, and the sign, in turn reflects the shape. Is the sign the building or building the sign?[11]

Within the discipline of architecture, Venturi, Scott Brown, and Izenour see their work to be consistent with emerging areas of inquiry, such as the search for underlying typologies and the larger search for meaning in architecture. They acknowledge the works of Charles Jencks, George Baird, and Alan Colquhoun as important influences, particularly the essays they wrote in *Meaning in Architecture*, published in 1969.[12] Ernst Gombrich's book *Mediations on a Hobby Horse* is also cited by Venturi, Scott Brown, and Izenour as an important influence.[13] Gombrich's thesis—that physiognomic forms are ambiguous, and they can only be interpreted within a particular cultural ambience—is consistent with Venturi, Scott Brown, and Izenour's belief that the symbols on the Strip conform to a conventional system of meanings that are not inherent in the forms themselves.[14]

However, what is of special interest to them is Colquhoun's interest in the typology of forms and how historical associations from the past become available to a designer's vocabulary:

> Alan Colquhoun has written of architecture as part of a "system of communications within society" and describes the anthropological and psychological basis for the use of a typology of forms in design, suggesting that not only are we not "free from the forms of the past, and the availability of these forms, and from the availability of these forms as typological models, but that, if we assume we are free, we have lost control over a very active sector of our imagination and of our power to communicate with others."[15]

Their primary aim is to rejuvenate this aspect of imaginative thought made dormant by modernist emphasis on functional aesthetics and to devise a methodology that would allow architects to analyze and evaluate the visibly vital architecture of the Strip. They want to remind architects that "architecture that depends on association in its perception also depends on association in its creation."[16] They argue that symbolism is essential to architecture, models from a previous time, or from existing cities, are source materials, and, most importantly, replication is part of the design process. For instance, they write that when designing a window, one starts not only with the abstract function of modulating light rays and breezes to serve interior space but also with the image of the window—of all the windows you know plus others you find out about. This approach, they argue, is symbolically and functionally conventional, but it promotes an architecture of meaning, which is broader and richer.

It is the unresolved ambiguity between a belief in underlying architectural typologies and associations that are constant (that repeat themselves from the past) and the Goodmanian search for the Strip's dynamic aesthetic that is open to infinite interpretations that weakens the book's potential to provide a cohesive vision.

Moreover, the book presents a loose array of photographs, diagrams, and notes on the casino strip meant to evoke the lived experience of the Strip. The techniques of representation are varied and experimental, and it is evident that there is a search for an analytical framework that will do justice to the new emerging environment. Charts offer photographs of all sides of the main casinos and gasoline stations and ninety-three frames of movie sequences capture movement. Other techniques such as miscellaneous reprints of tourist brochures are also experimented with in the book, along with a variety of maps. All these techniques are meant to challenge traditional two-dimensional modes of representation. However, despite the experimental edge of the whole project, a belief in abstraction is evident throughout the text and through the analytical diagrams. For instance, Venturi, Scott Brown, and Izenour argue that theirs is a study of method and not content, claiming that the analysis of a drive-in church would match that of a drive-in restaurant. In fact, they believe that analysis of one architectural variable in isolation from the others is a respectable scientific and humanistic activity, so long as it is resynthesized in design. Most of all, they clarify that they are approaching the problem of symbolism in architecture pragmatically from a practitioner's point of view, using concrete examples rather than abstractly through the science of semiotics or through a priori theorizing.

Furthermore, although the book makes a cogent argument for how past associations contribute to design, the methodology proposed in the book starts to come apart when one looks for interpretations of the study of history or of the practice of design. For instance, in one of the diagrams, the A&P parking lot is presented as a logical outcome in the evolution of vast spaces since the building of Versailles. The diagram compares various typologies that include Versailles, an

English garden, Broadacre City, Levittown, Highway Interchange, and the Strip. The various street symbols, architectural elements, and the ratio between space and signs are diagrammatically and chronologically mapped. In this comparison through history, in which one sees certain patterns disappear and others appear, a linear evolutionary paradigm is reinforced, and the architecture of small buildings and big signs emerges as a natural consequence of evolution through history. On the other hand, the analogies drawn are completely ahistorical; for example, the A&P parking lot is described as the parterre of the asphalt landscape, and grids of lampposts are likened to obelisks.[17] It is in such analyses that the book starts to loose its potential for providing a historical vision or methodological rigor.

Such frustration with the book's methodology is apparent in most reviews published at the time. While acknowledging the momentary brilliance of Venturi, Scott Brown, and Izenour's argument, most reviewers also criticize them for failing to provide a convincing methodology. Fred Koetter's review represents one such critique:

> After the fun, after the euphoria, after the diagrams and predictable points have been made, is the architect really serving society by the endorsement of such easy overtures to instant gratification? To be sure, the idea of strip development might certainly provide, by way of optimism, nimble abstraction and a variety of useful "models" for the general "structuring" of an automobile-driven urban pattern; but, at a certain point, the limits of the reference must be ascertained and the question must arise: can the literal extension of the it's-not-so-bad-if-you-look-at-it-right syndrome really transform obvious trash into a model for meaningful environment? But assuming momentarily a condition of semi-analytical detachment, what about the formal lessons of Las Vegas and its abstract lessons in "architectural communications"? . . . What is the architect to do with all that vitality? Is he to simulate it? Is he to run it through his analytical sieve and learn to produce less than fully animated caricatures of it? May he, in traditional way, use it to represent a version of "popular" vitality, to insinuate a recognition of front-line reality?[18]

On the other hand, contemporary theorists, particularly Jean-François Lyotard, Jencks, Hal Foster, and Fredric Jameson, have all focused on the book's postmodern laissez-faire approach and rhetoric. Neil Leach, in his *Anaesthetics of Architecture*, has criticized it for desemanticizing and aestheticizing architectural forms. Leach writes,

> it is in the abstract handling of form, and their refusal to engage the context of Las Vegas, that the real problems of the book emerge. In decontextualizing the forms of Las Vegas, they desemanticize them, setting up a pattern that is to haunt

them, as we shall see, in their builtwork.... It is this principle of aestheticization, then, that allows Venturi, Scott Brown, and Izenour to remain so oblivious to the sociopolitical questions at the heart of Las Vegas, to an aesthetisize it, and to adapt an approach that is epitomized by their celebration of the advertising hoarding.[19]

In such critiques lies the predicament of the postmodern moment. Can *Learning from Las Vegas* be seen as promoting anaestheticized advertising, or can it be seen as functioning aesthetically as a transformative moment? Are there ways one can distinguish between when aesthetic can be said to be functioning cognitively and when it can be said to be functioning anaesthetically—when images become insular? It is true that *Learning from Las Vegas* lacks a convincing normative framework or a broad vision. Its emphasis on creating an aesthetic awareness is intertwined with broadening social sensibility, yet the studio does not necessarily address the particular sociocultural economics of its setting.[20] And then there are places in the book where image making is uncritically embraced.[21] Yet it can be argued that *Learning from Las Vegas*'s brilliant polemic, which allows one to read the Strip as a system or systems of symbols, is a transformative moment when one relearns to see. Venturi and Scott Brown's call to withhold judgment does allow architects to recognize an aesthetic in the placement of neon lights, in the arrangement of parking lots, in the gasoline stations, and so forth. The aesthetic does not lie in the imagery of built forms, but in the recognition of the inflexion of buildings and billboards, in the recognition of the manner in which different typologies add density to the landscape, and in reading the repleteness of the various symbol systems. Such an aesthetic has the potential to constantly transform; it is difficult to paraphrase. If it is possible to discern moments when aesthetic functions cognitively and when it does not, then it can be argued that the polemic of *Learning from Las Vegas* functions most successfully in increasing our capacity to make discriminations and learn from the everyday. More importantly, as Scott Brown claims in relearning to accommodate the familiar, *Learning from Las Vegas* opens up our social sensibilities as well.[22]

Notes

I am grateful to Aron Vinegar and Michael Golec for their insightful comments on this chapter.

1. Robert Venturi, Denise Scott Brown, and Steven Izenour, *Learning from Las Vegas*, rev. ed. (Cambridge, Mass.: MIT Press, 1977), 153.
2. Nelson Goodman, *Languages of Art: An Approach to a Theory of Symbols* (Indianapolis: Hackett Publishing Company, 1976), 241.
3. Venturi, Scott Brown, and Izenour, *Learning from Las Vegas*, 11–13.
4. For more on the relationship between Goodman's infinite particulars and Aristotelian practical reasoning, see Ritu Bhatt, "The Significance of the Aesthetic in Postmodern Architectural Theory," *Journal of Architectural Education*, May 2000, 229–38.
5. Nelson Goodman, "Che cosa significa costruire, e quando e perche," *Domus* 672 (May 1986): 17–28.
6. Vittorio Magnano Lampugnani, introduction to "Che cosa significa costruire, e quando e perche" by Nelson Goodman, *Domus* 672 (May 1986): 17–28. Goodman is known to have respect for the deconstructionists. He saw his own work as a form of deconstructing language for achieving greater clarity and precision and eliminating spurious theories and issues. Goodman, e-mail communication with Curtis Carter, March 3, 2003.
7. Nelson Goodman and Catherine Elgin, "How Buildings Mean," in *Reconceptions in Philosophy* (London: Routledge, 1988), 42.
8. Goodman, *Reconceptions in Philosophy* (London: Routledge, 1988), 36.
9. Ibid., 40.
10. Venturi, Scott Brown, and Izenour, *Learning from Las Vegas*, 20.
11. Ibid., 73.
12. Charles Jencks, *Meaning in Architecture*, 1970.
13. E. H. Gombrich, *Mediations on a Hobby Horse and Other Essays on the Theory of Art*, 1965.
14. Ibid., 132.
15. Ibid., 131. It is important to note that in his 1967 review of *Complexity and Contradiction* in *Architectural Design*, Alan Colquhoun criticized Robert Venturi for failing to demonstrate the necessity for employing the formal structures adapted from past buildings. He was also critical of Venturi's Vanna Venturi House, which he said was a "learned game" in which "the self-circular semantic elements such as the string-courses and semi-circular windows" were composed in an "arbitrary grammar." Alan Colquhoun, "Robert Venturi," *Architectural Design XXXVII*, August 1967, 362.
16. Venturi, Scott Brown, and Izenour, *Learning from Las Vegas*, 129.
17. Ibid., 13.
18. Fred Koetter, "On Robert Venturi, Denise Scott Brown and Steven Izenour's *Learning from Las Vegas*," *Oppositions* 3 (May 1974): 100–101.
19. Neil Leach, *The Anaesthetics of Architecture* (Cambridge, Mass.: MIT Press, 1999), 63.
20. Denise Scott Brown, in "Learning from Pop," makes an argument that their approach has a strong social basis. Her concern was that architects working in a commercial society needed to be grounded in the "reality" of lower-middle-class American aesthetic values. Close study of the existing landscape might offer "formal vocabularies for today which are more relevant to people's diverse needs and more tolerant of the untidiness of urban life than the 'rationalist,' Cartesian formal orders of latter-day Modern Architecture." Denise Scott Brown, "Learning from Pop," in *A View from the Campidoglio: Selected Essays, 1953–1984*, ed. Peter Arnell, Ted Bickford, and Catherine Bergart (New York: Harper & Row, 1984), 27.
21. When criticized for image making, Venturi, Scott Brown, and Izenour defend themselves. They write, "please do not criticize us for primarily analyzing image: We are doing so simply because image is pertinent to our argument, not because we wish to deny an interest in or the importance of process, program, and structure or, indeed social issues in architecture or in these two buildings. Along with most architects, we probably spend 90 percent of our design time on these other important subjects and less than 10 percent on the questions we are addressing here: they are merely not the direct subject of this inquiry." Venturi, Scott Brown, and Izenour, *Learning from Las Vegas*, 90–91.

22. According to Denise Scott Brown, "Our social agenda was different from the modernists. We were not promoting an explicit social agenda, but the social concerns of our project were implicit. In fact we were making the argument that in opening aesthetic sensibilities one's social concerns shift as well." Denise Scott Brown, interview with the author, February 2003.

2

Format and Layout in *Learning from Las Vegas*

MICHAEL J. GOLEC

In 1972, Robert Venturi, Denise Scott Brown, and Steven Izenour published *Learning from Las Vegas*, a collection of studies designed by Scott Brown and drawn from the architects' Yale studio seminar on the Las Vegas Strip in the fall of 1968.[1] The book is packed with information graphics: aerial photographs, snapshots, signage, diagrams, all manner of maps, plans, elevations, sections, heraldry, graphs, sketches, charts, and lists. These graphic images—mostly influenced by media studies, sociology, urban studies, and pop art—visually reconstruct Las Vegas as the epitome of the commercial roadside environment. According to the authors, the Las Vegas Strip spontaneously disclosed its own patterns of use and value. How to transfer the vivid disorderliness, or semantic dimensionality, of the Strip to, or transform it into, the two dimensional format of a book was, however, a central problem for the authors.

Venturi, Scott Brown, and Izenour's initial intention was, in Scott Brown's words, to "do it deadpan," to allow Las Vegas to reveal itself and not to be upstaged by the design of the book.[2] Nevertheless, the art director for MIT Press, Muriel Cooper, had a different idea of what form *Learning from Las Vegas* should take. And, as it turned out, Cooper's design sensibility was not to the authors' liking. The disagreement surrounding the first edition's design prompted the 1977 publication of Scott Brown's redesigned and revised edition of *Learning from Las Vegas*. The reformatted 1977 edition—its miniaturization, its random placement of images, its conventional typographic layout—thoroughly dismantled Cooper's original design of *Learning from Las Vegas* and thus, I hope to demonstrate, rendered its visual form at odds with its textual content.

The potential visual potency of *Learning from Las Vegas*—the manner in which either the 1972 edition or the revised and redesigned 1977 edition mobilizes all kinds of informational devices to inculcate its audience—was nicely summed up in Venturi, Scott Brown, and Izenour's query: "How do you represent the strip as perceived by Mr. A rather than as a piece of geometry?"[3] Cooper's response, made manifest in her lively design, envisions the intensity of the Las Vegas Strip. Unlike Cooper, Scott Brown's response, articulated in her redesign for the revised edition—which according to her is more in keeping with the authors' original intention of "doing it deadpan"—attempts to maintain an aura of objectivity and a tone of scholarly dispassion. Scott Brown's design strategy of letting Las Vegas reveal itself through the uncolored presentation of data is in keeping with what the historians of science Lorainne Daston and Peter Galison have identified, in their "The Image of Objectivity" (1992), as the ideology of the nineteenth-century scientific atlas, a paradigm for scientific representation and mechanical documentation of nature.[4]

The nineteenth-century faith in objectivity, according to Galison, in his follow up article "Judgment Against Objectivity" (1998), was contested by the advent of twentieth-century subjective judgment, or "subjective evaluation." Subjective judgment, as Galison explains, is acquired through professional and aesthetic training that prepares one to make appropriate discernments and active decisions that mere mechanical documentation is incapable of performing.[5] Cooper's design judgments, informed by professional training, exemplify what the statistician and information designer Edward Tufte, in his book *Envisioning Information*, refers to as "escaping the flatland [of two-dimensions] and enriching the density of data displays."[6] According to Tufte, enhancing the impoverished flatland of two-dimensional informational graphics requires the *enhancement* of data—the creation of density, complexity, and dimensionality—so that experiences with information (as communication, as documentation, and as preservation) flow in a familiar way, a way that discloses to the reader something of his or her experiences of the three-dimensional world, the world that he or she bodily inhabits. The notion that a design should enhance data is in keeping with what Galison has referred to as a "judgment against objectivity," or a withdrawal from the early modernist faith in the veracity of unaided imaging.

The apparent incommensurability of subjective judgment and objectivity instantiated in the differences between the dynamic (or subjective) first edition and the deadpan (or objective) revised edition of *Learning from Las Vegas* is further complicated by the fact that Cooper's design is in keeping with the subject matter of the author's text. In fact, it is my contention that, in spite of Venturi, Scott

Brown, and Izenour's misgivings and Scott Brown's redesign, Cooper's design fully realizes the authors' desire to image the city in textual and visual representations that establish identifiable sets of schematic instructions to construct corresponding images of Las Vegas in the mind. It was, in fact, Cooper, not Scott Brown, who represented "the strip as perceived by Mr. A rather than as a piece of geometry."

This aspect of the origin and function of *Learning from Las Vegas*, however, has been largely ignored by commentators—chiefly Jean-François Lyotard, Umberto Eco, Charles Jencks, and, most famously, Fredric Jameson—who have concentrated instead on ways in which the book theorized a postmodern architecture. *Learning from Las Vegas* was at the crux of Jameson's *Postmodernism, or, The Cultural Logic of Late Capitalism*, in which he situated postmodernism "as a kind of aesthetic populism."[7] Aesthetic populism is certainly an acknowledged aspect of *Learning from Las Vegas*. Postmodernism, however, is not the operative paradigm of the book. Rather, as the various disassociations and intersections that exist between the design and publication of the 1972 edition and the redesign and revised publication of the 1977 edition bear out, the crux of *Learning from Las Vegas* is the critical tension that exists between Scott Brown's early modernist notions of objectivity and Cooper's late modernist notions of subjective judgment. To develop my argument that Cooper graphically realized the main thrust of Venturi, Scott Brown, and Izenour's *Learning from Las Vegas*, I draw upon two influential publications as well as on Venturi and Scott Brown's (with an emphasis on Scott Brown) early writings leading up to the publication of *Learning from Las Vegas* in 1972.

Images and Patterns

Kevin Lynch's *The Image of the City* first addressed envisioned information as it relates to mental pictures and experiences of the urban environment. Published in 1960, *The Image of the City* advocated an approach to urban planning that capitalized on the kinds of cognitive maps (or mental pictures) that visitors and native inhabitants formed by traversing the existing city (Boston, Jersey City, and Los Angeles were his case studies). Lynch considered "the visual quality of the American city by studying the mental image of that city which is held by its citizens."[8] The accumulation of mental images of the city had, not surprisingly, great imaginary potential, according to Lynch. Under these ideal circumstances, he wrote, "The common hopes and pleasures, the sense of community may be made flesh." The city had to be "visibly organized and sharply identified" before any comprehensive mental picture—or image—could arise. Only then could the city dweller invest the city with his or her "own meanings and connections," and thereby establish a sense of place.[9]

In addition to the precedent set by Lynch's *Image of the City*, Joseph R. Passonneau and Richard Saul Wurman's *Urban Atlas: 20 American Cities: A Communication Study Notating Selected Urban Data at a Scale of 1:48,000* was likewise a source of inspiration, or more likely an excuse to mull over the challenges inherent in escaping the flatland. Published in 1966, the *Urban Atlas*—a collection of maps juxtaposed with income and density distribution data—was reviewed by Scott Brown in the Spring 1968 issue of *Landscape*. Acknowledging the utility and elegance of the *Urban Atlas*, Scott Brown wrote, "A graphic representation of urban phenomena can help visually-minded people perceive and understand complex but ordered relationships in the city as no table or verbal description could."[10] The evocative use of graphic elements and layers of color in the *Urban Atlas* were, as far as she was concerned, an "important step in the development of an urban design and city planning theory and methodology."[11] Scott Brown focused her attention on the perceptual impact of the maps—the use of gradations of color and graphic devices to produce synoptic views of urban dynamics—contained within the atlas, comparing the design method to the sensorial affects of op art. For example, the saccadic pulsation—or eye-nerve vibration—of Bridget Riley's painting *Current* (1964) comes to mind. No doubt, *Current* is aptly named, because it causes an electrical shock-like jolt to the viewer's sensorium. But its pain-giving quality is only one aspect of the painting's total experience. As the art theorist Anton Ehrenzweig describes Riley's *Current*, a second aspect of the painting engenders "a voluptuous moment when the senses and skin tingle with a new warmth and sharpened awareness of the body and the world around."[12] Color theory, psychology, and physiology were all pertinent to, as Scott Brown stated in her review, "investigation of mapping methods and printing technologies."[13]

Although Scott Brown identified a number of positive attributes (she even went so far as to suggest that the atlas would be "a good buy for collectors of modern art"), she believed that the atlas failed on two points.[14] First, despite its affinities with op art, the *Urban Atlas* did not fully capitalize on the "eye's ability to read gradations in intensity quickly." And, second, although visually exciting, the atlas was static in its "one-shot character." To ratchet up the experiential component of the atlas, Scott Brown recommended the use of cinematography to show the dynamic patterning of the growth of the city.[15] Such an addition, she advised, would further invigorate an already affective graphic means of communicating the existing life of the urban environment.

The use of cinematography for the study of the city was first introduced in 1964 by Donald Appleyard, Lynch, and John R. Myer's *The View from the Road*, a monographic study that recorded, through the reproduction of motion picture cells, passing impressions from an automobile traveling on the highway. The experience of the highway, according to the authors, consisted of the perception of roadside detail, the sense of motion and space, the feeling of basic orientation, and the apparent meaning of landscape. The sequence of images that approximated a cinematic view described a brief trip on the Northeast Expressway through Boston "as it might impress a typical passenger."[16] Appleyard, Lynch, and Myer concluded that the speed and movement implicit in contemporary car culture could benefit the "desire to find visual means for pulling together large urban areas."[17]

The visual documentation of the existing urban environment was also a perceived characteristic of the pop art movement in the United States. In "A Significance for A&P Parking Lots, or Learning from Las Vegas," published in the March 1968 issue of *Architectural Forum* (later republished with revisions as the first section of *Learning from Las Vegas*), Venturi and Scott Brown took pop art to be an example of a tolerant approach to the "existing landscape." Combining a populist aesthetic with the advances proposed in *The View from the Road*, the article claimed that "creating the new for the artist may mean choosing the old or the existing. Pop artists have relearned this. Our acknowledging existing, commercial architecture at the scale of the highway is within this tradition."[18] Venturi and Scott Brown departed from the one-to-one equivalency of city to mental picture first proposed by Lynch in *The Image of the City*. Rather than contending, like Lynch, that the city had to be exceptionally organized in ways that were immediately apprehensible, Venturi and Scott Brown suggested that the city, regardless of its apparent organization or disorganization, retained latent patterns that could be discovered and disclosed by the architect-planner.

A year later, Scott Brown published "On Pop Art, Permissiveness, and Planning" in the May 1969 issue of the *Journal of the American Institute of Planners*. In Los Angeles, she proposed, the pop artist found both a subject and a catalyst: the existing city and a means to communicate. She wrote, "[Ed] Ruscha's *Thirtyfour Parking Lots* [1967], photographed from a helicopter, resemble [Allan] D'Arcangelo paintings: arrowed, tensioned, abstract diagrams where oil patterns on the asphalt reveal different stress from differing accessibility."[19] Ruscha, who wanted to report while at the same time to abstain from judgment, created a series of self-published books—*Twentysix Gasoline Stations* (1963), *Some Los Angeles Apartments* (1965), and *Every Building on Sunset Strip* (1966) are a few examples—that exposed the surfaces of the living city. Blunt in delivery, Ruscha's books were Okie-pop-minimal visions of vacant landscapes. In its random collection of aerial views of empty parking lots, Ruscha's *Thirtyfour Parking Lots* documented the commonly unseen. These images made visible what is usually invisible from the ground. For example, Scott Brown reproduced "Good Year Tires, 6610 Laural [sic] Canyon, North Hollywood." (She also reproduced "El Paso, Winslow Arizona" from *Twentysix Gasoline Stations* and "6565 Fountain Avenue" from *Some Los Angeles Apartments*.) The aerial photograph of the Goodyear Tires store shows a vast and unpopulated parking lot; it is long and narrow, almost too much so in relation to the proportionately small tire service center that the lot is intended to serve. The relevance of Ruscha's pop art images in general was that they furnished Scott Brown with instances of the materializations of the concealed relationship between the building and the parking lot. For her, Ruscha's picture evinced a "pattern in the sprawl."[20]

In 1971, Scott Brown contributed "Learning from Pop" to the December issue of *Casabella*, a special issue on "The City as an Artifact." In her most sustained discussion of the merits of pop art, Scott Brown explained that pop artists celebrated the existing environment—as it is rather than as it should be—and therefore pop art underscored the context in which the architect and planner could learn. Importantly, the "pop landscape"—supermarkets, parking lots, hot-dog stands, corner stores, warehouses, boulevards, driveways, alleys, and so on—could furnish the vital information required for future planning and subsequent building. It was, she wrote, "one of the few contemporary sources of data on the symbolic and communicative aspects of architecture."[21] Furthermore, Scott Brown recommended the application of new types of analytic techniques that could aggregate an abundance of repeated data into a comprehensible system. Film sequences like those reproduced in *View from the Road*, for example, could combine with conventional techniques such as Nolli maps, aerial photographs, and graphical comparative methods to systematically describe what Scott Brown perceived as the ever-evolving dimensionality of the existing city.[22]

Scott Brown's "Learning from Pop" was one part of a two-part dialogue with the architectural critic and historian Kenneth Frampton. Appearing in the same issue of *Casabella* and directly following Scott Brown's article, Frampton's "America 1960–1970: Notes on Urban Images and Theory" questioned the practical value of lessons learned from pop art and what he referred to as "Motopia" (i.e., Las Vegas, Los Angeles, Levittown, and so on). As far as Frampton understood, the two were not necessarily related. Unlike Las Vegas, for example, pop art exposed the brutality of a world (or, as Scott Brown might say, an existing environment) organized by the marketing principles of Madison Avenue. But as far as Frampton was concerned, this was by no means a positive attribute. The brutality of Madison Avenue was the brutality of pop art. The two were the same in their incessant appeals and stimulations. Indeed, as he observed, Ruscha's photographs were devoid of the kind of human warmth that "the life styles that these deculturated forms no doubt serve to support."[23] Rather than having a sincere affinity for his subject, Ruscha's images instead typified a "clinical" objectivity that was closer to institutionalized market research than it was to an authentic expression of a culture. (The question of how it was for Frampton that market research itself was not an authentic expression of a culture remained unanswered.) He further connected his criticism of pop art to Scott Brown's regard for new analytic techniques of research. Frampton asserted that a faddish fascination with imaging and imagining—an allusion to Lynch's influence—constituted a distraction from an actual "institutionalized vandalism" that an interest in the common and the "existing" wrought on culture. Frampton proposed that Scott Brown's populist presumptions were a form of coercion and that her "permissiveness"—her belief that the existing city held latent patterns that counted as empirical evidence of a kind of vernacular intelligence—masked the nascent hegemony of market capitalism under the purview of Madison Avenue.

Perhaps Frampton was correct to have raised his objections to Scott Brown's tolerant approach to the existing city and to urban planning. In her own defense, however, Scott Brown responded to what she considered to be Frampton's willful misreading of her article. Among many points of contention, Scott Brown, in her article "Pop Off: Reply to Kenneth Frampton," took the historian-critic to have suggested that "architects be radical about the wrong thing: not about using their skills to serve social innovation, but about revolutionary architecture." Contrary to Frampton's position, she took "social innovation" as implicit in pop art. She had this to say in "On Pop Art, Permissiveness, and Planning," a text that Frampton cited in his critique: "the best thing an architect or urban designer can offer a new society, apart from a good heart, is his own skill, used *for* society, to develop a respectful understanding of its cultural artifacts and a loving strategy for their development to suit the felt needs and way of life of its people. This is a socially responsible activity, it is after all, what [Herbert] Gans and the pop artists are doing."[24] Also, as Scott Brown understood him, Frampton distorted the Venturi and Scott Brown approach to architecture and urban planning, in Scott Brown's words, "by suggesting that we consider objects independently of their relationships. Our point is that architects tend to simplify relationships in the city; that Las Vegas is an object lesson in complex relationships."[25] Scott Brown's belief that architects and planners could learn from Las Vegas did not imply the wholesale reconfiguration of a city into a version of Las Vegas. Rather, Scott Brown argued that "learning to like Las Vegas for its body will help us to understand how to be gentle with the body of South Street [in Philadelphia] and hence with the lives of its occupants."[26] The benefits of corporeal experience, according to Scott Brown, like the "body" of Las Vegas, superseded the kind of armchair theorizing that she and Venturi took the European modernists to have engaged in, a kind of theorizing about urban spaces that was transplanted to the United States without consideration for the homespun intricacies of the lived context of its cities.

Scott Brown often implied or, as in the case above, explicitly referred to the body and its pleasures and displeasures. Her references to op art's sensorial effect in her review of the *Urban Atlas* counts as an example. Also, in "On Pop Art, Permissiveness, and Planning," she wrote, "The shiver that is engendered by trying to like what one does not like has long been known to be a creative one; it *rocks* the artist from his aesthetic grooves and resensitizes him to the source of his inspiration. . . . Here the jolt comes from the unexpected use of the conventional element in an unconventional way."[27] Alluding to both matters of taste and visceral responses to visual images, she described pop art as "a new horror-giving energy source."[28] And elsewhere, in response to the critic Allan Temko during the "Urban Renewal in America, 1950–1970" symposium in June 1971, Scott Brown stated, "There's something to be learned from Las Vegas and from Levittown, and there's something to be learned from Chartres. We are not giving the people of South Street Las Vegas or Chartres. Both are manipulative situations in a social sense, both are physical situations from which an architect can learn a great deal."[29]

The body and its vicissitudes, the physiology of perceptual experience, and the physicality of the city informed the production of *Learning from Las Vegas*. This was largely Scott Brown's doing, as demonstrated in her articles and reviews, and was compatible with her and Venturi's initial encounter with the Las Vegas Strip. In 1966, Scott Brown and Venturi drove a rental car across the arid Nevada sands and entered the neon city—U.S. Route 91, Las Vegas: "Dazed by the desert sun and dazzled by the signs, both loving and hating what we saw, we [Scott Brown and Venturi] were both jolted clear out of our aesthetic skins."[30] Indeed, sun and signs combined and created a shared state of mutual pleasure and displeasure. According to Scott Brown, the strip's full-on sensory assault effected a correlative epiphany with orgasmic inflections. Expectant, Scott Brown had visited Las Vegas a year earlier in 1965. On this later occasion, both she and Venturi were further primed for what they were about to meet on the highway by Tom Wolfe's *The Kandy-Kolored Tangerine-Flake Streamline Baby* (1965): "the neon and the par lamps—bubbling, spiraling, rocketing, and exploding in sunbursts ten stories high out in the middle of the desert." According to Wolfe, the electric stimulations of the strip made its visitors goofy, as did the "childlike megalomania" of gambling and overt sexuality of "the Las Vegas buttocks décolletage."[31] Both gambling and sex were (and are) the simultaneously pulsing draw and repellent of Las Vegas. In the glow of desert neon and the lowbrow glamour of gambling, Scott Brown and Venturi found beauty in a mean place.

Complexity

How then were Venturi, Scott Brown, and Izenour to preserve their experiences of Las Vegas, to translate them into a medium appropriate to their task, to learn to like Las Vegas for its body (with all of its accompanying shivers, jolts, and horrors), and to understand how to be gentle, loving, and respectful with the body of other cities and with the lives of their many inhabitants? Their chosen medium would have to exceed the restrictions of a conventional text with accompanying maps and plans, which, while conceptually adequate, would generally communicate close to nothing of actual experience.[32] Conventional architectural plans, flow charts, and statistical data arrays were, as the author's claimed, "static where it [the Las Vegas Strip] is dynamic, contained where it is open, two-dimensional where it is three dimensional."[33] On its own, a conventional map of Las Vegas would miss "the iconographical dimensions of experience."[34] Venturi, Scott Brown, and Izenour instead had to devise a superior way to graphically arrange the world so that it registered with the vivid sensations of a brutally physical and visually complex site like Las Vegas. The city had to be made flesh (to borrow a term from Lynch) in *Learning from Las Vegas* so that, some thirty years later, a reader's experience of the book would be something like having an experience of the city itself. *Learning from Las Vegas*, like Las Vegas, should mimetically jolt readers, make them shiver, and cause them some horror; it should envision the polymorphous pleasures of the body of Las Vegas so that the reader too might find beauty in a mean place. The solution boiled down to format and layout.

Format and Layout

Opened to lay flat at 21 × 14 1/8 inches (10 1/2 × 14 inches closed), the topography of *Learning from Las Vegas* and its typographic and graphic layout—the book's body, as it were—imply a subtle dimensionality where gray areas of text recede into the page and black areas of text lay across the page's surface. The main text very often runs across four columns of a five-column grid and is composed of 12-point text with 16-point leading Univers 45 Light with a ragged right margin (Figure 2.1). The book achieves tonal contrast by utilizing a secondary text that is composed of 12-point text with 14-point leading Univers 55 Roman with a ragged right margin. The book's axis of symmetry, established by the spine, is transgressed by the asymmetrical composition of each page. For example, the interplay of vertical 12-point text with 14-point leading, Univers 55 Roman, and the horizontal progression of four-color photographs mimics the push-pull of D'Arcangelo's *The Trip*, which occupies the lower left corner of the left page. And the orange-red arrow in D'Arcangelo's picture picks up the orange-red neon "(no) vacancy" sign pictured on the opposing page. Cooper's use of crosscutting elements in the layout of *Learning from Las Vegas* effectively demonstrates, for the reader, what the author's describe in their text: "A driver 30 years ago could maintain a sense of orientation in space. At the simple crossroad a little sign with an arrow confirmed what he already knew. He knew where he was. Today the crossroad is a cloverleaf. To turn left he must turn right, a contradiction poignantly evoked in print by D'Arcangelo."[35] Confounding students of "urban perception and imagability," *Learning from Las Vegas*'s format and layout—Cooper's emphasis of "heraldic symbolism," "physiognomic messages," and "locational signs"—gives form to the "noisy" communication system of Las Vegas.[36]

It should be said that Cooper's design contrivances were not new.[37] Indeed, the supreme modernist aspiration to immediacy through an adroit combination of image and text can be traced to Laszlo Moholy-Nagy's *Bauhaus Bucher* series, Herbert Bayer's "universal" typographic layout, and the German typographer and book designer Jan Tschichold's *Die Neue Typographie*—a manifesto-like primer for commercial typographers, first published in 1928. Because the studio seminar, conducted in the fall of 1968, included two graphic design graduate students, it is not surprising to discern the influence of Bauhaus and Neue Typographie-like sensibilities on the design of *Learning from Las Vegas* in the Yale seminar context. Indeed, with the dominating presence of preeminent practitioners like Paul Rand and Bradbury Thompson, Yale had long been the bastion of modernist graphic design. Central to Moholy-Nagy, Bayer, and Tschichold's new typographic system was that typography had too long followed out of date traditions; they recommended that typographers, acting like engineers, embrace their age and create a pared-down, dynamic typography and layout that reflected the age of advancing

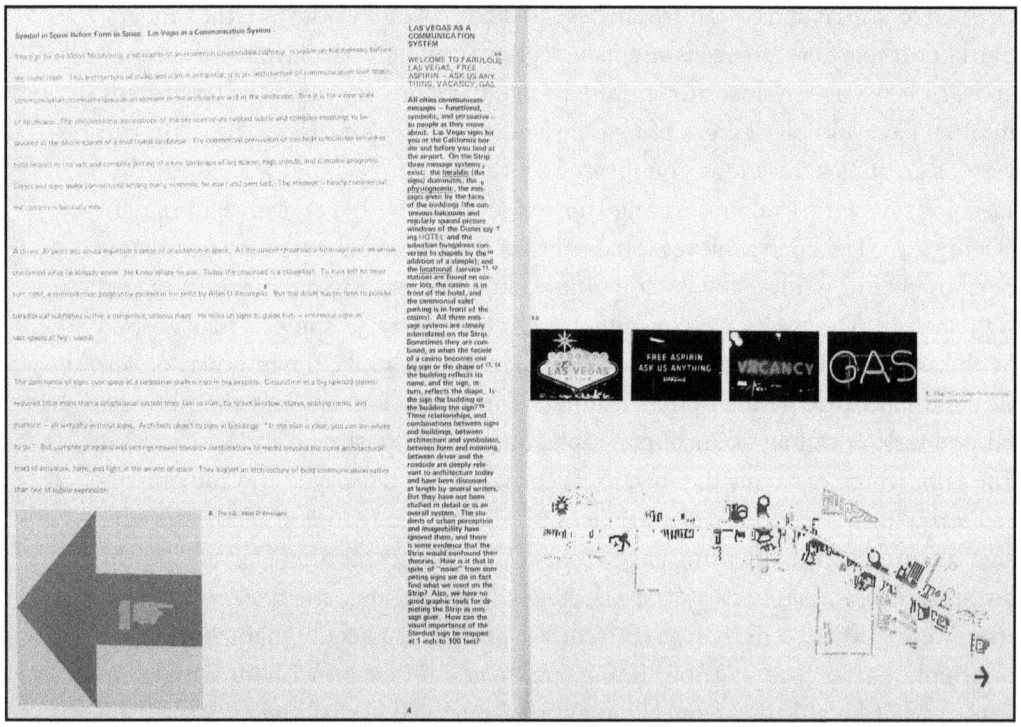

Figure 2.1. Spread from Robert Venturi, Denise Scott Brown, and Steven Izenour, *Learning from Las Vegas* (Cambridge, Mass.: MIT Press, 1972), 4–5. Muriel Cooper, Designer. Copyright 1972, Massachusetts Institute of Technology.

technologies. In particular, Tschichold meant to reinvigorate a staid profession by compelling the "new" typographer to adopt sans-serif typefaces and asymmetrical layouts. Many books on modern architecture pedantically followed Tschichold's example—as was the case with the Museum of Modern Art's *What Is Modern Architecture?* In this sense, *The View from the Road* also adopted the rigid layout prescribed by Tschichold (it too was an MIT Press book), but regardless of its intention to convey movement through the use of film sequences (and certainly exerting some influence on *Learning from Las Vegas*), it is rather static in its delivery.

Cooper's design of *Learning from Las Vegas* took up this modernist tradition by integrating text and image in such a way that as a reader pages through the book, he or she traverses the city of Las Vegas. *Learning from Las Vegas* achieved this through Cooper's assemblage of Venturi, Scott Brown, and Izenour's collection of images chosen from numerous sources and media, arranged and printed, and then bound into a book. Such a "confection," or an "assembly of many visual events," as Tufte would say, enlivens the book's information by envisioning what the author's text argues through the presentation of visual comparisons.[38] The mixture of images and the density of their compilation into book form conveys the complexity appropriate to an understanding of the Las Vegas Strip, but the book itself is not cluttered or confused. Indeed, despite the author's displeasure with the results, Cooper's design followed Venturi, Scott Brown, and Izenour's mandate to "find the system behind the flamboyance."

Learning from Las Vegas grants its reader a related view with a sequence of visual comparison charts that correlate individual building components with building types and sites. Distributed throughout the book, these charts are comparable to what Tufte refers to as "small multiples"—a design structure that is repeated for all images.[39] For example, the reader can compare casinos like the Sahara to the Riviera from a panorama, from the front, from the side, from parts, from the entrance, and from parking. In contrast to Cooper's visually active page spreads, the charts produced during the Yale seminar are constants that effectively boil down data into a coherent picture of Las Vegas. "The aim here," the authors explain, "is for designers to derive an understanding of this new pattern."[40] For the reader, then, a comprehensive pattern of Las Vegas is further enhanced by *Learning from Las Vegas*'s use of small multiples, a graphic system that enhances his or her visual reasoning. Indeed, charts in *Learning from Las Vegas* introduce a complementary visual informational structure—through comparison and selection—to the broader thematic complexity of the city of Las Vegas.

The apprehension of the city's patterns stems from perpetual comparisons of data maps: aerial photos of the upper strip; photos of undeveloped land; maps of asphalt; charts of autos, buildings, ceremonial space; Nolli's Las Vegas; charts of the intensity of communication by building type; their commercial use; churches; food stores; wedding chapels; and auto rentals. The authors compiled information that reflected economics, land use, activities on and around the Strip, movement (auto, mass transit, and pedestrian), volume and flow of traffic, and both business and recreation. This information was made manifest in maps of "comparative activity patterns," of "undeveloped land," of "ceremonial space," of "Strip messages" (at two scales), and of "illumination levels on the Strip." Cooper arranged strip message maps and the illumination levels map across a single spread. A large-scale "detail" map of the Strip with messages cuts across the upper halves of both pages, and a smaller-scale, though more expansive, map of the same information is directly below. Both message maps are followed by an even smaller-scale illumination-level map. The movement between scale and detail and between messages and illuminations creates an imagined view of the Strip based on empirical data. Although no one experiences Las Vegas from this perspective, such an information configuration elicits a series of "micro-readings" whereby the fine texture of the image—a sharpened resolution based on scale differentials—engenders a personalized experience related to everyday perception.[41] Here the reader locates areas of activity, a process that is further effected by the aggregate data displayed in each map and by the manner in which words overlap across the street map to exemplify messages enmeshed in the fabric of the city. Rather than obscuring the Strip with a convoluted method of display, this multilayered image aids the reader in imagining the complexity of the Strip.[42]

Cooper's design augments an unconventional use of conventional data displays like maps and charts with a dynamic approach to the use of photographs. Aerial photographs are extended by Ruscha-type elevation views of the Strip and *The View from the Road*-type cinematic reproductions. Drawing on lessons learned from *The View from the Road*, Venturi, Scott Brown, and Izenour were attentive to the Strip and the ability of its messages to control flow, direction, and speed.[43] Cooper's page layouts accentuate the velocity of flowing information. In these sequences, the camera and the car move steadily forward. As both camera and car move, a tension builds, growing in direct relation to the reduced cinematic field. The spatial narrative—animated, continuous, and flowing—foils the tradition of architectural montage, in which the sense of the city is created through juxtaposition and intervention.

There is a particular sequence of photographs in Cooper's expert layout, however, that produces a close approximation of an experience of the Strip (Figure 2.2). An admixture of color and black-and-white photographs, varying in size, creates a beguiling overview of the Las Vegas Strip. The photographs are not organized to convey a singular narrative through approximate movement. Rather, the photographs are ordered in such a way that they showcase the city and its patterns of activities. Swirling through the city from the air and from on the street, the reader's imagination is activated in kind. For the reader, size, color, and arrangement conspire to display the texture and detail of Las Vegas. The quickened and slowed pace of the composition and the condensed and expanded views of the photographs combine to transfigure *Learning from Las Vegas* into personalized and intimate "micro-readings" analogous to the diversity of everyday perceptions.

The nagging problem of translation, transferal, transformation, and the challenges of escaping the flatland still remain embedded in *Learning from Las Vegas*. There are moments when Cooper's layout does not quite live up to its program of envisioning Las Vegas. In a general sense, "Part II: Ugly and Ordinary Architecture, or the Decorated Shed" flattens out, and while the textual content certainly makes its challenging points, this portion of the book lacks the graphic boldness of the first part. More particularly, there are instances where the authors, as if the gravitational pull of doubt were pulling them toward the flatland, resort to loosely drawn arrows to signify (rather than embody) physical changes on the Strip and to direct the reader to significant points. These moments of pointing underscore Venturi, Scott Brown, and Izenour's ambivalence toward Cooper's design.

Figure 2.2. Spread from Venturi, Scott Brown, and Izenour, *Learning from Las Vegas*, 30–31. Muriel Cooper, Designer. Copyright 1972, Massachusetts Institute of Technology.

Like Lynch and the pop artists, Venturi, Scott Brown, and Izenour wanted to *image* the city. In one sense, the photographs, filmstrips, maps, charts, and other images that inhabit *Learning from Las Vegas* are, on their own, thought to be objective, automatic, and void of creative mediation. In this respect, *Learning from Las Vegas* evokes early modern atlases, which were, as Dalston and Galison remark, "manifestoes for the new brand of scientific objectivity," or "noninterventionalist," or "mechanical objectivity."[44] The idea of mechanical objectivity was antithetical to the subjectivity of the idiosyncratic and intimate, combating the subjectivity inherent to scientific and aesthetic judgments. Indeed, Venturi, Scott Brown, and Izenour intended such an objectivity with their initial notion of a deadpan use of new technologies to mediate between the city and the experience of the city in *Learning from Las Vegas*. Considering the content of the book and Scott Brown's early writings, it seems odd that Scott Brown's notion of permissiveness, her idea that, like pop art, the conventional could be handled unconventionally, and her early insights into graphic means to produce synoptic views of urban dynamics were at odds with Cooper's handling of the design problem inherent to envisioning Las Vegas. In fact, it now would seem reasonable to suggest that for both Scott Brown and for Cooper objectivity was second to the evocative force of subjective judgment. And it is no less reasonable to conclude that Scott Brown's prescriptive "learning to like" is more in keeping with the kind of training crucial to subjective judgment. Hence, it is Cooper's design of the first edition of *Learning from Las Vegas* that engenders in the reader's imagination by regenerating the heat of perceptual experience. Indeed, a critical component of the first edition of *Learning from Las Vegas* is how it builds its information density—its full array of data—by letting the reader form his or her own juxtapositions and mental palimpsests. In Cooper's hands, the graphic elegance and the spirited simplicity of the book engage the internal complexity of the mind, thereby exciting aesthetic pleasures. Las Vegas envisioned by *Learning from Las Vegas* through image variety and graphic juxtapositions means transgressing the limits of standardized grids, both in terms of the book and in terms of the city; it means opening a space for enjoyment; it means "trying to like what one does not like"; it means learning.

Learning Curve

There is always, however, a learning curve. Unfortunately, Las Vegas envisioned by the layout of *Learning from Las Vegas* only applies to the 1972 edition of the book. In 1977, MIT Press published Scott Brown's redesigned and revised edition of the book. It is my contention that the revised edition's greatly reduced format, its deletion of many graphic devices, and its pedestrian typographic layout handicapped Venturi, Scott Brown, and Izenour's joint effort to envision the Las Vegas Strip within the pages of Learning from Las Vegas. Nevertheless, as debilitating as the alterations to size, image content, and layout may have been, the existence of the revised edition underscores the visual potency of the first edition—the manner in which it mobilizes all manner of visual devices to inform its audience. While it is very difficult to measure whether or not all readers experience the first edition of Learning from Las Vegas in similar ways, it is fair to say that an experience of the first edition is distinct from an experience of the revised edition. The latter experience pales in comparison.

The alterations were made, according to "The Preface to the Revised Edition," because students complained about the first edition's price. Originally, the first edition cost twenty-five dollars, and the price quickly rose to seventy-five dollars.[45] No doubt, the larger format and four-color printing made for an expensive book. Given the authors' pedagogic intentions, it seems prudent that they would make adjustments to lower production costs so as to increase the books distribution among students of architecture. After all, a cost-prohibitive book was contrary to the populist intent of Learning from Las Vegas. Cost, however, was not the only determinant in Scott Brown's redesign. It was also the case that the authors were displeased with Cooper's design, a circumstance that they felt was imposed on them by the publisher. Scott Brown thus reformatted the book first to reduce its cost thereby making it available to students of architecture and urban planning and second to give it the scholarly aura that she and her colleagues had originally intended for Learning from Las Vegas.

Nevertheless, in an ironic twist, the compromises made in modifying the first edition of Learning from Las Vegas demonstrate the problematics of giving people what they want. By acquiescing to the gripes of architecture students and to their rigid view of how the material first produced in the studio should be reproduced, Venturi, Scott Brown, and Izenour effectively foiled their initial goal. On an experiential level, less can be learned from the 1977 edition than can be learned from the 1972 edition. To read from the former is to read from a markedly different book, a book that is far less ambitious in its ability to envision Las Vegas as "an object lesson in complex relationships."

Notes

1. The preface to the first edition explains in some detail the structure of the seminar. Robert Venturi, Denise Scott Brown, and Steven Izenour, *Learning from Las Vegas* (Cambridge, Mass.: MIT Press, 1972), xi.

2. Denise Scott Brown, telephone interview with the author, January 26, 2003.

3. Venturi, Scott Brown, and Izenour, *Learning from Las Vegas*, 15.

4. Peter Galison and Lorainne Daston, "The Image of Objectivity," *Representations* 40 (Autumn 1992): 81–128.

5. Peter Galison, "Judgment Against Objectivity," in *Picturing Science Producing Art*, ed. C. A. Jones and P. Galison with A. Slaton (New York: Routledge, 1998), 347.

6. Edward R. Tufte, *Envisioning Information* (Chesire, Conn.: Graphic Press, 1990), 2.

7. Frederic Jameson, *Postmodernism Or, The Cultural Logic of Late Capitalism* (Durham: Duke University Press, 1991), 2.

8. Kevin Lynch, *The Image of the City* (Cambridge, Mass.: MIT Press, 1960), 2. It seems to me that the study of mental imagery is a rather difficult task that belies something of the metaphysics of Lynch's project.

9. Ibid., 92.

10. Denise Scott Brown, "Mapping the City: Symbols and Systems," *Landscape* 17, no. 3 (Spring 1968): 22. See also Richard Saul Wurman and Joseph R. Passonneau *Urban Atlas: 20 American Cities: A Communication Study Notating Selected Urban Data at a Scale of 1:48,000* (Cambridge, Mass.: MIT Press, 1966).

11. Ibid., 23.

12. Anton Ehrenzweig, "The Pictorial Space of Bridget Riley," *Art International* 9, no. 1 (February 1965): 21.

13. Scott Brown, "Mapping the City," 24.

14. Ibid.

15. Ibid.

16. Donald Appleyard, Kevin Lynch, and John R. Myer, *The View from the Road* (Cambridge, Mass.: MIT Press, 1964), 34.

17. Ibid., 62.

18. Denise Scott Brown and Robert Venturi, "A Significance for A&P Parking Lots, or Learning from Las Vegas," *Architectural Forum*, March 1968, 37.

19. Denise Scott Brown, "On Pop Art, Permissiveness, and Planning," *Journal of the American Institute of Planners*, May 1969, 185.

20. Ibid., 186.

21. Denise Scott Brown, "Learning from Pop," *Casabella*, December 1971, 16.

22. Ibid., 17.

23. Kenneth Frampton, "America 1960–1970: Noted on Urban Images and Theory," *Casabella* 36 (December 1971): 36.

24. Scott Brown, "On Pop Art," 185. While attending the University of Pennsylvania in the late 1950s, Scott Brown studied with the sociologist Herbert Gans. See especially Herbert J. Gans, *The Levittowners: Ways of Life and Politics in a New Suburban Community* (New York: Pantheon Books, 1967).

25. Denise Scott Brown, "Pop Off: Reply to Kenneth Frampton," *Casabella*, December 1971, 41.

26. Ibid., 43.

27. Scott Brown, "On Pop Art," 185.

28. Ibid.

29. Quoted in Donald Canty, "Urban Renewal in America, 1950–1970: A Symposium," *Design Quarterly* 85 (1971): 26. Much like Frampton, Temko was especially derisive in his view of a kind of sentimentality and a conspicuous lack of sincerity in a knee-jerk-bleeding-heart-liberalism that assumed to give the "people" what they wanted.

30. Quoted in Lynn Gilbert and Gaylen Moore, *Particular Passions: Talks with Women Who Have Shaped Our Times* (New York: C. N. Potter, 1981), 310.

31. Tom Wolfe, *The Kandy-Kolored Tangerine-Flake Streamline Baby* (New York: Farrar, Straus, Giroux, 1965), 5.

32. On the inherent experiential plight of street maps, see Marc Treib, "Mapping Experience," *Design Quarterly* 115 (1980): 8.

33. Venturi, Scott Brown, and Izenour, *Learning from Las Vegas*, 15.

34. Ibid.

35. Ibid., 4.

36. Ibid.

37. For a detailed account of the relationship and design conflicts between the first and revised editions, see Aron Vinegar, "Chp. 5: Reducks, 1972, 1977," *I AM A MONUMENT: On Learning from Las Vegas* (Cambridge, Mass: The MIT Press, 2008), 111–71.

38. Edward R. Tufte, *Visual Explanations: Images and Quantities, Evidence and Narrative* (Chesire, Conn.: Graphic, 1997), 121.

39. Tufte, *Visual Explanations*, 28.

40. Venturi, Scott Brown, and Izenour, *Learning from Las Vegas*, 17.

41. Tufte, *Visual Explanations*, 37–38.

42. The ground rules were set earlier in Venturi's *Complexity and Contradiction in Architecture*, published in 1965 as the first in a series of the Museum of Modern Art Papers on Architecture. When Robert Venturi began to write *Complexity and Contradiction in Architecture* in 1962, modernism in architecture, as in many things related to art and design, counted as everything. The prevailing position was, according to Venturi, to idealize "the primitive and elementary at the expense of the diverse and the sophisticated." Knocking Ludwig Mies van der Rohe's much-quoted axiom, Venturi wrote, "The doctrine 'less is more' bemoans complexity and justifies exclusion for expressive purposes." The alternative was, for Venturi, inclusion for expressive purposes. He went on to state that "aesthetic simplicity which is a satisfaction to the mind derives, when valid and profound, from inner complexity." See Robert Venturi, *Complexity and Contradiction in Architecture* (New York: Museum of Modern Art, 1965), 16–17.

43. Venturi, Scott Brown, and Izenour, *Learning from Las Vegas*, 9.

44. Galison and Daston, "The Image of Objectivity," 81–82.

45. Denise Scott Brown, telephone interview with the author, January 26, 2003.

3

Photorealism, Kitsch, and Venturi

JEAN-CLAUDE LEBENSZTEJN • TRANSLATED BY VIVIAN REHBERG

To write, beneath the title
                    Photorealism, Kitsch and "Venturi"
a history of taste: not of its variations, but
rather of its trace-leaving vanishing, from
aesthetic feeling to its anaesthetized signs—

                                        a history, therefore, of distaste

                absence of taste, literally: here one was eating,
                or just about, shit made out of plastic: "Water,
                Vegetable Fat, Corn Syrup Solids, Sodium Case-
                inate, Mono and Di-glycerides, Sodium Citrate,
                Salt, Di-potassium, Phosphate, Carrageenin,
                Artificial Color and Flavor"[1]

(In all earlier dietary systems, flavor was considered to be an emanation of food, as indissociable from its substance as a sound can be from the violin that emits it. From then on, in the semblance of synthesized sounds, food was broken down into ingredients that could be artificially reconstituted, including flavor [and color], added as surplus, as the last and next to last components, the nonessentials required by your palates, still smitten with nature.

You had surely noticed they never told you what the flavor and color were made out of. Everything had a name, except those two ingredients: the inexpressible share? Yet, in that other product of substitution, *Soft Diet Blue Bonnet Imitation Margarine* [no era of deprivation would have dreamed of this ersatz of ersatz], the constituent ingredient of color and taste [which was the same] was clearly indicated: "Water, partially Hydrogenated Soy and Cottonseed Oils, Salt, Vegetable Monoglycerides and Lecithin, Potassium Sorbate, Sodium Benzoate [0.1 percent] and Calcium Disodium EDTA as preservatives, **Artificially flavored and colored (Carotene)**, Vitamins A and C added."[2])

(The history of (dis)taste began at a restaurant: Charlottesville, VA, around Christmas, 1974).

and chuckling from the fine-palated Frenchman—mustache, accordingly, pitying or ironic, not wanting to know that his tricolored plastic gastronomic shit contained, in somewhat local variations, the same disgusting things, minus their total acknowledgment on the plastic of the container

for disgust had ceased to be the intolerable coming back up via the shortest channel: everything was tolerable—that was the intolerable

history was being lived in the imperfect: anaesthetizing drugs, copiously distributed through the most diverse channels

televised insinuations, advertisements, s w e e t r o c k, department stores, Muzak, miniature artificial paradises, Jesus Freaks, Guru Freaks, plastic artifacts imitating the good old days—

proclaimed injunctions, subliminal or implicit, "Smile, you'll be happy"—

injected without your knowledge (since you were no longer feeling anything anyway), prevented you from sensing the evil, having destroyed pain and pleasure

the economy in question had left some pockets of enjoyment alive, but had lulled or killed the nerve that made enjoyment from them possible

replaced by their simulacra

triumph of the conspiracy—triumphant at being spontaneous: taste was obsolete, but they had put its signs in its place, supreme kitsch

—or their absence: impression left by this "mother and son" couple, then by this quartet of monsters that followed at the neighboring table in the restaurant

a burger joint expertly named Humpty-Dumpty

who seemed to be the unjustified victims of horrors, of mythic misfortunes, and seemed to bear, crushed

stooped bodies, hanging heads, drooping lips

the weight of these huge aches as if they felt nothing

; rather, a loss of taste, like at the dentist's, an immobilization of the mouth

taste drain

*

And so the photorealists tastelessly painted a tasteless world: mediocre sites, scrapped cars, nondescript individuals,

"I prefer the people to be not too 'interesting.'"[3]　　　　"I try not to pick interesting people"[4]

burger joints. They themselves could judge this world: love it, hate it, or both at the same time

"So I look at these things and I think, wow, that really looks terrific and it's subject matter that's never been dealt with before."[5]

"I think I would tear down most of the places I paint."[6]

"I love it and I hate it."[7]

; but the works were not letting anything of these appraisals show through. The same calm and blank gaze seemed to settle on all things and strike the spectator with lethargy in turn

"I don't enjoy looking at the things I paint, so why should you enjoy it?"[8]

Yet, these words caught your eye: "But in calmly painting the commonplace horror that grew denser with each step, come what may, photorealism gave off a violence more intense than any accusation: from *Candide* to Andy Warhol's *Accidents*, the resolution to evade judgment had proven itself, and it was enough for Richard McLean to show in the décor of a countryside under cellophane:

> by focusing on images of the urban environment Pop Art left the illusion of nature intact; photorealism spared nothing

, an elegant horse mounted and held by a pair of humans so devoid of grace that they provoked vague discomfort

> but the photographic source of these paintings, an American equestrian magazine, confirmed that it was not exaggerating, and the complacent pose

, so that you could, if you were so inclined, read in this highly neutral image, the Swiftian apologue of the Houyhnhnms and the Yahoos.

> "And if such spectacles, which in real life had ceased to move you, turned explosive in paintings and sculptures, it was because you had become accustomed to seeing artistic space as the final refuge in which to console yourself from the mediocre aggression of the outside world. Isolated and displaced in the purified setting of the art gallery, Duane Hanson's horrifying figures regained a violence that their frequent occurrence elsewhere had caused them to lose."

(Exceptionally, Hanson accepted the critical repercussions produced by his meticulous

> "New realist painting reflects everyday life. . . . But it is not like Pop Art, it is more reserved; it takes on the world with no comment. For me, this wasn't enough. I wanted to comment, and I have been reproached for trying to shock. As for me, I need to identify with lost causes,[9] with revolutions, etc. I am not satisfied with the world."[10]

illusions.)

*

Most reactions to photorealism are (for now, especially in France) dictated by taste—and therefore inadequate:

> "When one likes it, it is generally for the wrong reasons, and when one detests it, it is the same case."[11]

either by disgust from the right

> "Disgusting!"

or from the "left," aestheticizing or politicizing, but above all, moralizing, even when its judg-

> "Mediocratization."   "Censuring Cézanne."

> "Nixon's silent majority has found the art it deserves."

ment is not unsound

"Reflecting/prefiguring/propagating the neo-fascism of the technocratic age."[12]

or from a taste for revenge and consolation on the part of those who could never truly stand

> "The photorealists—the painters Morley, Estes, Eddy, Cottingham, Betchle [sic], Close, the sculptors Hanson and De Andrea—are expensive ($40,000–$120,000), but they are safe bets, according to the arts page of today's *Wall Street Journal*; while the scenes depicted are resolutely modern, the technique is traditional and one senses a return to the values of the métier."

Malevich and Newman, abstraction, art questioning art, the absence of guarantees, and the tiring gymnastics that one had to go through when one sought taste in contemporary art. Photorealism: a wholly restful modernism and the complacent prey of the ultimately brazen reaction.

Corroborating symptom: the revival (books, studies, "documentaries," exhibitions-rehabilitations) of Mac-Mahonian art against which heroic modernity had had to ardently struggle,

nuanced now with delicate irony under the salt-and-pepper mustache, not without the obligatory foreplay,

"Tongue-in-cheek."   "Documentary Interest."   "Kitsch."

"Putting Impressionism back into historical perspective."

which hardly conceals that, at bottom, you have still not digested Seurat—

but honest folks, they go straight to the point, they declare frankly, through the guise of the guest book, that the painting in the Luxembourg—Cabanel, Jules Breton, Glaize—was well painted, unlike today, unlike those horrors by Miró (in truth, too often horrors) hanging across the way in the halls of the Grand Palais.

(Return of the return: already around 1920, art had suddenly contorted when faced with the limitless unknown opened up by abstraction, which was symbolized by Malevich's white spaces. But the artistic reaction of the interwar period was not simply a matter of course; it went hand in hand with political reaction, such that we cannot easily untangle the ties that bound them together.

Same tidal wave yesterday, same reflux today, and the analogy might sound alarms over turns of events in political struggles. The recent fashion for the fascist years is disturbing in this respect, even when it appears in the highly aestheticized light of the retro: for we knew from a reliable source that the aestheticization of politics is itself an effect of fascism.

(Quote Benjamin.[13])

*

In photorealism, as in "Venturi's" architecture, one can discern an offensive against avant-gardism turned into institution, but an offensive internal to avant-gardism, one which demands that art keep flushing itself out: one goes and another takes its place. At times, in a "Less is a bore" impatient-distorted echo of Mies's[14] "Less is more," one had the impression of a: make way so I can get in there, not so discreet but nice all told in the candor, twisted or

> "Malcolm Morley put it that 'he was looking for a house in which no one was living'. . . . Realism became a way of getting away . . . in the sense that you didn't feel the ground was already broken."[15]

not, of the confession. Rarely has the desire for symbolic murder and the seizing of power

> "Abstract painting was a reaction to realism, and realism is a reaction to abstraction. It goes back and forth."[16]

been made so clear. Even dialecticized or coiled, the grandfather law cruelly makes its cuts.

| "By and large, what I call the 'grandfather law' is at work here—that is, a generation, with deliberate disregard for the views and feelings of the generation of its fathers and direct teachers, skips back to the preceding period and takes up the very tendencies against which its fathers had so zealously struggled, albeit with a new sense."[17] | "A closer inspection certainly soon shows that art even here did not return to the point at which it once stood, but that only a spiral movement would meet the facts."[18] |

(Spared from "Venturi's" blade: the kindly father, Louis Kahn).

The photorealists seemed to have abandoned most of the questions that had preoccupied painting since Cézanne: of tradition, of perspective, of discourse, of representation, of figuration, of the frame, of drawing, of "painting," of art, of its status, of its space. They made clean, overpolished, framed easel paintings representing scenes recognizable down to the detail or sculptures you might have mistaken for their model. But the grandfather law does not go without saying, and the violence, the breadth, and the success of this counteroffensive provided fodder for thinking about the forces that make and break the avant-gardes today. Accompanying conceptual art, an exemplary phenomenon of rejection:

> "The museum concept is not infinitely expandable. . . . The Museum as a building which houses works of art and organizes exhibitions is simply not adjustable to certain kinds of art."[19]

What a confession: would the Museum finally admit its limits?

If photorealism had a taste, it was the taste of disillusion. It made you aware that the avant-garde of the sixties, the one that called things into question, believed that anything went, lived off of a utopia by refusing to recognize the sites that guaranteed its own occurrence, and silently whispered this deal: "I do everything to draw you into my hallowing purview, because it will not be said that there exists a kind of art I cannot admit. But do not take advantage, my space and my tolerance are not without limits."[20]

*

Photorealism's neutrality was made out of indifference and ambivalence at the same time: neither A nor B and A and B. Taste, distaste, taste-drain.

"When Andy Warhol looks at a can of Campbell's soup, I don't know whether he likes it or hates it. I am not even sure that he knows himself. This ambivalence creates a tension. The same thing is true for our antenna up there. Is it love or is it hate? It's a little of the both of them."[21]

Television, canned soup, all kinds of canned things, hamburgers and their temples, vulgarity and stupidity reigned and repulsed; in a nutshell, fascinated, the meticulousness with which photorealism detailed the arsenal of mediocrity was the clearest indication of this fascination.

Ambivalence ricocheted back and forth. Oddly, the photorealists' works, like the world they reproduced, attracted and disgusted and neutralized taste and distaste. An ambivalence of effects, but also of causes, and if one loved and hated photorealism, it was not for "bad reasons" only, but for reasons simultaneously good and bad (or rather, all reasons of taste and distaste were simultaneously good and bad, but not equally). It was reactionary and avant-garde, smug and ambitious, discreet and rowdy: contradiction itself.

The contradiction was not derived from or reducible to some unity that would resolve it. It constituted the very spirit and the newest trait of photorealism and of "Venturi." In this, both of them were opposed to the interwar aesthetic, which was dominated as much in its avant-garde aspect (Mondrian) as in its neoclassical aspect (Brémond, Valéry) by the principles of essentialization and purification. Mondrian's pure plastic art could allow for opposites (vertical/horizontal, color/absence of color), but their opposition had to be regulated, harmonized through the very purity of the opposition (even if the results extended beyond the principles and produced a tension between the finite and the infinite, the calculated and the improbable, the principle and the result).[22] Nowadays, the heterogeneous, the impure, the unresolved contradiction have become positive forces, accepted in the most diverse fields of aesthetics and knowledge. Therefore, as opposed to classical interpretations of art history, which attempted to reduce Leonardo's *Last Supper* to the inimitability of meaning, to a moment, to a point of view, Leo Steinberg proposed to show "how it appears in a climate which finally accepts pictorial symbols as multiple signs."[23] Counter to German Social Democrats of the late nineteenth century who "evidently believed that history advances *on the other side*, the 'good,' that ... of contradiction *reduced to its purest design* (the contradiction of Work and Capital)," Althusser, in his essay "Contradiction and Over-determination," insists upon the capital importance of the circumstances, exceptions, and specifics that can make or break a struggling revolutionary movement:

> "All of the important political and theoretical texts of Marx and Engels . . . offer us the subject of a first reflection on these so-called 'exceptions.' The fundamental idea emerges that *the Work-Capital contradiction is never simple, but that it is always specified by the concrete historical forms and circumstances in which it is practiced.*"[24]

In opposition to the architectural orthodoxy of the fifties (Mies, Johnson, Skidmore), "Venturi" defended the rights of complexity and contradiction in architecture:

> "I like elements which are hybrid rather than 'pure,' compromising rather than 'straightforward,' ambiguous rather than 'articulated,' perverse as well as impersonal, boring as well as 'interesting,' conventional rather than 'designed,' accommodating rather than excluding, redundant rather than simple, vestigial as well as innovating, inconsistent and equivocal rather than direct and clear."[25]

Thus photorealism: the greatest proximity between sign and object and the greatest distance. Spatial illusionism and absolute flatness. A decidedly reactionary style, erasing years of unrelenting artistic battles, and a general appearance—coldness, absence, no expressionism whatsoever, rejection of all figurative hierarchy—that was as characteristic of the avant-garde of the sixties as it was of Meissonier. If not more: for the properties of photorealism—no texture, no movement, no emotion, no life, especially no style—appeared to be an unexpected outcome of Reinhardt's[26] abstract dogmas, minus the abstraction,

painters playing the subject against art and art against the subject in turns.

"It seemed the only way you could get away from style and 'Art' was to paint things as they really looked."[27]

"I have no interest in the subject as such, satire, social commentary or anything which can be connected to the subject. I like the light of Corot. There is only Abstract Painting. . . . I accept the subject as a by-product of the surface."[28]

What good is the by-product, you asked; why not undertake this program in rigorously abstract terms, like Ad Reinhardt wanted; and what is this need to dress modern art up in the flashy rags of the past? Photorealism threw the question back at you: why give synthetic milk the appearance and taste of natural milk?

The sense of values revolted inside you. How can one of the most elevated faculties of the mind be compared to some roadside restaurant stench? Must art please everyone at all costs, and had not Malraux repeated time and again that art has a sacred essence, that it is irreducible to history, to the contingencies of consumption, to the circulation of merchandise?

Here, photorealism handed over one of the possible keys to its approach: art (even if its pricing does not follow the general rules of profit) is a form of merchandise like any other. By withdrawing its production from the circuits of capitalist production (linked to the need to dispose of its products without excessive delay), the avant-garde provided the latter with a supplement of soul it was lacking. Photorealism silently acknowledged that the latest stage of an increasingly ravenous capitalism left nothing intact, that the

> Fuseli, even on the eve of the Revolution:
>
> "149. Art among a religious race produces relics; among a military one, trophies; among a commercial one, articles of trade."[29]

witnesses for the defense who trumpeted the alibi supported, through their denial, the extent of its influence.

*

Marx remarks somewhere that periods of swift transformation are precisely those in which men hang fearfully onto their past. The past, one might add, can also take the form of nature in the frightened consciousness that experiences history as an uprooting, an accelerated distancing from the natural origin. Therefore, the second half of the eighteenth century reacts to the industrial revolution by a return to antiquity and a return to nature.

Now that the merging of businesses, with the help of their technological apparatus, was relentlessly transforming the places you frequented, your ways of life, your behaviors and thoughts, nostalgic denial made for one of the greatest themes of modern advertising and decoration. Crafts, ecology, and the exposed beam brightened the leisure hours of the young executive. Just like Mrs. Smith, washing machine X washed its secret with clear water. Yogurt Y (promoted by the doubly archaic picture of Vermeer's *Milkmaid*) was made out of whole milk, just like in the olden days, and you could admire this exacting use of grammar: the list of ingredients informed you in tiny letters that it, indeed, included "whole milk," but also powdered skimmed milk (strange battle around the milk). American televisions and refrigerators started to hide their advanced technology behind a rustic, mass-produced, exterior (called the Mediterranean style over there).

The mimicry of plastic substances went so far as to imitate the modern imitations of the past. That is how *Blue Bonnet* imitation margarine was served in little pots made out of flexible, imitation Arcopal-plastic decorated with neo-rococo designs, while the grandmotherly headdress, which served as its reassuring emblem, hugged the young face of an ideal housewife, whose features, hairstyle, and makeup instead suggested the aesthetic of family magazines dating from just a few years back.

The combined recourse to the past and to nature enhanced the desirability of a product that was benefiting its producers more than anyone else, for in the end the only justification for synthetic milk was that it costs less and keeps better. The added taste and color topped the chemistry and justification with nature.

Artifice imitated the effects of an altogether different organic process, like exposed beams made out of Styrofoam and painted chocolate brown that supported nothing but warmed up the concrete surface of the ceiling (an excess of artifice replacing nature's share). One of the most undeniable motivations of kitsch was this sort of imitation, sticking together and unsticking the past and future, nature and artifice, the organic and the synthetic, form and content.

*

Kitsch is not merely bad taste, but isolated, studied, aestheticized, collected bad taste: object of an ambiguous interest. It was in vain that Dorfles condemned it irrevocably in the name of taste: his book was above all a book of images intending to bewitch. The text, botched,[30] and the captions

> "An example of facile and grotesque reproduction: the effort to identify the inimitable blue of one of Cézanne's paintings with the blue of a sport shirt."[31]

were reminiscent of pornographic films with documentary pretensions, the accusatory commentaries of which played a part in the necessary rhetoric endorsing the voyeur's pleasure.

Dissociate, beforehand, the objects of kitsch and the sentiment of kitsch: "An object, a spectacle, are not kitsch in themselves, but are only so by virtue of gaze for which they were not, as a rule, destined." There was nothing kitsch about Louis Mariano for the public who paid dearly for the pleasure of admiring him at the Théâtre du Châtelet, nor probably for himself. Kitsch cannot be intentional, unless it changes its nature: then it becomes *camp* (Mae West). But the sense that endows a certain object with the quality of kitsch is not itself kitsch either. Rather, kitsch exists in the relationship of object to the sense.

The objects of kitsch are vulgar, so judges the sense of kitsch: schlock and the counterfeit copy falsifying the authenticity of what they imitate. They multiply the signs of quality they are utterly lacking: taste, culture, distinction. That is why the Mona Lisa is an inexhaustible source of kitsch, as is the Venetian palace rebuilt or transported to southern California. They can even (like the extraterrestrial invaders in the film *Invasion of the Body Snatchers* who take over human bodies while maintaining their human appearance) take the place of the object for which they provide the simulacra. Such was the fate of Saint-Paul-de-Vence, a real village in Provence transformed without a hitch into a fake Provençal village, or of Colonial Williamsburg, an authentic U.S. colonial town transformed into a Disneyland-style spectacle.

The sense of kitsch supposes wholly contradictory qualities. It apparently knows the norms of taste and the degree of admiration that is appropriate to allot to each

> "A kind of deviation or degeneration of what must be considered as the 'norm' of man's ethic and aesthetic attitude."[32]

"Can we put Orpheus and the Beatles in the same sphere? Moses and Hitler? Knights-errant and athletic heroes?"[33]

thing. Here we find the same old couplings determined by an everlasting hierarchy: original and copy, originary and derivative, truth and lie, full and empty, depth and surface: exterior that does or does not deceive about its interior.

The taste for kitsch does not overturn these values. The supercool connoisseur, appreciating kitsch, collecting its objects, secures a certificate of good taste and distinction. And humor. Like a sense of humor, the sense of kitsch knows how to distinguish between the serious and lighthearted, good and bad, the intended and unintended. The

"The empty incarnation of an inauthentic feeling."[34]

value of authenticity is the basis for all its criteria, even though it seemed to suspend this value."

*

Kitsch proceeded by degrees: third, nth, second at the very least. But the nth did not disregard the n-first, nor did the third the second, or the second the first. In other words, the connoisseur of kitsch liked the objects of kitsch through direct affinity, just like their naïve consumer; but he was ashamed of doing so. That is why the taste for kitsch occurred by preference among intellectuals or semi-intellectuals of petit-bourgeois origin, whose stints in high school or at college had provided access to legitimate culture. The second degree conveyed petit-bourgeois attachments and the effort to sever their ties at the same time—the conflict between familial culture and school culture that facilitated advancement.

The first scenes in *Female Trouble*, the film by John Waters (a child of Baltimore's middle class who spent time at college, then in petty crime, and finally making movies), crudely revealed how the petit-bourgeois sentiment of kitsch was taking root. The same went for those hideous housewives and the clean and sinister decors of the suburbs the photorealists tossed at you in abundance. And their polished technique

"I can identify with my subject matter: I like it and I hate it. There is a realization that my roots are there. It deals with a very middle-class lifestyle which I tried to get away from when I was younger. But eventually I had to admit to myself that that was who I was and, like it or not, had to deal with it."[35]

rendered the ideal of the middle-class aesthetic, which could only appreciate art when it was establishing itself on a surefire tradition and making itself visible through conscientious work with quantifiable and estimable results.[36]

But the photorealists' art was not the art of the middle class, which preferred to

"Open, in your home, a window onto 'something else.'"[37]

feed its imagination with whatever its décor lacked: undergrowth, exoticism, and nudity. And if it assumed its aesthetic values—tradition and polish—it was to put them at a distance. Middle-class taste found itself represented, as did its way of life. Photorealist style presented itself as the citation of a style that was not its own (since it did not have any): a draining of the subject and a draining of style. Even so, photorealism was pleasing, but in degrees, like kitsch: to the middle class it offered the reassuring image of its norms; to its elite bourgeoisie, their duplication, loaded with critical effects.

The duplicity was more clearly acknowledged with regard to "Venturi," whom two administrations accused, over the course of the same week, of being "insufficiently social" and "too political"[38] (in the official parlance, political is a negative epithet for the social). He fought alongside the population of South Street, a black ghetto in Philadelphia, against administrative authorities who wanted to run an expressway through it and to chase out the inhabitants; yet he agreed to compete for the *National Football Hall of Fame*, the ideological program of which (complacently cited in *Learning from Las Vegas*)

> "Honoring [football heroes] permits the reaffirmation, during a time [1967] of long hair, beards, and beatnik revolt on the campus, of the Foundation's conviction that football is the biggest and best classroom in the nation for teaching leadership." [39]

would make any self-respecting liberal architect shudder in horror yet had stirred "Venturi's" architectural verve.

Obviously, he was taking pleasure in rankling the American architectural institution, which vomited him up as the architect of the silent majority: proclaiming himself to be the "supporter of the rights of the middle-middle class to their own architectural aesthetics,"[40] wallowing pleasurably in kitsch,

> "In designing the building we have done our best to give it a grand and imposing look. Our first idea was to make a pure symbol out of it and to reproduce the Eiffel tower in the Mojave desert on a scale of seven-eights. . . . That would have given the city a world wide celebrity."[41]

offering as models of modern architecture shopping malls and residential suburbs, whose little houses with lawns mowed every Sunday represented, he asserted "the aspirations of nearly everyone: of ghetto dwellers just as of the white silent majority."[42]

(Indeed. "Venturi," so preoccupied with complexity and contradiction, seemed to have quite firm ideas about nearly everyone's aspirations. Supposing that were true, could one not imagine other reasons behind this taste: the absence of other models, the openness to media hype and the dominant ideology with regard to housing? Was it necessary to reaffirm, against "Venturi's" populism, that "mass" culture, which is disseminated through channels that do not belong to the people, is not a popular culture? A good portion of the masses vote for reactionary governments at the service of interests that frustrate and exploit them: does this mean that these masses are naturally inclined to reaction? To fascism? To racism? Do contradictions not exist within the groups that make up the middle classes? [Moreover, must one speak of *a* middle class?] Is there no distance between their desires and their needs? Is the taste for bad taste innate? If the middle classes and the fraction of workers who, more or less, share its tastes and its way of life, listen to Waldo de los Rios's fortieth symphony rather than to Mozart's, is it not because they feel excluded from the good taste and culture that has purchase on Mozart and are attempting to approximate them via this derisive means of access?)

*

"Consumer" society

> this formula, so complacently accepted, even by those who profess to fight against what it stands for, should be dismantled: it insinuates that the value that structures it is a use-value. This is not at all so. Capital aims at producing not goods of consumption but surplus-value, and its concern is disposing of the merchandise that serves to produce it (surplus-value). The term "consumer society" obeys the tactics and ideology of advertising: suggesting to the consumers that they want just what one wants to make them buy.

had the effect of transforming cities, lands, seas, and practically everything into a trash bin. As appreciation left behind great quantities of residue, the question of recycling arose. A necessity, in turn, made into profit: salvage and retrieval companies could transform waste and pollution into capital gain.

The sense of kitsch was a minor manifestation of this process of trashification and recuperation. It selected out from the mass of rubbish a certain number of objects that the second degree granted a second wind. Antique statuary, turned into a kitsch object at Caesars Palace in Las Vegas, acquired letters of cultural nobility thanks to "Venturi's" use of it. From Rome to Las Vegas and back again,

"Los Angeles will be our Rome, and Las Vegas our Florence."[43]

the cycle was closing. Perhaps you would see it take off again soon. The revolution of nostalgias sped up so swiftly (the thirties in 1970, the forties in 1973, the fifties in 1974) that it was not unlikely to see the seventies and retro, already abandoned in the trash bins of culture, come back into style several years later. A retro of retro, a kitsch of kitsch, risked occurring if history did not change its course.

But the sense of kitsch could only allow itself selective recuperation. It had to rummage through the flea market to find its true happiness and to set it up in a décor bearing the stamp of good taste. Isolation—sorting and displacement—brought about the metamorphosis: a simply hideous object in a 1930s middle-class interior increased in value in an antique dealer's during the seventies or in the culturalized pages of Dorfles's book.

Kitsch offered only a limited view of the recycling in progress. Everything had become liable for recuperation, and the exploitation of workers had learned how to profit from revolutionary bywords, or so-called ones—May 1968 recycled as "1975, woman is liberated. She wants to work," which a temping agency informed you ad nauseam (disguising its interest as information).

Photorealism staggered under the blow: it made visible a generalized kitsch, reproduced the integral recuperation. The trashified universe was restored bit by bit, the technique of

> "I am painting the world bit by bit by recycling garbage into art. Everything is useful, everything is a fit subject for art."[44]

disaggregation playing a double game: parodying academic squaring and, at the same time, representing scrapping and recycling. Morley's undertaking revealed that the most exalted products of Western culture had not escaped the dump. Raphael's *The School of Athens* or Vermeer's *Artist's Studio* had entered the factory and were served up anew in the form of gigantic postcards. And Morley's tableau vivant *The Last Painting of Vincent Van Gogh*

> a reproduction made by hand, very blotched, of the *Wheat Field with Crows*, set up on a false stand with a palette, a can of paint, a rag, and reproduction of a pistol of the era at its feet.

brought to mind a similar "kitsch" scene from Minnelli's film *Lust for Life*, reproduced in Dorfles's book.[45] But redemption came after the fall: art turned into rubbish, and the rubbish turned back into art. The cycle could start over again (Morley calling his mimic).

All this offered only the image of recuperation; the real trash was out of its reach. Before long, photorealism was just adding new objects. The architect was functioning elsewhere; "Venturi" proposed the most intelligent and most ambitious recycling of the trash-environment. Instead of lamenting the ugliness of the urban and suburban landscapes, car culture, and the misdeeds of capitalism, "Venturi" accepted those unavoidable

> "What did we learn in Las Vegas that could be of service to us on South Street? . . . That beauty could emerge from the existing fabric and that it was better to look for a latent order from the inside than to impose a facile order from the outside."[46]

facts as his base material. Just as well to confront them, to draw an order from this chaos—not an ideal one, but the only one possible:

> "In another reality, in a society which would have taken seriously the dwellings of the poor, no architect would have been able to affirm that it was necessary to maintain this zone rather than to construct new lodgings in it for it inhabitants. But such a choice didn't exist."[47]

The lesson to learn from the existing fabric, anarchic and without beauty, was manifold (*learning from*, key terminology in "Venturian" recycling). First, judgments made in the name of taste do not produce explanations of the taste for bad taste. And, anyway, who guaranteed you that your condemnation of current bad taste was worth more than the

> "Many people like suburban houses. This is the compelling reason for learning from Levittown."[48]

judgments borne during the classical age against medieval taste or popular taste? "Venturi's" analyses comparing the parking lot at Caesar's Palace to Saint Peter's square in Rome and its blue and gold mosaic to the tomb of Gallia Placida[49] confused humanist

> "The conventional shed of a high-rise Howard Johnson motel is more Ville Radieuse slab than palazzo, but the explicit symbolism of its virtually pedimented doorway, a rigid frame in heraldic orange enamel, matches the Classical pediment with feudal crest over the entrance of a patrician palazzo, if we grant the change in scale and the jump in context from urban piazza to Pop scrawl."[50]

values of taste and culture, undermining the certainties of the cultivated intellectual, of the kitsch specialist or modernist architect.

What did Las Vegas teach, exactly? Not merely a new monumentality,

> "Chapels without the nave."[51]

or new forms of enlargement,

> The sign of Caesar's Palace: "a freestanding, pedimented temple façade was extended laterally by one column with a statue on top—a feat never attempted, a problem never solved in the whole evolution of Classical architecture."[52]

but a new order of problems concerning architectural semiotics. Commercial architecture, which signified in a declarative way (the restaurant or the store had to announce itself effectively to the motorist approaching at a great speed), supplied two types of signs: the *decorated shed* (a nondescript building preceded by a more conspicuous sign meant to draw attention to it) and the *duck* (so named by "Venturi" for its paradigm: a restaurant shaped like a duck to indicate this fowl was served inside).[53] Now these models have a retrospective value. There are ducks and decorated sheds all throughout the history of architecture: the gothic cathedral is a duck in its floor plan (the symbolic Latin cross) and a decorated shed in its façade

> "Chartres is a duck (although it is a decorated shed as well), and the Palazzo Farnese is a decorated shed."[54]

, which is relatively independent from the main body of the building it draws attention to.

But does not modern architecture, contemporaneous with abstract art, distinguish itself precisely through its refusal to signify? Without a doubt; but it expresses. What? Architecturality, newness, monumentality, the factory style, which served as its model at the onset of the century. Refusing to denote its functions, it connotes values. Its signs, instead of being acknowledged and clearly circumscribed, are diffuse and shameful. And Rudolph's heroic buildings or megastructures are nothing in the final analysis but

"When modern architects righteously abandoned ornament of buildings, they unconsciously designed buildings that were ornament. In promoting Space and Articulation over symbolism and ornament, they distorted the whole building into a duck."[55]

"The Boston City Hall and its urban complex are the archetype of enlightened urban renewal.... It is too architectural. A conventional oft would accommodate a bureaucracy better, perhaps with a blinking sign on top saying I AM A MONUMENT."[56]

disguised ducks.

In opposition to the "heroic and original architecture" of the modernist tradition, "Venturi" drew one last lesson from average, "ugly and ordinary" architecture: specifically, the values of the ugly and the ordinary. And from these improbable models, "Venturi" drew an "ordinary" architecture—extraordinary in its mixture of aggressiveness and invisible elegance, of lightness and insolence (almost a game of Tinkertoys)—"an architecture of the 'second glance,'"[57] whose overlooked qualities recalled the mortifying experience, repeatedly recounted during the classical age, of the connoisseur who passed in front of Raphael's Vatican frescos without noticing them, because their perfections were such that they cancelled themselves out.

But the ordinary has limits, and "Venturi" himself found the lawn ("it isn't our work") of the fire station he built in Indiana "perhaps too ordinary."[58]

(A *too* loaded with avowals. One does not easily get rid of architecture, style, and taste in general. Is it not an overabundance of taste that allows "Venturi" to draw such gracious architecture out of bad taste; and is not his ordinariness as connoted a sign as Rudolph's heroicity and originality? If the patent architecturality of modern architecture is a disgraceful symbol, what can be said about "Venturi's" modest architecturality, hidden in its secret compartment? Recycled, the ugly and the ordinary become signs in turn: noble signs of ignoble signs of noble signs.)

Cultural recycling is nothing new. After expunging paganism, the Christian Middle Ages reused some of its tenacious myths (the hardy remnants of paganism were left to populate the sewer of Christian Hell), or some material debris was diverted from its original function (destroyed temple columns transformed into church columns).[59] Yet it was the religious ideology of antiquity, and not its aesthetic, that found itself tossed into history's scrapheap. Actual kitsch appeared to be linked to the industrial revolution: observe Lequeu's cowshed, Beckford's Fonthill, and the Royal Pavilion in Brighton. In 1773, the architect William Chambers, using terms that strangely echo "Venturi's" arguments, suggested, in the exotic voice of a fictional Chinaman, recycling the scenes of misery and of death that abounded at that time in the English countryside. It was not a question of embellishing this landscape, since industrial capitalism could only develop out of the ugliness and misery it sowed there at every turn. But the moors and the shacks, the gallows and the famished beasts, the "lugubrious and terrifying" traces left by the industrial revolution could be reconverted into spectacles of terror of the most sublime sort. Into a garden, hardly cheerful no doubt, which had the strength, the audacity, or recklessness to convert a misery of the most real and immediate kind into its own representation through the artifice of framing.

> "England abounds with commons and wilds, dreary, barren, and serving only to give an uncultivated appearance to the country, particularly near the metropolis: to beautify these tracts of land, is next to an impossibility; but they may easily be framed into scenes of terror, converted into noble pictures of the sublimest cast, and, by an artful contrast, serve to enforce the effect of gayer and more luxuriant prospects. On some of them are seen gibbets with wretches hanging *in terrorem* upon them; on others, forges, collieries, mines, coal tracts, brick or lime kilns, glass-works, and different objects of the horrid kind. What little vegetation they have is dismal; the animals that feed upon it, are half-famished to the artist hands; and the cottagers, with the huts in which they dwell, want no additional touches, to indicate their misery: a few uncouth straggling trees, some ruins, caverns, rocks, torrents, abandoned villages, in part consumed by fire. Solitary hermitages, and other familiar objects artfully introduced and blended with gloomy plantations would compleat the aspect of desolation and serve to fill the mind, where there was no possibility of gratifying the senses."[60]

> "Is not Main Street all right? Indeed, the commercial strip of a Route 66 almost all right?"[61]

Capitalism had learned the art of accommodating its leftovers. What it still had to learn was how to recuperate all of its scraps, without remainder.

However, a taboo object, withdrawn from the all-purpose recycling, remained: the cadaver. A holy horror presently sealed the dead in concrete, prohibiting decomposed human matter from blending with the earth, from entering into the composition of plants,

> as the Marquis de Sade requested in his will: do everything necessary so that I may be transformed into oaks.[62]

and from reforming, among others, the flesh of the living. "Venturi" made the California City Cemetery look like a country club.[63] Chambers was representing the violent death of criminals (converting it into its own spectacle, "of the sublimest cast"). "Venturi" disguised death, but displayed the disguise, recycling for its own sake the space where death had been kept out of recycling.

*

Figures of disaggregation, allotment of places and duties, "everything in its place"—

The ideological machine made its cuts; the fallen scraps remained: Blacks, Arabs, homosexuals, druggies, madmen, delinquents—all those who did not fit in with its views or bend to its values.

They were allowed to exist on the condition that they stood in their own shame, in the enclosures that had been arranged for them: asylums, prisons, residential homes, nightclubs. Freedom under watch, as long as they served capital gain, locked up if nonrecuperable. It was vital for the dominating class to maintain those cordoned-off spaces, to prevent them from communicating with each other and the whole of mankind it exploited or oppressed.

In its own way, avant-garde art was one of these ghettos. After having long excluded it, the official culture finally noticed that it would be more profitable to neutralize it while reserving a tiny institutional place for it. Winks at avant-garde, "research" broadcasts, a center for art and culture. The still "revolutionary" avant-garde figures were softening, however. They were willing to sleep with Holofernes, but they first cried that they were going to cut off his head, "to subvert from the inside"[64] the institutions they had just been named to lead.

In any case, over the past hundred years, what action could an artist take, if not a limited one? They could withdraw, produce with their sights on something better, keep repeating that "we are passing through a tunnel—*the times*,"[65]

but not without venting this regret: "The constellations shine initially: how I might wish that in the obscurity which assails the blind horde, as well as points of brightness, such a thought momentarily would be fixed, in spite of those sealed eyes not distinguishing them—for the fact, for exactitude, so that it be said."[66]

But during the flourishing years of the avant-garde (1910–30)—when this word had meaning—artists cherished the dream of enlightening the masses, of inserting art into

> "The whole triangle is moving slowly, almost invisibly forwards and upwards. Where the apex was today the second segment is tomorrow. . . . Every segment hungers consciously or, much more often, unconsciously for their corresponding spiritual food. This food is offered by the artists, and for this food the segment immediately below will tomorrow be stretching out eager hands."[67]

> "At a time when so much attention is paid to the collective, to the 'mass,' it is necessary to note that evaluation, ultimately, is never the expression of the mass. The mass remains behind yet urges the pioneers to creation. . . . One serves humanity by enlightening it. Those who do not see will rebel, they will try to understand, and will end by 'seeing.'"[68]

> "a task of urgent necessity—to avoid man becoming a slave to the machine, by protecting the mass production of the machinist anarchy and by returning life and meaning to him."[69]

their lives, of guiding them out of the tunnel. Dictatorships broke the dream. After the Nazi era, it became clearer than ever that avant-garde artists would not transform the environment and would not lead the masses to salvation. The social-democratic illusion of the Bauhaus had hoped to harmonize capital and work, erasing the class struggle through an act of philanthropy,

> "for it certainly is a question of philanthropy: ameliorating the quality of life for the masses through the mass production of *gestalted objects*, that is to say, solid, functional, inexpensive, and attractive."[70]

But the reality of this (the class struggle) signified its political failure (to be convinced of this, it sufficed to look at any everyday consumer artifact). After all, the owners of the means of production—who, to increase profit, did not retreat from layoffs, accelerations of pace, accidents in the workplace, pollution, and manufacturing defects, which were hushed up even when they endangered the life of the user—were not about to amuse themselves producing "solid, functional, inexpensive and attractive" objects to please the Bauhaus and raise the level of the masses.

The situation had backfired: instead of removing art from its walls to insert it into the ongoing production, they had created museums of decorative art in which quality products initially destined for use rather than contemplation came to be stranded. And while the Center for Industrial Creation was going strong in its designer offices, junk was flourishing even more than ever outside.

The more "art" there was in the museum, the less there was elsewhere. The architecture issued from the Bauhaus made nothing but splendidly isolated monuments to

> "The 'total' design in the style of the Bauhaus had to be accompanied by public and private social programs. This is not the case in America today, and the ideals of the Bauhaus, along with the existing great dreams of architectural urbanism, will function, as they did on South Street, to betray rather than to defend the social goals which gave them birth."[71]

the glory and good taste of big capital. And it had no desire to stop the trashification of the environment, one of its necessary and profitable effects. Proposing the simple development of the existing site was still too much to ask of it, and "Venturi" complained with hue and a cry about having no commissions.[72] Even though he was appropriately concerned about concessions and compromises, nobody wanted any of it, and he was doomed to the fate of all good architects: programming new cities, building a few buildings here and there, an oasis of elegance in the middle of a desert they could not manage to enhance but that nevertheless secured their ready-made place in the history of architecture.

"Venturi's" structures undoubtedly figured among the most interesting of their time; however, they were far from equivalent to his ambitions, and the glaring light he cast on the weakness of the architect within the game of forces at play was his most original contribution.

> "Ironic convention . . . recognizes the real condition of our architecture and its status in our culture. Industry promotes expensive industrial and electronic research but not architectural experiments, and the federal government diverts subsidies toward air transportation, communication and the vast enterprises of war or, as they call it, national security, rather than toward the forces of the direct enhancement of life. . . . Architects should accept this modest role, rather than disguise in what might be called an electronic expressionism. . . . The architect who would accept this role as combiner of significant old clichés—valid banalities—in new contexts as his condition within a society that directs its best efforts, its big money, and its elegant technologies elsewhere, can ironically express in this indirect way a true concern for society's inverted scale of values."[73]

In its own way, photorealism also asked about the effectiveness of art and especially of the avant-garde. Instead of abolishing the distance between artistic imagery and mass-cultural imagery, media technology had exaggerated it. Pop art presented itself as an attempt to build a bridge between the two types of imagery. But the commercial image (mass-produced and mass-consumed, ephemeral, industrial, anonymous) was simply imitated by the still individual, precious, elitist artistic image. What did a Warhol silk screen, an edition of two hundred sold at art prices, have in common with the million copies of the five-cent newspaper that served as its model? Warhol had surely succeeded in using his name to break through the walls behind which the avant-garde was still in circulation; despite this, they were not disrupted.

Photorealism proceeded differently. Somewhat like "Venturi," it located itself on the positions of the middle-class public excluded from avant-garde culture: mistrust of intellectualism, conformity, respect for artistic tradition. Beneath this exterior (not exactly a disguise), it placed within reach some of the sharpest biases of modern art.

> "The hope of understanding the public mind is not entirely ignoble. The wish to close the gap between the public vision and the artist's vision is a contemporary priority."[74]

However one might judge the tactic of compromise in art, this was a nonnegligible performance.

*

This duplicity hinged on the equivalence of the sign to its object or, rather, to its surface: Chuck Close's faces show not the interiority of a being, but the accidents of an epidermis, enlarged to the scale of a lunar landscape. The thin layer of paint sticks to the skin of the model. The gaps in representation are reduced to the minimum: the reviews of Waters's film *Pink Flamingos* insisted on the fact that during the shooting, the protagonist (a three-hundred-pound transvestite) had truly swallowed the dog turd we saw her eating on the screen.

It seems the signifier is in a bind and must reckon with the most old-fashioned conventions, worn to the point of transparency. The rhetorical arsenal of Waters's films (framing, editing, camera movements) is one that even commercial cinema has no use for anymore. And it is the moment when the kind of painting truly cherished by the middle class discovers the stylization and the virtues of the visible stroke that photorealism takes over the decried value of the copy and (with the exception of Morley) the polished technique Baudelaire condemned over 130 years ago.

Now the excessiveness of the reaction is anchored in the avant-garde. Against the dominant aesthetic ideology, which sees in art an imitative divergence, the expression of a creator, a supplement of soul added to the real—the modern ersatz of religion—the art of Jasper Johns, Warhol, Frank Stella, and Ed Ruscha acquired new energy from literality.

Photorealism, in contrast, effects a literal illusion. Morley's painting in particular produces the appearance of an illusion that it just as quickly short-circuits. Take his painting *Regatta*:[75]
A very enlarged (121 × 247 cm) representation of a personalized check with a few sailboats on water visible on it, framed, obliterated by all the (printed and handwritten) inscriptions that make up the check proper, including Morley's huge signature,

> signing the check and not the painting: another
> very different signature signs the latter

which is overlaid by the bank's red stamp
("Paid")

recalls a Jasper Johns with two secret compartments: the aquatic image obliterated by the check obliterated by the stamp,

all of it obliterated by the rage of painting that, through its very visible marks, annuls, while still maintaining, the group of signs and their erasures.

(The idea also recalls the fake check Duchamp sent to his dentist Tzanck in 1919 as payment for treatment: the entire avant-garde symbolically summoned under the guise of nostalgia.)

Literality denying art and style is still an effect of art, but of a modest art, wiping away most of the values it contains

"Although our buildings seem ordinary they are not at all ordinary, but rather, we hope, they are of a very elaborated architecture, very carefully designed from each square inch to the total proportions of the building."[76]

"Stylelessness is also a style, they forget that."[77]

that connote presence: personal style, transcendence, the creator, the name of the artist.

> "For some time, I have hoped to affirm that the name of 'Robert Venturi,' when it functions to describe a written or architectural production of the firm Venturi and Rausch . . . is unjust for those who have contributed their ideas and their creativity[78] to our staff. . . .
>
> "I find that the role of the cultural hero (even in its modern form of anticultural anti-hero) is a backward, romantic theme just as out-of-date today as is an 'original' and 'heroic' architecture. . . . Our firm has a better aspect as it is in reality: a group of strongly pronounced individualities, who share the same enthusiasm and work together, and not a pyramid with the Architect at the top."[79]

(It remains, despite Venturi's denial [and he alone signed this remark about the name], that the trade name "Venturi" still had a mythic value [thus the quotation marks]. It showed that one cannot so easily rid oneself of patronymic values and that the architect's production was, for better or for worse, caught in a hierarchical division of labor. A single protest is not enough to push away the insistent forces of economy and ideology).

*

During this time, the most critical peak of the avant-garde (for the metaphor of the spiritual triangle was still valid) was dreaming of a nonreligious art: escaping the values of taste and style, the sites that institutionalized art (museums, concert halls, universities, magazines), and the kinds of audiences selected by these sites. Now this art existed in its way, but you were not seeing it (so it was not art), so insipid, lukewarm, and imperceptible was its presence: it was MUZAK!, the sonorous monster that was gliding above you in Woolworth's, train stations and airports, office building elevators, and soon after in factories and cafeterias, in all places of work and leisure.

In the arts as in nature, rot is the laboratory of life. In the postromantic and expressionist dissolution of the tonal system resides the seed of Webern's music. In the sewer of Muzak resides the possibility of an ephemeral, anonymous art, without appropriation, without style, without disguised rituals, without presence, without place because it was in all places, without public because it was heard by all publics, without subject because the subject was broken up for want of a differential field suitable for constituting a subject.

Muzak surely lacked "quality," but more specifically, it lacked the strength to expose all this; for Muzak was functional, exploitative, anesthetic. It aimed at lubricating in order to ease the way, to get you to produce or to purchase more. Its strength, which could have been liberating, served to make you stupid.

Photorealism had some of Muzak's traits, plus the discreet implication of a critique at work. The limit was its own limit: it glided peacefully into artistic spaces without trying to break them down, without asking itself about the conditions of possession and dispossession of cultural goods.

*

Photorealist painters in the strict sense painted after photographs. This was not a new practice, and one could follow its evolution from Francis Bacon back to Delacroix. But the use they were making of it was distinctive.

The photo offered them several advantages. It facilitated the execution of the painting, no reticence in admitting it.

> "I usually use photographs. It's too difficult to paint from the object."[80]

It stabilized the moment and movement. It contained a series of messages that the eye could not perceive all at once (a window, the reflection on the window, and what one sees through it). It made it possible to "see reality in all of its awkwardness, and all of its randomness."[81] An instrument introduced from the sewer, it desensitized the painter to the object.

> "The trouble with painting from the object is that you might fall in love with some part of it."[82]

More specifically, it made the data (like the blur of peripheral vision) it was made out of,

> "I think we know what a blur looks like only because of photography. It really nailed down blur."[83]

but could not discern, perceptible. It introduced a tension between its modernity and the archaism of painting, folding one era of figurative technology down on top of the other. And another tension between the two dimensions of its site of production and the three it was representing. On the one hand, it accentuated the artificiality of the scene it reproduced and, on the other, the literality of painting. The flat image represented a flat image

> "We attempt to eliminate that difference [between what represents and what is represented] as much as possible and resort to the camera to do it."[84]

at the same time as the spectacle of which it was the image.

The literality of the photorealist painters, who were using the photograph, was thereby similar to that of sculptors, who were not using it. This was the case with Jasper Johns, who used painting only to represent flat objects—targets, flags—and sculpture only to represent objects in relief—beer cans, light bulbs; the two- or three-dimensional equivalence of representing and the represented was the rule. There could be interplay between the two and three dimensions, but only on the condition that it also existed in the represented object: *New York Foldout* by Morley[85]

> a huge painting (183 × 907 cm) laid out as a folding screen on the ground, and representing a series of postcards opening out representing scenes of New York

, preserved the double status of its model: a flat object in a deep space, images of deep spaces on flat surfaces.

In the works of most of the painters, the painting's referent was ambiguous: photo or reality? But some of them exposed double representation and lifted all doubt by

> "Let's say that I painted a man fishing. I wanted this picture to be read as the image of an image of a man fishing. This it doesn't have this activity as an object, but rather the imagistic activity which this subject allows to establish."[86]

integrating elements that could only belong to a photograph into their canvases. Morley, above all, scratched out representation, damaged it with all sorts of evidence: reproductions of the margins of the photo, of its back side folded over (the only case of true illusionism?), of the inscriptions that were added to it, juxtaposition of two different images, like a post card with two scenes. In his painting *Racetrack*[87]

> reproduction of an advertising photograph for a tourist agency, representing a racetrack in South Africa, surrounded by a large white margin and accompanied by an inscription

, two large strokes of paint obstructed the scene, the photo and the painting

> "The X was not part of the gridded design: it was added, affixed instantaneously, painted on plastic, reversed and pressed against the surface, it was printed over the painting like a monotype."[88]

, associating in a single refusal modern fascism and the naturalness of illusionistic art, as if the depoliticization of touristic gaze and the blindness to the signifier were, in middle-class representation, the effect of one and the same lack of sight.

(It should have been remarked in passing that all these artists did not comprise a school, a style of a system as homogenous as these and other lines seemed to imply. The ambiguities of photorealism were converted into different perspectives. Morley, with Hanson, distinguished himself through a decidedly political point of view; Estes, through the "magic of light"; Eddy because of a Greenbergian formalism ["the integrity of the picture plane"]; Close through his interest in the "the process of transmitting information."[89] Generally, while conserving the two terms of their ambivalence, the photorealists could expose either their academic side [like Bechtle and so many others] or their avant-garde side [like John Clem Clarke, Close, and especially Morley, who stood out for the ambition of his program touching upon the principles of representation].)

What's the point of this work?

The photorealists could have joined two reproductive techniques together by using photosensitive canvas, for example, like Warhol had. They did not do so, and mostly they did not even project the photograph onto the canvas. They were content to square it, to paint it bit by bit with a myopic eye. (Morley even painted upside down so the image would not interfere.) This nostalgic respect for the handmade and for laborious technique provided middle-class taste with proof of work well done, but it simultaneously accentuated the absurdity of the enterprise and the irony of bestowing such worthless

> "Using substances that cannot be manipulated or molded (sculptors Jed Nelson and Fumio Yoshimura), they build their work part by part—carving, grinding, and gluing with consummate skill—to make it look like a factory-made, mass-produced object stamped out on an assembly line."[90]

subjects with this luxury of details, of rigor, even of "true poetry."[91] Why take such pains to

> constant reference to Vermeer: literal with Morley, Clarke or George Deem,[92] omnipresent with Estes. But the worthlessness of the subject did not serve here to exalt the values of painting. Not in a noticeable way. Literality cut short all effects of overtaking or transfiguration.

reproduce something that, all things considered, a photo could reproduce better, or, as the public rumor asked, "if it looks so much like a photo, why paint it?"[93] Now this was the most unexpected function of photographic mediation: the paintings seen in the flesh, and not reproduced (supplement of representation) in the guise of the photo of a painting of a photo of something, gave the strange, incomprehensible, perhaps unjustifiable impression that painting came as an additive, like the taste of synthetic milk. To paraphrase Blanchot, painters found themselves in this increasingly comical situation of having nothing to paint, of having no means to paint it, and were constrained by an extreme need to keep painting it. Like the subject, painting was there for no reason, a useless extra whose role was to add nothing to nothing and to say it in silence.

Once representation had been pushed aside, what had prevented abstract painting from dissolving into nonart was the reinforced insistence of the principles of "presence" and of "inner need."

> "In every great serious work one sublime and calm expression resonates: 'Here I am!' Recognition or denigration vanish. Nothing else remains but the eternal sound of these words."[94]

Photorealist works, on the contrary, seemed to declare not only the superfluity of their presence but also the need for this superfluity and the superfluous, not of abstract art, but of the values of need and presence that formed its core and kept it alive. By refusing to accentuate the signs of art, photorealism cleared away a floating signifier detached from its own reasons for being there and, as if split in turn into two instances, a signified of the signifier (the *Here I am!* now pushed aside) expressing the pushing aside.

Or an insignifier.

Perhaps there would be someday, and in spite of itself, the most abstract art in the semiotic of the semiotics it had perhaps half-opened. The photorealist drain contributed its discrete share to the never-ending story of representation.

Notes

In reprinting this text we have tried to keep as close as possible to the original composition and layout while mindful of the challenges presented by changes of typeface and format for this publication. (Eds.)

1. These are the ingredients of the American brand of artificial powdered milk *Instantblend*. The author of these lines had not read William C. Seitz's article on photorealism ("The Real and the Artificial: Painting of the New Environment," *Art in America*, Nov.–Dec. 1972, 58–72) before writing. Seitz's article began by citing the composition of a similar artificial milk, which has a slightly different formula: "Corn Syrup Solids, Vegetable Fat, Sodium Caseinate Solids, Dipotassium Phosphate, Sodium Silico Aluminate, Polysorbate 60, Sorbitan Monosterate, Artificial Flavor and Color."

2. Highlighted in boldface type in the text.

3. Richard McLean in Linda Chase, Nancy Foote, and Ted McBurnett, "The Photo-Realists: 12 Interviews," special issue on photorealism, *Art In America*, Nov.–Dec. 1972, 83. Short extracts from these interviews appeared in French in *Opus international* 44–45 (on *Realisms*), June 1973, 38–47. It is regrettable that this series of interviews was not included in *Super Realism*, the critical anthology edited by Gregory Battcock (New York: E. P. Dutton & Co., 1975).

4. Duane Hanson, cited in Kirk Varnedoe, "Duane Hanson: Retrospective and Recent Work," *Arts Magazine*, January 1975, 67.

5. Ralph Goings in Chase, Foote, and McBurnett, "12 Interviews," 89.

6. Richard Estes, ibid., 80.

7. Robert Bechtle, ibid., 74.

8. Richard Estes, ibid., 80.

9. ("But let's wait until the end.")

10. Duane Hanson, in Duncan Pollock, "The Verist Sculptors: 2 Interviews," *Art in America*, Nov.–Dec. 1972, 99.

11. Don Eddy in Chase, Foote, and McBurnett, "12 Interviews," 81.

12. See Jean-Claude Lebensztejn's chapter, "Photorealism, Kitsch and Venturi," in this book,

13. Walter Benjamin, "The Work of Art in the Age of Its Technical Reproducibility: Second Version," in *Walter Benjamin Selected Writings*, vol. 3, 1935–38, eds. Howard Eiland and Michael W. Jennings (Cambridge, Mass.: Harvard University Press, 2002), 101–33; and "André Gide et ses nouveaux adversaries," in Walter Benjamin, *Poésie et revolution* (Paris: Denoël, 1971), 217–21.

14. Robert Venturi, *Complexity and Contradiction in Architecture* (New York: Museum of Modern Art, 1966), 16–17.

15. Robert Bechtle in Chase, Foote, and McBurnett, "12 Interviews," 73–74.

16. Richard Estes, ibid., 79.

17. Walter Friedlaender, *Mannerism & Anti-Mannerism in Italian Painting* (New York: Schocken Books, 1966), 54.

18. Heinrich Wölfflin, *Principles of Art History* (New York: Dover, n.d.), 234.

19. William Rubin (the effective curator of the Museum of Modern Art in New York, curator of exhibitions and author of texts on Frank Stella, Dada and Surrealism, etc.) in *Artforum*, October 1974, 53–54. One should read the entire interview from which these lines were taken; although it is clearly stated that "Mr. Rubin insists on emphasizing that his opinions do not necessarily constitute the official policy of the museum," one cannot help but draw a parallel with the reorganization of museums after the crises that shook the entire American museological institution in 1971 (strikes, authoritarian deinstallations, exclusions and resignations). And one should remind oneself that the board of trustees of the Museum of Modern Art (in a word, big capital investing art and investing in art), without even having to give orders to Mr. Rubin, might have had something to do with it.

20. A few examples: When invited by the Guggenheim in 1971, Daniel Buren exhibited two works, including a striped canvas measuring 20 meters by 10 meters, not on a wall, but in the center of the building, occupying the large column of air that had remained empty up until that point. It was removed upon the request of certain participants, who complained that the canvas made their work invisible ("intrusive-obtrusive drapery"). That same year in the same place, Hans Haacke planned to show a series of photographs taken of New York apartment buildings accompanied by text stating their location and financial transactions concerning them: it was suggested that this exhibition "could have discomfited

certain religious institutions which were implicated" as owners of slums and brothels. [Sam Hunter and John Jacobus, *American Art of the 20th Century* (Englewood Cliffs, N.J.: Prentice-Hall,1973), 452.] The exhibition was cancelled upon the request of the director, and one of the museum curators resigned. In 1974, Haacke was invited to participate in the exhibition *Projekt 74* (with the promising subtitle "Kunst bleibt Kunst" ["Art Remains Art"]), at the Wallraf-Richartz Museum in Cologne. He proposed to exhibit a painting by Manet in the Museum's collection accompanied by a panel presenting the social and economic status of each of the former owners of the painting and the prices they paid (see Carl R. Baldwin, "Haacke: *Refusé* in Cologne," *Art in America*, Nov.–Dec. 1974, 36). Unfortunately, the panel concerning the last purchaser, Hermann J. Abs (president of the Museum's Kuratorium, who had gathered the funds so that institution could acquire the painting and offer it to the Museum on the occasion of the first anniversary of Adenauer's death on April 18, 1968), stated that this person had occupied important financial positions during the Third Reich, then had spent time in prison before playing an active part in the economic miracle in postwar Germany. Haacke's project was refused. Several artists took down their works as a sign of protest. Buren added to his own contribution a photocopy of Haacke's panels as well as the inscription "art remains political." This addition was removed by the museum authorities.

What pushes the Museum to its limits to the point at which, losing its cool, it forbids artists from exhibiting and provides even greater publicity (for what other impact can an avant-garde exhibition have?) to the information it is trying to suppress? It is not only the content of the information or the damage it might cause

> there are still many former Nazis who want to give works of art to the museums, as the director of that museum specified in his letter to Hans Haacke: they should not be discouraged

it is the inadmissible fact that the information is provided within its walls. What the museum cannot tolerate is the laying bare of its inner workings: specifically, that the role of the
In a letter to Hans Haacke, Dr. Keller, director of the Wallraf-Richartz Museum, stated,

> "A museum knows nothing about economic power: it does, indeed, however, know something about intellectual and spiritual power." (Cited in C. Baldwin, "Haacke," 37).

Museum consists precisely in cutting art from other instances; sheltering it from the history raging outside. How could it accept that the price art pays for its pricelessness would be spread on its walls for all to see, along with the profitable operations that give rise to the circulation of its "treasures," the links between artistic institutions and big capital, and the reactions that are known to change with the wind?

21. Denise Scott Brown (Robert Venturi's wife and partner), in John W. Cook and Heinrich Klotz, *Questions aux architectes* (Brussels: Mardaga, 1974) (referring to the golden antenna—ornamental, not functional—that originally crowned Guild House, the senior citizens' home in Philadelphia built by Venturi and Rauch).

22. Meyer Schapiro, "On Some Problems of Semiotics of Visual Arts: Field and Vehicle in Image-Signs," *Semiotica* 1, no. 3 (1969): 223–42.

23. Leo Steinberg, "Leonardo's *Last Supper*," *The Art Quarterly* XXXVI, no. 4 (1973): 302.

24. Louis Althusser, *Pour Marx* (Paris: Maspéro, 1965), 97, 104.

25. Venturi, *Complexity and Contradiction*, 22.

26. Ad Reinhardt, "Twelve Rules for a New Academy," *Art News*, May 1957; partially reprinted in G. Battcock, ed., *The New Art*, rev. ed. (New York: Dutton, 1973), 167–70.

27. Robert Bechtle, in Chase, Foote, and McBurnett, "12 Interviews," 73.

28. Malcolm Morley, statement published in the catalogue of the IX Biennale de Sao Paulo, 1967, 89.

29. Heinrich Füssli, *Aphorisms*, in *The Life and Writings of Henry Fuseli*, ed. John Knowles (1788; repr. London 1831), 3:116.

30. The same remark held true for Udo Kultermann, *New Realism* (New York: New York Graphic Society, 1972).

31. Gillo Dorfles, *Kitsch* (London: Studio Vista, 1969), 177.

32. Ibid., 291.

33. Ibid., 41.

34. Ibid., 82. Dorfles finds Italian fascism kitschier than Nazism because it is less "authentic" (42).

35. Robert Bechtle, in Chase, Foote, and McBurnett, "12 Interviews," 74.

36. See Roland Barthes, "L'art vocal bourgeois," *Mythologies* (Paris: Seuil, 1955), 189–91; Charles Rosen and Henri Zerner, "L'antichambre du Louvre ou l'idéologie du fini," *Critique*, October 1974, 865–66.

37. Advertising leaflet for Alt reproductions on canvas or wood.

38. Robert Venturi, Denise Scott Brown, and Steven Izenour, *Learning from Las Vegas* (Cambridge, Mass.: MIT Press, 1972), 130.

39. Cited in Venturi, Scott Brown, and Izenour, *Learning from Las Vegas*, 116.

40. Ibid., 106.

41. Ibid., 186. This is the main building of the California City Civic Center. In the end, "Venturi" opted for a cube measuring 90 feet per side (in reference to Claude-Nicolas Ledoux's model).

42. Ibid., 107.

43. Ibid.

44. Malcolm Morley, in *Arts Magazine*, Summer 1972, 37

45. Compare Battcock, ed., *Super Realism* (the cover) or *Arts Magazine*, February 1973, 63, and Dorfles, *Kitsch* (English edition), 194.

46. Venturi, Scott Brown, and Izenour, *Learning from Las Vegas*, 130.

47. Ibid., 126.

48. Ibid., 106. Levittown is the "Venturian" paradigm of the middle-class residential suburb, which was fully built in several American states by Levitt & Son promoters, not by architects. Six years prior, Venturi's opinion of Levittown was much less favorable: "From such false coherence real cities will never grow." Venturi, *Complexity and Contradiction*, 59.

49. Venturi, Scott Brown, and Izenour, *Learning from Las Vegas*, 48.

50. Ibid., 77.

51. Ibid., 47.

52. Ibid., 75.

53. Ibid., 64.

54. Ibid.

55. Ibid., 109.

56. Ibid., 99.

57. Ibid., 112.

58. Ibid.

59. Voir Meyer Schapiro, "On the Aesthetic Attitude in Romanesque Art," in *Romanesque Art* (New York: Braziller, 1977), 1–27.

60. Sir William Chambers, *A Dissertation on Oriental Gardening (Second edition) with an Explanatory Discourse by Tan Chet-Qua of Quang-Chew-Fu* (London: Griffen, 1773), 130–31.

61. Venturi, *Complexity and Contradiction*, 102.

62. The "*Cinquièmement, enfin*," of the will and testament should be cited in its entirety. Failing that, it should be read and reread, in Gilbert Lely's "Vie de Marquis de Sade," in de Sade, *Œuvres complètes* (Paris: Cercle du Livre Précieux, 1966), 11, 631–32, or in André Breton's *l'Anthologie de l'humour noir* (Paris: Sagittaire, 1940). But, contrary to Breton, it is acceptable not to find any manifestation of humor in this paragraph of the will and testament (perhaps just a humor that undoes all of the oppositions on which humor functions): the insistent recurrence of wood (wooden coffin . . . wood seller . . . woods of my land . . . wooden thicket . . . the aforementioned wood . . . spread above the acorns . . . *hylé*, matter) gloriously quashes the "spirit" of men, which is worth little compared to the wooden thicket that could not give a damn about the fate of its memory.

63. Venturi, Scott Brown, and Izenour, *Learning from Las Vegas*, 187.

64. Pierre Boulez, interviewed by Jacques Lonchamp, *Le Monde*, January 10, 1974.

65. Stéphane Mallarmé, "L'action restreinte," in *Œuvres complètes* (Paris: Pléiade), 371.

66. Mallarmé, "Conflit," *Œuvres completes* (Paris: Pléiade), 359.

67. Wassily Kandinsky, *Concerning the Spiritual in Art*, trans. M. T. H. Sadler (New York: Dover, 1977), 6–7.

68. Piet Mondrian, "Plastic Art and Pure Plastic Art," *Circle*, rev. ed. (1937; repr. London: Faber & Faber, 1971), 44.

69. Walter Gropius, "My Conception of the Bauhaus Idea," in *Scope of Total Architecture* (1935; repr. New York: Collier Books, 1962), 20

70. Eric Michaud, "Le 'projet social' du Bauhaus. *Gestaltung*: la question du pouvoir," *Traverses*, 2 (November 1975): 86.

71. Venturi, Scott Brown, and Izenour, *Learning from Las Vegas*, 131.

72. See Cook and Klotz, *Questions aux architectes*, 422–23.

73. Venturi, *Complexity and Contradiction*, 51–52.

74. H. D. Raymond, "Beyond Freedom, Dignity and Ridicule," in *Super Realism*, ed. Battcock, 134.

75. Reproduced in the exhibition catalogue *Hyperréalistes américains*, Galerie des Quatre Mouvements, Paris, Oct.–Nov. 1972, 52–53. Kim Levin makes the comparison with Duchamp and also with Johns in "Malcolm Morley: Post-Style Illusionism," in *Super Realism*, ed. Battcock, 182.

76. Robert Venturi, in Cook and Klotz, *Questions aux architectes*, 423.

77. Duane Hanson, cited in Kirk Varnedoe, "Duane Hanson," 68.

78. Return (in his modern form) of the old artist.

79. Venturi, Scott Brown, and Izenour, *Learning from Las Vegas*, xii.

80. John Salt, in Chase, Foote, and McBurnett, "12 Interviews," 88.

81. Ralph Goings, ibid.

82. John Salt, ibid.

83. Chuck Close, ibid., 76. It should have been mentioned that the blur recorded by the camera does not obey the same rules as peripheral vision and that making the blur visible comprised a kind of fantastic abstraction, since the gaze cannot fix itself upon it.

84. Robert Bechtle, cited in Linda Chase, "Existential vs. Humanist Realism," in *Super Realism*, ed. Battcock, 85.

85. Reproduced in Battcock, ed., *Super Realism*, 45.

86. Richard McLean, in Chase, Foote, and McBurnett, "12 Interviews," 83.

87. Reproduced in Kultermann, *Hyperréalisme* (Paris: éditions du Chêne, 1972), pl. 124, and (cropped) in *Opus International* 44–45 (Fall 1973): 31.

88. Kim Levin, "Malcolm Morley," in *Super Realism*, ed. Battcock, 180.

89. Cindy Nemser, "An Interview with Chuck Close," *Artforum*, January 1970, 55.

90. Kim Levin, "The Ersatz Object," in *Super Realism*, ed. Battcock, 104.

91. Gerrit Henry, "The Real Thing," in *Super Realism*, ed. Battcock, 8 (about Estes).

92. See Kultermann, *Hyperréalisme*, pl. 73–75.

93. Cited in Linda Chase, "Existential vs. Humanist Realism," in *Super Realism*, ed. Battcock, 82.

94. Wassily Kandinsky, conclusion to *Du spirituel dans l'art* (Paris: éditions du Beaune, 1951), 103.

Theory as Ornament

KARSTEN HARRIES

Not long ago, I stumbled on the University of Nottingham's announcement of a program "designed to cater to the growing demand for courses that explore the potential contribution to the design process of an advanced theoretical input. As is evident in the work of several avant-garde architects, theoretical debates may often provide powerful design tools in the studio."[1] The announcement did not surprise me: for some time now, theory has come to play a significant part in advanced architectural design. And even if interest in theory may be waning just a bit as the winds of architectural fashion continue to shift, this is still a good time for architectural theory. Just consider the schools of architecture that have invested in theory and the architects who have explicitly embraced and contributed to theory in a sense that very much includes philosophy. References to Martin Heidegger and Jacques Derrida, Michel Foucault and Gilles Deleuze have become an expected part of architectural discourse.

As the University of Nottingham's announcement suggests, architecture theory today is not just theory about architecture; it has become part of architecture. The boom enjoyed by theory in today's architecture world is intimately connected with this blurring of the boundary that once separated the theory and the practice of architecture. Such blurring is a phenomenon that theorizing about architecture has to recognize, question, and try to understand if it is to do justice to the place and practice of architecture in today's world.

A philosopher may well find this development both pleasing and puzzling: how are we to understand the fact that just when philosophy would appear to be becoming ever more peripheral in our modern world,[2] architects are embracing it with a fervor never seen before? Think of such thought-provoking crossings of the gulf that normally separates philosophy and architecture as Peter Eisenman's and Bernard Tschumi's collaboration with Derrida on the one hand and Mark Wigley's *The Architecture of Deconstruction*[3] on the other! How are we to understand the place theory has come to occupy in avant-garde architecture?

This embrace of theory by architecture demands thoughtful consideration: What need does architecture have for theory? What sort of theory? The fact that today there should be such widespread interest in "architecture theory" is hardly self-explanatory. Chemists do not worry much about the question, "What is chemistry?" They seem to know what they are doing and why they are doing it. And can something similar not be said of all disciplines certain of their way? Artists, on the other hand, are very much preoccupied today with just what it is that they are doing, so much so that it has become impossible to establish a clear boundary that separates production of art from theorizing about art. Theory has become part of art. This fact calls for further theory. And has architecture not earned her place among her sister arts in this respect, too?

A historian would have to recognize the contribution made by *Learning from Las Vegas* to this development. There can be no question that it helped reorient the discussion of architecture away from traditional aesthetic concerns and toward issues of communication. To be sure, this assertion is put into question by the unequivocal affirmation by Robert Venturi and Denise Scott Brown in their 1992 statement, "Personal Approaches and Positions Toward Contemporary Architectural Practice," of an architecture defined in traditional Vitruvian terms as "firmness + commodity + delight," an architecture they here oppose to a currently fashionable "architecture derived from literary criticism, semiotics, philosophical theory, psychology, strange ideas about perception." In that programmatic statement, they support "theory as support for architecture," but oppose "theory as a substitute for architecture," support "architecture as the subject of theory," but oppose "architecture as the victim of theory." However, the thought-provoking remark on the present state of architecture that begins this 1992 statement would seem to recognize their contribution to a development they came to find questionable:

> One way to describe our view of where architecture is today is to simply observe that the "Gentle Manifesto" in *Complexity and Contradiction in Architecture* and the position expressed in *Learning from Las Vegas* have been embraced within mainstream architecture and theory in the last few years, but embraced in a way that is somewhat perverse and ignores warnings accompanying the original

messages—granted that authors and theoreticians of much architecture today would deny any influence, perverse or positive, derived from those sources or any parallel, ironic or otherwise, between their approach today and ours of the mid '60s and early '70s.[4]

That appropriations of both books should so often have been one-sided and "somewhat perverse" was indeed only to be expected, given their complexities and contradictions coupled with a striking rhetoric that invited simple slogans that seemed to speak to the needs of an architecture world that had come to find modernism wanting and struggled to address that want.

The "linguistic turn" in architecture and, more especially, architecture's embrace of theory are part of that struggle and demand to be understood as such. And pointers toward such an embrace could be found in both *Complexity and Contradiction in Architecture* and *Learning from Las Vegas*. In this chapter, I will explore some of these pointers, quite aware of the warning that such a focus is one-sided and fails to do justice to what mattered most to the authors and especially to their world-open, undogmatic pragmatism. Challenging an already shaken modernism, *Learning from Las Vegas* especially helped to recall architecture to the pleasures of decoration and to a more sympathetic and thoughtful engagement with the vernacular, with a visual language shaped by an enormous increase in physical and spiritual mobility and by a culture of ever noisier clamors for attention, not only promising both ever more freedom and a devaluation of the binding but also confining significance of place. That this twofold challenge has helped shape today's built environment is beyond doubt. Beyond doubt, too, is that such an increase in freedom is shadowed by disorientation and skepticism.[5]

But what interests me here is something else: the way the authors of *Learning from Las Vegas*—Robert Venturi, Denise Scott Brown, and Steven Izenour—challenging modernist preconceptions with their words and work, invited a still ongoing reconsideration of the relationship of building and words—and that includes but does not reduce to a reconsideration of the relationship between architecture and theory. That such a reconsideration did not always lead architecture and theory in directions they welcomed has become clear in retrospect.

The opposition voiced in 1992 to an architecture derived from literary criticism invites consideration of how such criticism once figured in and helped shape Venturi's own evolving reflections about architecture. Consider, for example, his boundary-crossing appropriation, in the Preface to *Complexity and Contradiction*, of T. S. Eliot's discussion of analysis and comparison as tools of literary criticism:

> These critical methods are valid for architecture, too: architecture is open to analysis like any other aspect of experience, and is made more vivid by comparisons. Analysis includes the breaking up of architecture into elements, a technique I

frequently use even though it is the opposite of integration, which is the final goal of art. However paradoxical it appears, and despite the suspicions of many Modern architects, such disintegration is a process present in all creation, and it is essential to understanding. Self-consciousness is necessarily a part of creation and criticism. Architects today are too educated to be either primitive or totally spontaneous, and architecture is too complex to be approached with carefully maintained ignorance.[6]

Quite in keeping with a long tradition going back at least to Aristotle's *Poetics*, Venturi, too, here declares integration the final goal of art. But if a work of art is to keep our interest, must not integration triumph over and therefore presuppose complexity and contradiction? With approval, Venturi thus cites the literary critic Cleanth Brooks, who in *The Well Wrought Urn* insisted, "If the poet . . . must perforce dramatize the oneness of experience, even though paying tribute to its diversity, then his use of paradox and ambiguity is seen as necessary. He is not simply trying to spice up, with a superficially exciting or mystifying rhetoric the old stale stockpot. . . . He is rather giving us an insight which preserves the unity of experience and which, at its higher and more serious levels, triumphs over the apparently contradictory and conflicting elements of experience by unifying them into a new pattern."[7] The difficulty is how to distinguish, confronted with particular examples, between "trying to spice up, with a superficially exciting or mystifying rhetoric the old stale stockpot" and "triumphing over the apparently contradictory and conflicting elements of experience by unifying them into a new pattern," how to distinguish between a superficial dressing up of what remains all too familiar and work that succeeds in creating something new and convincing, while addressing the real contradictions and conflicts that burden our experience.

Venturi has no difficulty demonstrating how readily the literary critic's problem is transferred from poetry to architecture, where mannerism and baroque offer especially striking examples. But how are we to identify today the conflicts that require resolution? As long as the nature of these conflicts remains ill defined, it will be impossible to draw a convincing distinction between a rhetorical spicing up of the same old stockpot and more genuine creation.

Venturi's rhetoric of analysis pulls the reader toward fragmentation and complexity. This rhetoric is given a special note by the way the boundaries that would seem to separate the creative artist from the critic, architecture from literature, are blurred here. Such blurring invites reflection: Does such blurring offer a strategy to escape the superficiality deplored by the critic? Or does it perhaps invite such superficiality? Or should the very distinction between genuine creation and superficial rhetoric be left behind, along with the modernist critique of the superficiality of ornament that the authors of *Learning from Las Vegas* were to challenge with such vigor?

Venturi's appeal here to a leading exponent of New Criticism in support of his own architectural agenda is a bit surprising—doubly so, given the evolution from *Complexity and Contradiction in Architecture* to *Learning from Las Vegas*. There would seem to be tension between the aesthetic ideal suggested by Brooks's title, *The Well Wrought Urn*, and the direction indicated by *Complexity and Contradiction*, leading toward an understanding of the work of architecture as a decorated shed. Does the way *Learning from Las Vegas* celebrates decoration not turn its back on the kind of unity figured by a well-wrought urn? Is decoration here not experienced as an addendum to a functional building that, while it may have its own significance and aesthetic appeal, no longer needs to stand in an essential relationship to the latter?[8]

But what I would like to address here is something that links *Complexity and Contradiction* and *Learning from Las Vegas*: the suggestion that the methods valid for literary criticism are also valid for the making of architecture, that buildings are like texts, that both depend for much of their meaning on already established symbols. According to the authors of *Learning from Las Vegas*, "Basic to the argument for the decorated shed is the assumption that symbolism is essential in architecture and that the model from a previous time or from the existing city is part of the source material and the replication of elements is part of the design method of this architecture. That is, architecture that depends on association in its perception depends on association in its creation" (131).[9] In keeping with this understanding of architecture, the authors of *Learning from Las Vegas* thus introduce a paragraph titled "A Significance for A&P Parking Lots, or Learning from Las Vegas" with this quote from Richard Poirier's "T. S. Eliot and the Literature of Waste":[10]

> Substance consists for a writer not merely of those realities he thinks he discovers; it consists even more of those realities which have been made available to him by the literature and idioms of his own day and by the images that still have vitality in the literature of the past. Stylistically, a writer can express his feeling about this substance, either by imitation, if it sits well with him, or by parody, if it doesn't. (72)

Important here is the distinction between what a writer "thinks he discovers" and what is available to him only as mediated by the words of others, be it as literature or as everyday talk. The quoted passage invites the question, just what images in literature—and not only in the literature of the past, but in today's literature and everyday talk—"still have vitality"? How are we to distinguish what is vital from what is stale? Consider the image of Tanya, featured on the cover of *Learning from Las Vegas* and illustrated once more in the body of the book: does it strike us as vital or as stale? Today we may well experience the pictured billboard first of all as a nostalgic invocation of a more innocent Las Vegas, representative of an age still blind to the need to confront and question the supposed omnipotence of the automobile (52). I find the sign interesting as re-presented by the authors, that is, in the context of a book published by the MIT Press. But were I to actually meet such a Tanya, plastered on a billboard on some hot roadside, I would wish her away. Just what is it that this Tanya has to teach me today? To accept and enjoy the symbol and what it symbolizes instead of longing to actually discover and really know another human being? To settle for signs and simulacra rather than demand to lay hold of reality?

Both Poirier and Eliot return in *Learning from Las Vegas*, joined now by James Joyce:

> Pop artists have shown the value of the old cliché used in a new context to achieve a new meaning—the soup can in the art gallery—to make the common uncommon. And in literature, Eliot and Joyce display, according to Poirier, "an extraordinary vulnerability . . . to the idioms, rhythms, artifacts, associated with certain urban environments or situations. The multitudinous styles of *Ulysses* are so dominated by them that there are only intermittent sounds of Joyce in the novel and no extended passage certifiably is his as distinguished from a mimicked style." Poirier refers to this as the "decreative impulse." Eliot himself speaks of Joyce doing the best he can "with the material at hand." Perhaps a fitting requiem for the irrelevant works of Art that are today's descendants of a once meaningful Modern architecture are Eliot's lines in "East Coker":
>
> That was a way of putting it—not very satisfactory:
>
> A periphrastic study in a worn-out poetical fashion,
>
> Leaving one still with the intolerable wrestle
>
> With words and meanings. The poetry does not matter. (72)[11]

What Poirier has to say about the "decreative impulse" invites comparison with what Venturi has to say about analysis, understood as "a breaking up of architecture into elements," a process said to be essential to both the appreciation and the creation of architecture. Significant in the cited passage is the reference to Andy Warhol's soup can. What lets us consider it a work of art? As Arthur Danto has pointed out, it is no longer the material object and its aesthetic properties. What matters is rather the way the soup can's dislocation and re-presentation occasions a play of thought, a play also with the philosophical question, just what is it that makes art *art*? Danto speaks of a "philosophization" of art.[12] Theory here becomes part of both the creation and the appreciation of art. *Learning from Las Vegas* suggests that architects have much to learn from Warhol's "philosophization" of art.

Many a recent work of architecture seems somehow naked and mute without its accompanying theory, like a shed stripped of its ornament. To fully appreciate a building such as Guild House in Philadelphia, we have to understand how this building with its six stories plays with the urban vernacular, a modernist formal vocabulary, and the tripartite organization of a palazzo. The discussion in *Learning from Las Vegas*, which compares the explicit "ugly and ordinary" symbolism of Guild House to the implicit "heroic and original" symbolism of Paul Rudolph's Crawford Manor in New Haven, provides a helpful guide to appreciating the significance of the building. Our first impression of Guild House may well be that of an all too ordinary, not very beautiful building. But that look, we learn, was intended. "The technologically unadvanced brick, the old fashioned, double-hung windows, the pretty materials around the entrance, and the ugly antenna not hidden behind the parapet in the accepted fashion" were meant to be at home with the "rather *pretty* and ordinary" plastic flowers bound to turn up in these windows (93). This self-conscious, ironic, and somewhat condescending turn to the stale and ordinary is of course supposed to be anything but stale. Its artistic re-presentation is to give it a new significance and life. The ordinary offers material to the architect's creative play in a way that invites thoughts not of Keats's well-wrought urn—this ageless but "Cold Pastoral"—but of a very different sort of urn: Marcel Duchamp's *Fountain*. This fountain's subversive play with both plumbing and art invites comparison with the way Guild House, too, plays not only with the ordinary but with architecture: "The pretensions of the 'giant-order' on the front, the symmetrical palazzolike composition with its three monumental stories (as well as its six real, stories), topped by a piece of sculpture—or almost sculpture—suggest something of the heroic and original. It is true that in this case the heroic and original façade is somewhat ironical, but it is this juxtaposition of contrasting symbols—the appliqué of one order of symbols on another—that constitutes for us the decorated shed—not architecture without architects" (93–100). I will have to return to the significance of the way the authors of *Learning from Las Vegas* here explicitly distance themselves from Bernard Rudofsky's "frankly polemic" nostalgic celebration of seemingly ageless old-world vernacular building in his *Architecture Without Architects* (1964).[13] Guild House does not invite us to dream of an architecture that is the product of anonymous builders supported by the collective wisdom of generations in tune with the rhythms of nature. In keeping with Jean-François Lyotard's understanding of postmodernism,[14] nostalgia has given way to a playfulness that may strike us as arbitrary and willful. But the result does become interesting once we explore the contrapuntal play with both architecture and its history and the vernacular. The pleasure we take in such a work is very different from the pleasure we take in a well-wrought urn. Decoration here is not meant to be understood as a beautiful addendum to a functional shed. What matters is rather the way decoration provides us with pointers to the different symbolic orders that are here made to collide. A full appreciation of that collision requires an awareness of the colliding codes. If we are to recognize Guild House as a major work of architecture, we need to supplement what we see with theory. This theoretical supplement lets us experience the building not as beautiful or true but as interesting.[15] Such theory depends on words, which acquire an ornamental function.

Something similar could be said of quite a number of the most widely discussed architectural works of the past three or four decades—consider, for example, works by Eisenman or Michael Graves. Words here serve to augment the meaning of a building not just or even primarily in the form of conspicuous signs but as called forth by thoughtfully placed markers that invite the knowing to engage in playful theorizing. The inventiveness of such play lets us appreciate the architectural significance of the work.

Part of the significance of Guild House is that it continues to raise the question, just what is it that makes some structure a work of architecture as opposed to a mere building? And it raises this question in a way that invites reflection on the part words have played and perhaps should continue to play in establishing this difference. The building resists interpretation of this difference in terms of the simple addition of beautiful decoration to a functional shed: is it not rather the introduction of elements that demand a more thoughtful response that makes this a work of architecture? Has such thoughtfulness not become a necessary part of the pleasure we take in what deserves to be considered a work of architecture? What do invocations of beauty still matter? Guild House, at any rate, raises the at-bottom philosophical questions: What is architecture? What was it? What should it be today? Uncertainty about the essence and future of architecture is not a recent phenomenon. What is new is that works of architecture should so self-consciously question and play with the essence of architecture.

The early nineteenth century already wondered in what style it should build. Such uncertainty belongs with Georg Wilhelm Friedrich Hegel's famous pronouncement in the introduction to his *Lectures on Aesthetics*: "Art is and remains for us, on the side of its highest destiny, a thing of the past. . . . What is now aroused in us by works of art is, over and above our immediate enjoyment, and together with it, our judgment. . . . Therefore the *science* of art is a much more pressing need in our day than in times in which art, simply as art, was enough to furnish a full satisfaction."[16] Art in its highest sense, Hegel asserts, has come to an end. And a sign of this is the fact that art as just art can no longer give us a full satisfaction, that to give us moderns such satisfaction, it requires the aid of theory. Theory is to return to art a voice it has lost.

Hegel speaks here of art in general, but what he says of art is especially true of architecture, the art Hegel places at the very origin of art. We should thus expect that works of architecture, too, as opposed to merely functional buildings, today need the aid of theory if they are to give us a full satisfaction. Theory here does not mean theorizing that in some fashion serves the production of architecture, for example, by analyzing the pressing problems some building should address or the means, materials, and technologies available to the builder—not that Hegel would have questioned the importance of such theorizing. But to really speak to us moderns, even the greatest works of the past need to be illuminated by texts that allow us to understand how they once satisfied what Hegel took to be the highest function of all art: to provide, like religion and philosophy, not so much physical as spiritual shelter. It is the productive tension between these two very different requirements that architecture in what Hegel took to be its highest sense had to confront and resolve.

I wrote "once satisfied" using the past tense because, if Hegel is right, we heirs of the Enlightenment look no longer to art, but to theory, for such spiritual shelter. We live in an age that has made thought expressed clearly and distinctly the proper custodian of whatever meanings should preside over our lives. For that very reason, we are bound to associate art and architecture in their highest sense with the past. Appropriate to our spiritual situation is an understanding of the work of art as a source of a purely aesthetic pleasure that leaves our deepest spiritual need unsatisfied. With the loss of its former ethical function, the work of architecture comes to be understood as a well-built, functional building to which a pleasing aesthetic component has been added. This may sound like a recasting of the Vitruvian architecture = firmness + commodity + delight. But what gives delight, the aesthetic component, now no longer attempts nor has the power to provide that spiritual shelter that the temple and the cathedral once offered.

Just as many artists have found it difficult to settle for such an understanding of art that may seem to reduce it to high-class entertainment, many architects, including Venturi and his associates, have found it difficult to accept an understanding of the work of architecture as just a decorated shed in this aesthetic sense. And it is more than nostalgia that supports such unwillingness to leave Hegel's thesis of the end of architecture in its highest sense unchallenged, because presupposed by that thesis is his conviction that reason alone is able to provide heirs of the age of reason with all the spiritual shelter we need. But does such conviction today not also belong to a past that cannot be recovered? Gone is the optimism of the Enlightenment, and once again we demand that architecture also addresses our need for spiritual shelter. This, at any rate, is how I would want to understand Venturi and Scott Brown's "ARCHITECTURE AS ELEMENTAL SHELTER AND BACKGROUND FOR LIVING."[17]

But even if we have lost the Enlightenment's confidence in the power of pure reason to build us our spiritual home and once again demand that architecture speak to us of what matters, it is difficult to dismiss Hegel's assertion that to give us moderns full satisfaction such work must be supplemented with theory. And why should architects leave such theorizing to philosophers burdened by unreasonable demands for rigor and claims to truth? Why not insert theory into architecture by supplementing functional sheds with signifying elements born of and inviting theoretical reflection?

The architectural community's love of theory today invites comparison with the love of ornament of a hundred years ago, and it also invites reactions that parallel Adolf Loos's condemnation of such ornament: must we not understand recent efforts to make theory actually part of the architectural work as just another nostalgic and futile attempt to hold on to a significance architecture can no longer possess in this age shaped by science and technology, as just another symptom of the death of architecture in what was its highest sense? Hegel would have us accept that death as part of humanity's coming of age.

Do such reflections help us to understand what has made the architecture world so receptive to the ideas advanced in *Learning from Las Vegas*? Quite aware that the catchy expression "decorated shed" may seem to suggest the very opposite, I have nevertheless argued that such receptiveness has much to do with a nostalgia that finds it difficult to let go of thoughts that architecture should be more than a matter of dressing up mute, functional buildings in aesthetically pleasing finery that says little. Architecture should speak, and *Learning from Las Vegas* promised to return to architecture its lost voice, emphasizing that symbolism is essential to architecture. But does architecture recover that essence when dressed up in symbols drawn from the past and the present? Does such re-presentation preserve the original power of such symbols?

Considering the architecture of his day, Friedrich Nietzsche observed in *Human, All Too Human* that "stone is more stone than it used to be" and that "the meanings of forms have been forgotten and materials and their visual qualities are stressed." He was thinking of Victorian architecture; it, too, was laden with borrowed symbols. Such borrowing, he felt, anticipating modernist critiques of these decorated sheds, could not restore to architecture its lost voice. For that we had to look elsewhere. But "we have outgrown the symbolism of lines and figures, just as we have been weaned from the sound effects of rhetoric, and have not drunk this kind of mother's milk of education from the first moment of our lives."[18]

Does the re-presentational collage approach to symbolism suggested in *Learning from Las Vegas* promise to restore to us what Nietzsche thought had been lost? Not that we are able to return to the still-confident, operatic eclecticism (in comparison to our own) of Victorian architecture. As Lyotard suggests, our freer postmodern relation to history, nature, and culture demands a more ironic, more playful appropriation of whatever it was that allowed architecture to speak in the past.

But what is now to bind our freedom and render it nonarbitrary? What should architecture say and in what language? We have become, to borrow Venturi's own phrasing, too educated, too self-conscious, to be able to appeal in modernist fashion to architecture's proper voice. Such education has brought us a new appreciation of the beauties of the theatrical architecture of the nineteenth century: what modernism had scorned as decadent today speaks of an innocence many of us have come to envy. Is bad faith strongly held not better than no faith at all? But our postmodern self-consciousness makes it difficult for us to settle for such faith, it demands irony.

I have suggested that the climate of receptivity that helps to explain the ways in which *Learning from Las Vegas* was appropriated and misappropriated has much to do with a nostalgic longing, tinged with irony, for an architecture that, challenging the perceived muteness of so much of modernist building, would once again speak and say something significant. Such a mixture of irony and nostalgia also feeds the hunger for theory that has spread through the architectural community and especially our schools of architecture. Might theory not help architecture to recover its lost voice?

In the introduction to her widely used anthology *Theorizing a New Agenda for Architecture: An Anthology of Architectural Theory 1965–1995*, Kate Nesbitt also interprets the recent proliferation of theorizing as a reaction to architectural modernism, to an architecture that by the1960s "had been reduced to formulaic repetitions of the canonical works of the Modern Movement."[19] The modern movement did, of course, produce its own share of theory. Countless programs and manifestos testify to the modern movement's refusal to accept the decorated sheds of the nineteenth century as the fitting architectural expression of the modern age, their borrowing in keeping with Hegel's pronouncement that architecture in its highest sense had come to an end. A striking expression of this refusal is Lyonel Feininger's cover for the Bauhaus program, showing a Gothic cathedral in modernist forms. Walter Gropius's Wagnerian text invites comparison with Heidegger's Nietzschean call for a modern repetition of the Greek temple in his "The Origin of the Work of Art."

Can we today be confident that architectural modernism was wrong when it defined itself in opposition to the decorated sheds of the nineteenth century? Should that reason that gave us our science and technology and with them an altogether new freedom not also suffice to provide a humanity that has come of age with the spiritual shelter human beings require—shelter that finds its appropriate architectural expression in naked walls and right angles? The founders of the Bauhaus, like so many architects of that defiantly optimistic generation following the self-destruction of Old Europe in the First World War, still dreamed of a purer architecture able to found genuine community even as it would allow for the realization of utopian dreams of freedom and pleasure, dreams that then tended toward thoughts of a socialist paradise. The Second World War and what followed have shattered such defiant dreams over and over. Was it because their very content was incoherent?

Translated into America and recast as the International style, architectural modernism lost the wonderful but naïve ethical pathos that originally supported it and transformed itself into its own caricature, producing countless buildings that were increasingly boring and mute. We cannot blame the translation from old Europe to the United States for this devolution. The modern movement had to end in uncertainty because it overestimated the power of reason and underestimated the power of history to provide human beings with adequate psychological shelter.

Such uncertainty called for reexamination, called for more theory, theory that, calling modernist expectations into question, looked beyond architecture to words, especially to the words of theory, to restore to architecture the voice it had lost, somewhat in the way the builders of a much earlier age looked beyond architecture to the Word, especially to the words of theology, to discover what mattered most profoundly. According to Nesbitt,

> During this time of reexamination of architecture (and of cultural modernity), the influence of extradisciplinary paradigms increased, notably literary paradigms such as semiotics and structuralism. Communication theory and phenomenology presented additional ways to approach the crisis of meaning within architecture. In response to the loss of socially-motivated engagement with the world, Italian Marxism and the Frankfurt school offered political critiques of architecture. No single theory dominated the discourse as academic architects borrowed new thoughts from other disciplines. This pluralist, revisionist period can be general characterized as postmodern.[20]

In her preface, Nesbitt places special weight on the publication of Venturi's *Complexity and Contradiction*, which is said to have "radically changed attitudes to modern architecture."[21] In this estimate, she followed one of her mentors at Yale, Vincent Scully, who prides himself in having had the wit, in the introduction he wrote for that book, to have called it "the most important writing on the making of architecture since Le Corbusier's *Vers une architecture*, of 1923."[22]

Although Venturi's book did have an enormous impact, we must keep in mind that by then the modernist paradigm had been undermined in more than one way. Just two years before, the Museum of Modern Art had published Rudofsky's *Architecture Without Architects: A Short Introduction to Non-Pedigreed Architecture*, which "a whole generation of architects took . . . as its point of departure for the attempt to escape from modernist formalism."[23] There is, of course, a striking difference in tone and, more especially, a strikingly different assessment of the importance of theory. As already mentioned, Rudofsky dreamed of an architecture firmly embedded in ageless ways of dwelling and building. Such a dream is of building that has no need for theory, no need for words—an architecture tendered eloquent just by its silence. Theory here would have us leave theory behind. Venturi was of another mind. Written mostly in 1962 and published in 1966, *Complexity and Contradiction* belongs with Warhol's soup can or his *Brillo Box* of 1964, a work that, following the example set by Duchamp, calls into question the identification of the work of art with what presents itself to the eye. As Danto points out, the question, why is Warhol's *Brillo Box* art while that in the supermarket is not? could no longer be answered by the object alone; it required philosophy.[24] Theory becomes an essential part of the work of art.

In this respect, Warhol had a precursor not only in Duchamp but also in Philip Johnson, the éminence grise of architectural postmodernism. Consider Charles Jencks's assessment of the significance of Johnson's *Glass House* of 1949:

> The building was provided by Johnson with an "explication de texte" so that the Modern Movement could follow the allusions (among the twenty-seven were—Le Corbusier, Van Doesburg, Malevich, Mies, Ledoux and Schinkel). These historical programme notes published in the *Architectural Review* were helpful for a full architectural experience, but the real significance of the house was as a social gesture. All of a sudden architectural journalism had become part of the object. Marshall McLuhan, Tom Wolfe, and Robert Rauschenberg were pre-empted here. The social celebration of architecture through photographs was suddenly as significant as the building. Soon Rauschenberg could 'paint a portrait' by merely saying: "This is a portrait of Iris Clert, if I say so." But Johnson was the first to realize the implications of a sophisticated audience and new means of communications for the architectural tradition.[25]

The way that theory today has so often become part of architecture is here prefigured. Prefigured is what we can call "an architecture of the built word."

"An architecture of the built word"—the expression should remind the reader of Tom Wolfe's characterization of American abstract expressionism as an art of the painted word, a characterization that still provides us with a valuable lens through which to look at recent art and architecture. Published in 1975, *The Painted Word* captured well how the art world by then had changed. Wolfe writes of having been jerked alert by something he read in a review by Hilton Kramer of the work of seven realist painters: "Realism does not lack its partisans, but it does rather conspicuously lack a persuasive theory. And given the nature of our intellectual commerce with works of art, to lack a persuasive theory is to lack something crucial—the means by which our experience of individual works is joined to our understanding of the value they signify."[26] Kramer's claim recalls Hegel's assertion that to give us a full satisfaction art has to be assisted by theory. And does this not also hold true of works of architecture? As ornament was once supposed to do, theory today helps to alleviate what, following Milan Kundera, we can call the unbearable lightness of too much recent architecture. Presupposed by such love of theory is a legitimate sense that something is missing in what gets built today.

Wolfe seized on the words "to lack a persuasive theory is to lack something crucial." They opened his eyes to the fact that, despite its claim to have freed itself from literary meanings, modern art had in fact "become completely literary: the paintings and other works exist only to illustrate the text."[27] Was it not words that really mattered? Wolfe delighted in poking fun at artists who had become mere illustrators of "the Word," the word of critics such as Clement Greenberg, Harold Rosenberg, and Leo Steinberg. There is the suggestion that in becoming such illustrators they averted their eyes from what Leonardo da Vinci and those who followed him had discovered and developed, betraying the grand tradition of Western art. How different, Wolfe suggested, was the example set by science, which built on what the past had achieved!

Wolfe's mention of da Vinci raises the question: why single out a Renaissance painter? Does the Renaissance stand here for a decisive break in the history of art? Medieval painters at any rate were painters of "the Word," now capitalized with greater justice, for "Word" here meant not the words of some critic or theorist but holy scripture. The replacement of scripture by the critic's words demands further consideration, but I want to underscore the obvious: from the very beginning, Christian art and architecture served the Word. Such service shaped such art. The Renaissance did not put an end to that tradition—think of the art of the Counter-Reformation! Modern art and architecture's turn away from the Word invites understanding as the exception rather than as the rule. And if in the sixties artists and architects demonstrated a renewed interest in words, in theory, should this not be interpreted, perhaps, and with greater justice than the return to decoration as a return to the mainstream of Western art and architecture?

In this connection Duchamp deserves special recognition as the artist who more decisively than any other prefigured the postmodern reaffirmation of the primacy not of perception but of words, of texts. Was he not right to challenge that emphasis on materiality, on the physicality of painting, which he thought Gustave Courbet had introduced into modernist painting? And does his example not hold an important lesson for architects, too? Is this not one thing we can learn from *Learning from Las Vegas*?

Duchamp does indeed invite description as an artist of the Word, although confronted with his *Fountain* we may want to strike the capitalized singular. Duchamp himself spoke of a provocation. The title, so interestingly at odds with what it names, underscores such provocation. But to be provocative, this work of art requires spectators who both recognize this piece of plumbing and presuppose that art has certain boundaries. Duchamp's *Fountain* challenges these boundaries. Like so much modern art and architecture, this is art about art, presupposing and inviting theorizing about art. More especially, it challenges an understanding of art that celebrates the artwork's material presence. What it asserts instead is that what matters is not the physical object, not its special aura, but the fact that it was chosen and the ideas governing that choice. Such art substitutes the words chosen by the creative artist-critic for the word of God.

Duchamp's turn to an "intellectual," "literary" art may be understood as a refusal to accept the end of art as Hegel understood it or as a defiant attempt to return to art that voice modernism would deny it. I have suggested that any such attempt has to challenge the primacy of perception, has to place itself in opposition to an approach that understands works of art as first of all "visual products." Duchamp hints at what now matters when he invokes chess, at which he excelled: this new art is like such a cerebral game. The beauty of its moves is to be grasped by the mind, not the eye. Can such play still be considered art? The reception of Duchamp's *Fountain* demonstrated the willingness of the art world to apply the term "art" to creations that please, not because of their visual appearances, but because of the play of ideas they occasion. And such play is inescapably also a play of words. Words now become constitutive of the aesthetic object.

This invites a reconsideration of Nikolaus Pevsner's understanding of the work of architecture as a functional building transformed by an aesthetic addendum into a work of art. Duchamp and the many artists and architects who followed his example demand a reconsideration of the nature of this addendum. What now matters is no longer the transformational power of beauty but the insertion of markers into a work that will occasion interesting thoughts—thoughts especially about architecture and its past, present, and future. Instead of that harmonious interplay of understanding and imagination in which Immanuel Kant sought the source of aesthetic pleasure, we now have a play of reason that lets us judge what is before us as interesting. The successful introduction of such markers demands an inventive, thoughtful architect who is able to substitute the Word that once illuminated Western architecture with words sufficiently engaging to make us want to play along. Guild House can serve as a test case.

Following Kundera, I have spoken of the unbearable lightness of much recent architecture. Following Hegel, I have suggested that much art and architecture today seems naked unless dressed up in words by some interpreting text. It is in the need to cover such nakedness that efforts to make theory part of architecture, to transform it into a strange kind of ornament, have their foundation. But without the support of something able to take the part of that Word that once presided over Western art and architecture, such theory has to degenerate into a play that, while it may entertain, leaves us cold and homeless in our world. Modernist architects looked to socialism for a substitute. Such hopes have been shattered.[28] As a result, theorizing has taken an aesthetic turn. The way some of today's most talked about architects have transformed theory into a strange kind of ornament suggests once again that architecture has lost it way. And such a loss of way, as Aristotle and Ludwig Wittgenstein knew, inevitably awakens more theory—theory that needs to consider carefully the road traveled, to inquire into turns taken and rejected and also into the destination, in order to help us decide where to go now. Such theory will also have to return to the question of the relationship between building and word and address it in a way that will resist the currently fashionable ornamentalization of theory. Theory is needed today to prevent architecture (and also theory itself) from becoming, as Venturi and Scott Brown put it, "the victim of theory." Pointing in so many different directions, *Learning from Las Vegas* continues to furnish such theorizing with an ambiguous—and, for that very reason, challenging—point of departure.

Notes

1. University of Nottingham Porstgraduate Prospctus, http://www.nottingham.ac.uk/prospectuses/postgrad/information.php4?inc=course&code=009548 2/22/02 (accessed February 22, 2002).

2. See Karsten Harries, "Philosophy in Search of Itself," *What Is Philosophy?*, ed. C. P. Ragland and Sarah Heidt (New Haven, Conn.: Yale University Press, 2001), 47–73.

3. Mark Wigley, *The Architecture of Deconstruction: Derrida's Haunt* (Cambridge, Mass.: MIT Press, 1993).

4. Robert Venturi and Denise Scott Brown, "Personal Approaches and Positions toward Contemporary Architectural Practice," typescript dated April 16, 1992, with the header "For *Harvard Architectural Review*."

5. See Aron Vinegar, "Skepticism and the Ordinary: From Burnt Norton to Las Vegas," *Visible Language* 37, no. 3 (October 2003): 288–311.

6. Robert Venturi, *Complexity and Contradiction in Architecture*, 2nd. ed. (New York: The Museum of Modern Art, 1977), 13.

7. Ibid., 20, citing Cleanth Brooks, *The Well Wrought Urn* (New York: Harcourt, Brace and World, 1947), 212–14.

8. See Karsten Harries, *The Ethical Function of Architecture* (Cambridge, Mass.: MIT Press, 1997), 70–81.

9. All page references in this chapter are to Robert Venturi, Denise Scott Brown, Steven Izenour, *Learning From Las Vegas*, rev. ed. (Cambridge, Mass.: MIT Press, 1977).

10. Richard Poirier, "T. S. Eliot and the Literature of Waste," *The New Republic*, May 20, 1967: 21.

11. The cited passages are from Poirier, "T. S. Eliot and the Literature of Waste," 20, 21; T. S. Eliot, *The Complete Poems and Plays, 1909–1950* (New York: Harcourt, Brace and Company, 1958), 125; and T. S. Eliot, *Four Quartets* (New York: Harcourt, Brace and Company, 1943), 13.

12. Arthur C. Danto, *Encounters and Reflections: Art in the Historical Present* (New York: Noonday Press, Farrar Straus Giroux, 1990), 334.

13. Bernard Rudofsky, *Architecture Without Architects: A Short Introduction to Non-Pedigreed Architecture* (Garden City, N.Y.: Doubleday, 1964), n.p.

14. See Jean-François Lyotard, "An Answer to the Question: What is Postmodernism," in *The Postmodern Explained. Correspondence 1982–1985*, trans. Don Barry, Bernadette Maher, Julian Prefanis, Virginia Spate, and Morgan Thomas (Minneapolis: University of Minnesota Press, 1993), 1–16.

15. On the interesting in architecture, see Karsten Harries, "Modernity's Bad Conscience," *AA Files* 10 (Autumn 1985), 53–60.

16. Georg Wilhelm Friedrich Hegel, *Introductory Lectures on Aesthetics*, trans. Bernard Bosanquet, ed., intro. and commentary by Michael Inwood (London: Penguin, 1993), 13.

17. Robert Venturi and Denise Scott Brown, "Personal Approaches and Positions."

18. Friedrich Nietzsche, *Menschliches, Allzumenschliches*, I:218.

19. Kate Nesbitt, ed., *Theorizing a New Agenda for Architecture: An Anthology of Architectural Theory 1965–1995* (New York: Princeton Architectural Press, 1996), 12.

20. Ibid., 12.

21. Ibid.

22. Vincent Scully, "Note to the Second Edition," in *Complexity and Contradiction in Architecture* by Robert Venturi (New York: Museum of Modern Art, 1966), 12.

23. Andrea Bocco Guarneri, *Bernard Rudofsky* (New York: Springer, 2003), 121.

24. Danto, *Encounters and Reflections*, 5.

25. Charles Jencks, *Modern Movements in Architecture* (New York: Doubleday Anchor, 1973), 206–7.

26. Hilton Kramer, quoted in Tom Wolfe, *The Painted Word* (Toronto: Bantam Books, 1976), 4. See also Karsten Harries, "The Painter and the Word," *Bennington Review* 13 (June 1982), 19–25.

27. Wolfe, *The Painted Word*, 6.

28. See T. J. Clark, *Farewell to an Idea: Episodes from a History of Modernism* (New Haven, Conn.: Yale University Press, 1999), and my review article in *The Art Bulletin* 83, no. 2 (June 2001), 358–64.

5

Mobilizing Visions: Representing the American Landscape

KATHERINE SMITH

> The highway has rammed itself through our lives and we shall never be the same again. . . . Artists, by engulfing the highway and its paraphernalia into our cultural tradition, help us through their translation to see ourselves as we really are.
>
> —DENISE SCOTT BROWN AND ROBERT VENTURI, "THE HIGHWAY"

This statement from Denise Scott Brown and Robert Venturi's essay for *The Highway* at the Institute of Contemporary Art in Philadelphia confirms that in 1970 they were already making connections between art and architecture and suggesting that artistic representations might mediate and even redefine reality—showing us who "we really are"—in ways that could facilitate changes in perception. Visionary goals—finding new ways of looking at and learning from the American landscape—were central to *Learning from Las Vegas*, which they published just two years later with Steven Izenour. Paradoxically, they stake out their new perspective on old ground, asserting that "learning from the existing landscape is a way of being revolutionary for an architect. Not the obvious way, which is to tear down Paris and begin again, as Le Corbusier suggested in the 1920s, but another, more tolerant way; that is, to question how we look at things."[1] This approach is one they see in, and share with, contemporary art. In *Learning from Las Vegas*, they link their own objectives for innovation with a similar sort of revolutionary, yet at once retrospective, vision that they locate in pop art. They relate the pop artists' conceptual strategies to their own in the first pages of the text as they specifically declare, "For the artist, creating the new may mean choosing the old or the existing. Pop artists have relearned this. Our acknowledgment of existing, commercial architecture at the scale of the highway is within this tradition."[2]

The architects use pop art, through both literal illustrations and textual allusions, to contextualize their emerging theories of architectural symbolism and to bolster their own representational strategies. While there are clear affinities between pop art's and Venturi, Scott Brown, and Izenour's embrace of the existing American vernacular, the architects' general comments about pop art in *Learning from Las Vegas* focus on the use of common subject matter in uncommon ways. As they write, "Pop artists used unusual juxtapositions of everyday objects in tense and vivid plays between old and new associations to flout the everyday interdependence of context and meaning, giving us a new interpretation of twentieth-century cultural artifacts. The familiar that is a little off has a strange and revealing power."[3] The architects' understanding of the importance of pop art's content, its immediate evocation of cultural associations, and its provocative alterations in scale and context have directed aspects of their theories and designs.[4]

The single example of pop art reproduced in *Learning from Las Vegas*, Allan D'Arcangelo's *The Trip*, instantiates the potential complexities of the Strip environment and the attendant mechanisms of perception to which Venturi and Scott Brown were specifically responding. D'Arcangelo's print accompanies the following statement: "A driver 30 years ago could maintain a sense of orientation in space. At the simple crossroad a little sign with an arrow confirmed what he already knew. He knew where he was. Today the crossroad is a cloverleaf. To turn left he must turn right, a contradiction poignantly evoked in the print by Allan D'Arcangelo. But the driver has no time to ponder paradoxical subtleties within a dangerous, sinuous maze. He relies on signs to guide him—enormous signs in vast spaces at high speeds."[5] The print formally plays out the disorientation the architects describe. The red arrow, which dominates the composition, points left, while a smaller, yellow-orange hand, finger extended, aims right, simultaneously indicating opposite directions through complex messages delivered simultaneously but differently and mediated by the relative sizes, linear articulations, and color effects of the two primary elements. This image is clearly not a literal illustration of the sort of highway cloverleaf they describe but instead an evocation of the "paradoxical contradiction" of moving, or being instructed to move, in two directions at once.

The inclusion of this image demonstrates the extent to which Venturi, Scott Brown, and Izenour understood not just the material dimensions but also the compositional complexities of some pop art and its relevance to the contemporary landscape. While D'Arcangelo's print might intimate the importance of signs and the potential risk of distracted vision, the architects' use of the image especially reflects an impulse similar to the one corroborated by Donald Appleyard, Kevin Lynch, and John R. Myer in their studies of the contemporary experience of highway travel and their assertions of the need for new ways to represent elements of this landscape. In *The View from the Road*, they describe an experience of the highway:

> While the road makes a dynamic impression on the driver and his passengers . . . [b]oth . . . are likely to be an inattentive audience, whether through the compulsion to watch only a small part of the scene, or conversely through the very freedom to let attention wander. . . . Yet at the same time both are a captive audience who cannot avoid remarking, even if only subconsciously, the most dramatic events of a scene which is too mobile and too dangerous to be ignored. . . . The modern car interposes a filter between the driver and the world he is moving through. Sounds, smells, and sensations . . . are all diluted in comparison with what the pedestrian experiences.[6]

This type of contemporary vision necessitates the eye-catching devices in roadside architecture, which Venturi, Scott Brown, and Izenour were examining and whose symbolism they were theorizing in *Learning from Las Vegas*, specifically in their concept of the "duck" and the "decorated shed," which they count foremost among prominent and legible sign systems embodied in vernacular architecture.

The following chapter focuses on the aesthetic strategies from pop art that influenced Venturi, Scott Brown, and Izenour's own images of architectural forms and urban spaces. In the two studios at Yale that preceded *Learning from Las Vegas*—on the commercial environment of Las Vegas in 1968 and on the domestic architecture of Levittown in 1970—they emphasized the art of Ed Ruscha and Claes Oldenburg in particular, whose work informed the objectives of their architectural studios and also influenced the visual format and presentation of *Learning from Las Vegas* and *Signs of Life: Symbols in the American City*, a related exhibition organized at the Renwick Gallery, Smithsonian Institution, in 1976. Oldenburg's sculpture and Ruscha's photography paralleled, even as they anticipated and influenced, Venturi and Scott Brown's conceptualizations and representations of city spaces. The emphasis on three-dimensionality and overscale in Oldenburg's sculptures and on flatness and façade in Ruscha's art already identify central concerns of the "duck" and the "decorated shed," respectively, providing reciprocal and complementary relationships between their art and Venturi and Scott Brown's own research. While the architects' use of these pop precedents embraces parallels in exaggerated scales and vernacular content, it also exceeds merely formal qualities to suggest the ways that some pop art does not simply represent the subject matter of daily life but attempts to replicate the lived experiences of the depicted environments.

Positioning Pop: A Critical Account

The architects' numerous statements about pop art in *Learning from Las Vegas* and elsewhere lend concrete form to their stated affinity with the 1960s art scene. Pop art was so central to the architects' approach that references to this style were already apparent in their individual writings by the end of this decade. In the introduction to *Complexity and Contradiction in Architecture*, for instance, Vincent Scully describes Venturi's understanding of pop art in ways that are strikingly similar to the architects' comments in *Learning from Las Vegas*, quoted earlier. Scully asserts that Venturi

> is one of the very few architects whose thought parallels that of the Pop painters—and probably the first architect to perceive the usefulness and meaning of their forms. He has clearly learned a good deal from them during the past few years, though the major argument of this book was laid out in the late fifties and predates his knowledge of this work. Yet his "Main Street is almost all right," is just like their viewpoint, as is his instinct for changes of scale in small buildings for the unsuspected life to be found in the common artifacts of mass culture when they are focused upon individually.[7]

Scully refers here to the final paragraph of *Complexity and Contradiction*, where Venturi references pop art and forestalls the lessons to be learned in Las Vegas. As he writes, "Some of the vivid lessons of Pop Art, involving contradictions of scale and context, should have awakened architects from prim dreams of pure order.... And it is perhaps from the everyday landscape, vulgar and disdained, that we can draw the complex and contradictory order that is valid and vital for our architecture as an urbanistic whole."[8] Similarly, Scott Brown's statements in articles such as "On Pop Art, Permissiveness, and Planning" echo Venturi's earlier claims about the significance of pop art for architectural theory. As Scott Brown notes, "the best thing an architect or urban designer can offer a new society, apart from a good heart, is his own skill, used *for* the society, to develop a respectful understanding of its cultural artifacts and a loving strategy for their development to suit the felt needs and way of life of its people. This is a socially responsible activity; it is, after all, what [Herbert] Gans and the pop artists are doing."[9] And again she reiterates in "Learning from Pop" that "[t]he urgency of the social situation, and the social critique of urban renewal and of the architect as server of a rich narrow spectrum of the population . . . have been as important as the Pop artists in steering us toward the existing American city and its builders."[10] These ideas about pop art, which the architects had already expressed separately, find collective endorsement, salient expression, and comprehensive context in *Learning from Las Vegas*.[11]

Certainly, their thoughts also reflect contemporary critiques of pop art, which stressed the integral relationship between this style, its subjects, and the American landscape. Andy Warhol, recalling a road trip from New York to California in 1963, for example, famously claimed, "The farther west we drove, the more Pop everything looked on the highways. Suddenly we all felt like insiders because even though Pop was everywhere—that was the thing about it, most people still took it for granted, whereas we were dazzled by it—to us, it was the new Art. Once you 'got' Pop, you could never see a sign the same way again. And once you thought Pop, you could never see America the same way again."[12] Similarly, John Rublowsky's 1965 book on New York pop, with photographs by Ken Heyman, affirms the necessary link between pop subjects and city spaces both through evocative photographic layouts that juxtapose pop images with their urban counterparts and through written statements that tie the characteristic styles and subjects of various pop artists to the urban landscape, like Venturi, Scott Brown, and Izenour's project: "The voluptuous shape of a hamburger; the simplicity and directness of a comic-strip panel; the eye-stopping design of a can of soup; the naïvely surrealist vision of a billboard; the cold, gaudily efficient look of a 'Hollywood' bath; the garish exuberance of a highway strip development. . . . Their work has explored a hitherto-neglected area of reality, and the sensitivity of their vision has given us new esthetic vistas."[13] Critical accounts of West Coast pop likewise contend that "the question for Southern California, is not so much whether the area was/is ripe for Pop, but whether the whole ambience . . . is not preemptively Pop in itself."[14] And in *Learning from Las Vegas*, Venturi, Scott Brown, and Izenour indeed compare Las Vegas signage and this artistic style: "the need for high-speed communication with maximum meaning" makes the signs "Pop Art."[15] While their comment alludes to the clear similarities between the familiar subjects and large scales of roadside signs and pop works, this statement also makes an implicit connection between the importance of an image's immediate identification and legibility, specifically, because of the kind of mobilized and distracted perception that defines vehicular travel—an understanding that operates at the core of the architects' use of Pop art.

Upscale Objects: Seeing "What Claes Oldenburg Did for Hamburgers"

As Venturi and Scott Brown were formulating their ideas about pop art's significance for architecture, Oldenburg was similarly pondering the place of his increasingly large-scale sculptures in urban landscapes. Known for his enlarged representations of everyday objects, Oldenburg began his *Store* sculptures in the early 1960s, continued with larger vinyl and canvas works on similar subjects in the mid-1960s, and quickly translated such pieces into proposals for public monuments. Oldenburg was following a trajectory that, by the end of the 1960s, would intersect with Venturi and Scott Brown's thinking about vernacular architecture and urban design.

For Oldenburg, as for Venturi and Scott Brown, studying the architecture and urban spaces of the American West was a galvanizing opportunity. During the 1960s, Oldenburg took several trips to Los Angeles and made increasingly secure connections between his sculptures and the commercial environment. On Oldenburg's first trip in 1963, Dennis Hopper photographed *Giant Blue Shirt with Tie* (1963) in front of a Mobil station, a location in which the sculpture becomes, on its wheeled clothing rack, an ironic analogue for the absent automobile. Its placement within the contemporary city seems a more appropriate context than the Dwan Gallery, where this work was otherwise displayed. Placing his sculptures in an urban environment rather than in an art gallery likely helped to generate the artist's proposals for object monuments like *Proposed Colossal Monument for Ellis Island, New York: Frankfurter* (1965), and *Proposed Colossal Monument for Park Avenue, New York: Good Humor Bar* (1965), which he continued in subsequent years.

Oldenburg also saw in Los Angeles examples of extant commercial architecture from the early twentieth century, buildings that, through their sculptural emphasis, take on the forms of their products, from foodstuffs and animals to clothing and machinery. These structures, like Oldenburg's sculptures, are enlargements of everyday objects—hot dogs and doughnuts, owls and pigs, hats and igloos—whose appearances were intended to inculcate an immediate and perceptual link between the overall imagery, the building's function, and the business's goods.[16] During his time in Los Angeles in 1968, Oldenburg conceived and executed a series of works—lithographs and accompanying notes—that records the artist's evolving experiments with architectural form. As his *Notes* clarify, the objects in Oldenburg's lithographs can be understood in relation to the history of commercial American architecture as he specifically perceived it in Los Angeles. He explains, "There was a time when Los Angeles was the world capital of aggrandized objects, but now, even the last of the great Spotted Dogs has disappeared. Common structures, like diners, stole grandeur by imitating zeppelins. Buildings may be 'dressed' in colorful patterns or plainly, depending on the taste and services."[17] Oldenburg's "body buildings" include office buildings in the form of women's thighs, a tunnel entrance in the shape of a nose, and a diner with the outline of a knee. While these subjects reflect the artist's contemporaneous interest in anatomical fragments, the former also bears a particularly striking resemblance to

Sanderson's Hosiery, a shop dominated by a woman's leg and foot, confirming, like Oldenburg's description, their link to specific structures within the Los Angeles landscape.

Oldenburg was implicitly calling for a reintroduction of recognizable symbolism in architectural design—for him, an artistic strategy based on some of the buildings that Scott Brown also studied and documented during her research on vernacular architecture in Los Angeles in the mid-1960s. Furthermore, Oldenburg commented in an interview in 1968, "A friend who is a student of architecture at Yale told me that the kind of objects I choose are the closest thing to symbols available in our time. Architects find it difficult to design monuments today, he said, because they can't find appropriate symbols."[18] Oldenburg's statement conveys knowledge, if indirect, of Venturi and Scott Brown's emerging theories and at least derives from an impulse similar to the one that compelled Venturi, Scott Brown, and Izenour's study of Las Vegas.

One of the illustrations in *Learning from Las Vegas*, a tourist brochure providing an aerial view of the strip, includes several examples of enlarged objects like the thunderbird on the eponymous sign and the enormous candles in front of the Flamingo, which are not unlike Oldenburg's own monument proposals. While Oldenburg's art is not actually illustrated in *Learning from Las Vegas*, Venturi, Scott Brown, and Izenour explicitly compare the Strip's signage to Oldenburg's sculptures when describing the Caesar's Palace sign: "Although not so high as the Dunes Hotel sign next door or the Shell sign on the other side, its base is enriched by Roman centurions, lacquered like Oldenburg hamburgers, who peer over the acres of cars and across their desert empire to the mountains beyond."[19] The architects are referring to Oldenburg's multiple hamburger sculptures from the early 1960s. Works like *Hamburger, Popsicle, and Price* (1961–62), *Two Cheeseburgers with Everything (Dual Hamburger)* (1962), and *Hamburger with Pickle and Tomato Attached* (1963), all painted with enamel, have a surface sheen analogous to the luster of the centurions. *Floor Burger* (1962) (Figure 5.1), made of canvas and covered with loose, painterly drips, has a layered appearance that also evokes the idea of lacquer included in the description of Caesar's Palace. Even more significant than this textual allusion to Oldenburg and the surface articulation of his objects, however, is the scale of Oldenburg's *Floor Burger* and its similarity to the photograph of the Burger House, a hamburger stand in Dallas reproduced in *Learning from Las Vegas*. Uncannily related to Oldenburg's large-scale rendition of the same subject, this fast-food restaurant in the shape of its product is itself a precedent for the artist's monument proposals. Oldenburg's parallel explorations of vernacular architecture and the relevance of his work to Las Vegas imagery extend well beyond the look of the Caesar's Palace sign. Indeed, Oldenburg's allusive appearance in the text confirms a deeper influence between artist and architects.

Figure 5.1. Claes Oldenburg, *Floor Burger*, 1962. Canvas filled with foam rubber and cardboard boxes painted with acrylic paint, 132.1 × 213.4 cm. (Art Gallery of Ontario, Toronto [purchased 1967].)

Floor Burger is specifically relevant for Venturi and Scott Brown's theories because this work, like Oldenburg's other similarly large, soft sculptures such as *Floor Cake* (1962) and *Floor Cone* (1962), reconceives the process of viewing as embodied and, ultimately, theatrical in the same way that Michael Fried describes minimalist (or literalist) sculpture in "Art and Objecthood." According to Fried, "the experience of literalist art is of an object *in a situation*—one that, virtually by definition, *includes the beholder.*"[20] This situational aspect, for Fried, is intensified by a work's scale, contributing to the viewer's physical and psychic responses to the work and heightening his or her awareness of the spatial conditions of its location. Because of its size—approximately four by seven feet—*Floor Burger* manifests the anthropomorphic qualities that Fried locates in minimalist art, promoting a more fully bodily interaction and encouraging an understanding of viewing as a kind of encounter. Oldenburg's display method also induces contingent relationships—physical and psychic—between the sculptural object and its audience. When Oldenburg exhibited such works at the Green Gallery in 1962, for instance, he installed them, as their titles suggest, directly on the floor and away from the wall. Without even a pedestal to designate a separate space for the work apart from the spectator's own, *Floor Burger* insinuates itself into the gallery in a way that constitutes vehement "presence," not only demanding visual attention but also potentially redirecting the spectator's path, fulfilling Fried's notion that literalist works "*confront* the beholder—they must, one might almost say, be placed not just in his space but in his *way*."[21] By altering the visual field and the perception of the gallery space, Oldenburg's sculptures, like Fried's literalist objects, thus affect a more subjective experience in ways different than his early, enlarged, but still relatively small sculptural objects. As Fried asserts, "Something is said to have presence when it demands that the beholder take it into account, that he take it *seriously*—and when the fulfillment of that demand consists simply in being *aware* of it and, so to speak, in acting accordingly."[22] Because Oldenburg's upscale pieces command space and challenge the viewer in both optical and bodily terms, they attract notice in ways that Fried was suggesting in minimalist practice and that Venturi and Scott Brown were similarly theorizing for the sculptural buildings in American vernacular architecture.

In the studio projects preceding *Learning from Las Vegas*, Venturi and Scott Brown tie their emerging ideas to Oldenburg's through allusions to his art, especially his hamburgers, while their comments in the studio notes substantiate their shared notions of the significance of Oldenburg's art for their own projects. In the Levittown studio, Scott Brown outlines several tasks, including "The Oldenburg Interpretation." This section of their studio reinforces the architects' views that successful symbolism involves an innovative representation of the familiar and that a nonjudgmental approach facilitates a renewed understanding of the contemporary urban environment. For this topic, the architects direct their students to "do for housing what Oldenburg did for hamburgers" and explain, "Oldenburg has essentially made us look at hamburgers in another way because he has portrayed them in an unusual way: big, lacquered and in an art gallery. Does he hate them or love them and should we? Probably he feels some of both, but that doesn't matter—at least not yet. The first thing is the shift in vision and understanding which an Oldenburg can induce, and the re-interpretation and re-classification of our cultural artifacts which he provides."[23] This statement addresses exactly the alterations in scale, appearance, and context that Venturi, Scott Brown, and Izenour articulate more generally, in terms of pop, in *Learning from Las Vegas*. They locate in Oldenburg's sculptures the alterations in scale, treatment of surface, and changes in context that inflect both their description of the Caesar's Palace sign and their general comments about pop art in *Learning from Las Vegas*. Moreover, Oldenburg's "re-interpretation and re-classification of our cultural artifacts" is essentially generalized in *Learning from Las Vegas* as pop's "new interpretation of twentieth-century artifacts," while their claim that "the familiar that is a little off has a strange and revealing power" is conversely specified from pop overall to

Oldenburg in particular, as his art clearly influences several of the architects' later sculptural designs.[24]

Oldenburg's works, whether his large-scale sculptures, his proposed object monuments, or the representational architecture in his lithographs, mirror the kind of sculptural forms that Venturi, Scott Brown, and Izenour designate in *Learning from Las Vegas* as the "duck." Although Venturi and Scott Brown have identified the relevance of Oldenburg's art for the commercial landscape, their project notes for several design competitions in New York in the late 1970s and early '80s specifically acknowledge a nexus between their designs and Oldenburg's sculptures. The Westway Urban Design Project (1978–85) includes sculptures of oversized apples as plinth decorations, while the Times Square Plaza Design (1984) places a single, similarly large apple on the roof of an information kiosk. The apple, over ninety feet in diameter, would dominate the southern area of Times Square and the building on which it rests. The apple holds, for Venturi, a recognizable relation to Oldenburg's large-scale works: "This design proposes a Big Apple for Times Square: a piece of representational sculpture which is bold in form yet rich in symbolism . . . realism with a diversity of associations. It is popular *and* esoteric—a Big Apple symbolizing New York City and a surrealistic object evoking René Magritte or a Pop-art monument in the manner of Claes Oldenburg."[25] In a later plan for a band pavilion at Battery Park in New York (1989), Venturi, Rauch, and Scott Brown resurrect the enlarged apple and this time transform it from decorative object into functional architecture. As Venturi explains, it "is somewhat like the representational sculpture of Claes Oldenburg but is also architectural and provides shelter," the proposal that comes closest to the architects' so-called duck.[26]

More than any other pop artist, Oldenburg created sculptural objects that exist in dialogue with Venturi and Scott Brown's architectural projects. While statements in the Levittown studio and *Learning from Las Vegas* suggest the architects' specific knowledge of his art, later projects affirm the attention they paid to, and the lessons they learned from, his sculptural practice. Oldenburg's work generally maintains a discourse around the architects' "duck," which they oppose to the "decorated shed," and thus specifically complements the assimilation of Ruscha's facades to Venturi and Scott Brown's own.

"The Moving Eye": Experiencing Ed Ruscha's Photographic Practice

While Oldenburg's sculptures and monument proposals proposals paralleled Venturi, Scott Brown, and Izenour's research and even influenced later designs, Ruscha's photography functioned as an early conceptual and artistic precedent for the architects, shaping their research on and representations of Las Vegas and other city spaces. In the preface to *Learning from Las Vegas*, Venturi singles out

Ruscha, acknowledging "the Pop artists" collectively while adding parenthetically, "particularly Edward Ruscha."[27] Scott Brown had discovered Ruscha's photography in the mid-1960s when she was teaching at the University of California, Los Angeles, and creating her own photographic archive of the vernacular architecture in the city.[28] During this decade, Ruscha produced photographic books such as *Twentysix Gasoline Stations* (1963), *Some Los Angeles Apartments* (1965), *Every Building on the Sunset Strip* (1966) (Figure 5.2), and *Thirtyfour Parking Lots* (1967), which similarly accumulate examples of architectural typologies in Los Angeles.

Scott Brown's first published statements about Ruscha's art and his instructive approach to contemporary urban forms in "On Pop Art, Permissiveness, and Planning" give early evidence of the centrality of Ruscha's method for the architects' own. In this article, which reproduces single photographs from three of Ruscha's books—a gas station, an apartment building, and a parking lot—Scott Brown writes at length about Ruscha's photography and in so doing articulates the ways that his style would anticipate thoughts about pop art in *Learning from Las Vegas*. She begins with a historical overview and claims, as she and her coauthors would reiterate in *Learning from Las Vegas*, that architects and urban designers "are beginning to look for new, more receptive ways of seeing the environment."[29] She situates Ruscha's work within this current attitude and describes the prescient viewpoint in his photographic images:

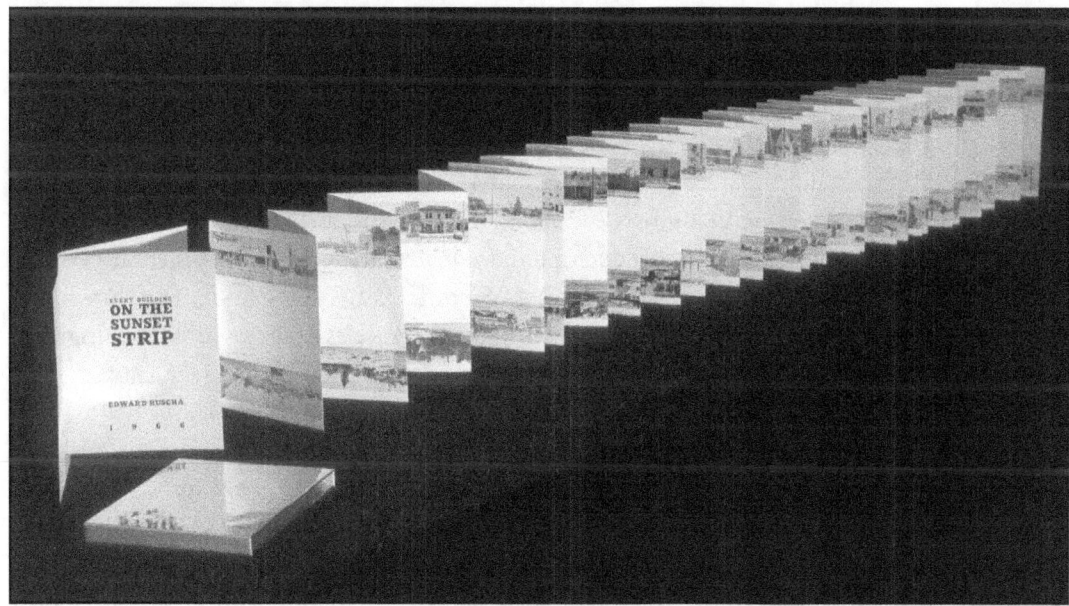

Figure 5.2. Ed Ruscha, *Every Building on the Sunset Strip*, 1966. Photographic book, black offset paper folded and glued, 7.1 × 5.6 × 0.4 in. (Copyright Ed Ruscha. Courtesy of Gagosian Gallery, N.Y.)

But architects and urban designers are, in fact, Johnnies-come-lately on this scene and can learn from others. From Edward Ruscha, for example. His *Twenty Six Gasoline Stations* are photographed straight: no art except the art that hides art. His *Some Los Angeles Apartment Houses* are end-of-the-world, bridge-playing, walk-up, R–4, togetherness type, with the Tiki at the doorway and a pool in the patio. Ruscha's *Thirty Four Parking Lots*, photographed from a helicopter, resemble D'Arcangelo paintings: arrowed, tensioned, abstract diagrams where oil patterns on the asphalt reveal differential stress from differing accessibility. His *Sunset Strip*, a long, accordion fold-out, shows every building on each side of the Strip, each carefully numbered but without comment. Deadpan, a scholarly monograph with a silver cover and slip-on box jacket, it . . . suggests a new vision of the very imminent world around us.[30]

Scott Brown's comments draw attention to Ruscha's subjects and style as well as to the ways the resulting images might serve to produce information about vernacular architecture captured through seemingly objective vision. With the exception of the *Every Building on the Sunset Strip*, whose alternative format Scott Brown describes, Ruscha's books of gas stations, apartment buildings, and parking lots arrange black-and-white photographs as individual or paired images, and the two-page spreads include few, if any, textual interruptions. In this way, the framing of each subject, in both the photographic composition and the book's general layout, seems to impose little distinction between representation and reality through seemingly casual, almost snapshot-like images, or an "art that hides art."[31]

Ruscha has explained his technique and its effect in similar terms, claiming, "Instead of going out and calling a gas station 'art,' I'm calling its photograph art. But the photograph isn't the art—the gas station might be. The photograph is just a surrogate gas station. The photograph by itself doesn't mean anything to me; it's the gas station that's the important thing. . . . [W]hat I was after was no-style or a non-statement with a no-style."[32] In another statement, the artist contends, "The camera is used simply as a documentary device, the closest documentary device; that's what it's all about. . . . I like facts, facts, facts are in the book. The closest representation to an apartment house in *Some Los Angeles Apartments* is a photograph, nothing else, not a drawing, because that becomes somebody else's vision of what it is, and this is the camera's eye, the closest delineation of that subject."[33]

In the Levittown studio notes, Scott Brown again references Ruscha's approach and here more clearly explicates the relevant effects of his documentary method as she expounds on the ways that the artist's style could support the studio members' research goals: "What new techniques are required to document new forms? We should aim to dead-pan the material so it speaks for itself. Ruscha has pioneered this treatment in his monographs (*The Sunset Strip, Some Los Angeles Apartments*). It is a way to avoid being upstaged by our own subject matter. It can lead too, toward the methodical rigour which will be required of architectural formal analysis once it is recognised as a legitimate activity."[34] As Scott Brown's comments indicate, the architects engaged not just Ruscha's subject matter but also his deadpan style, inasmuch as the transparency, or "realism" of the artist's straightforward documentation of vernacular architecture bolstered their theoretical approach.[35] Ruscha's method provided a specific way, as they put it in *Learning from Las Vegas*, of generally "looking nonjudgmentally at the environment."[36]

Ruscha's subject matter in *Twentysix Gasoline Stations*, *Some Los Angeles Apartments*, and *Every Building on the Sunset Strip* focuses on building façades in a way that anticipates the "decorated shed" and the architects' interest in symbolic communication more generally. As Ruscha has commented in *Every Building on the Sunset Strip*, "All I was after was that store-front plane. . . . It's like a Western town in a way. A store-front plane of a Western town is just paper, and everything behind it is just nothing."[37] He has reiterated elsewhere, "Los Angeles to me is like a series of store-front planes that are all vertical from the street, and there's almost like nothing behind the façades. It's all façades here—that's what intrigues me about the whole city of Los Angeles—the façade-ness of the whole thing."[38] Just like Ruscha's photographs of gas stations and apartment buildings, most of which were shot frontally from a position on or across the street, the accumulated façades along the Sunset Strip become a collection of architectural surfaces. Ruscha's concentration on façades in strip architecture especially demonstrates his shared perception of and interest in the symbolic nature of building fronts, which, as the architects suggest, exists at the foundation of vernacular American architecture. Statements in *Learning from Las Vegas* reveal a parallel consideration. As the architects likewise specify, "The false fronts of western stores . . . were bigger and taller than the interiors they fronted to communicate the store's importance and to enhance the quality and unity of the street. But false fronts are of the order and scale of Main Street. From the desert town on the highway in the West of today, we can learn new and vivid lessons about an impure architecture of communication."[39] Because the "decorated shed" is something of a box with applied ornament that emphasizes only one of its sides—the one facing the road—its decoration reiterates a kind of flatness and exposes a formal quality that underscores the significance of Ruscha's *Every Building on the Sunset Strip* as artistic precedent for Venturi and Scott Brown.[40]

Unlike the designs of Ruscha's other publications, which isolate individual images, *Every Building on the Sunset Strip* sutures discrete photographs together to depict the continuous architectural façades along this Los Angeles landmark, as if viewed sequentially through the car's side windows. The twenty-seven-foot, accordion-pleated publication gives the impression of a fragmented but continuous passage. Within the series of images, divisions between adjoining photographs are often perceptible. These subtle ruptures between images, as well as the segmented folds of the book's single-page layout, create relatively distinct zones within the unidirectional path, somewhat compromising but not completely undermining the notion of an uninterrupted route, clearly reinforced by the paper's considerable length. As in Ruscha's other books, textual remarks are minimal: addresses are numbered; cross-streets are labeled. Both sides of the road are visible as buildings face each other, as on the street, across the white area down the center of the book.

In *Learning from Las Vegas*, there are two illustrations that bear Ruscha's name: "An 'Edward Ruscha' elevation of the Strip" (Figure 5.3) and a "Piece of South Street 'Ruscha,'" which represent the Las Vegas Strip and the architects' plan for the Philadelphia Crosstown Community, respectively.[41] The captions of both illustrations make clear their appropriation of Ruscha's art, and the compositions take on the format of *Every Building on the Sunset Strip*, which he made with a motorized camera from the back of a truck and has described as "continuous motorized photos."[42] When photographing Las Vegas and its signage, Venturi, Scott Brown, Izenour, and their students employed both view and movie cameras. In a two-step process used to record the length of the Strip, they attached movie cameras to the

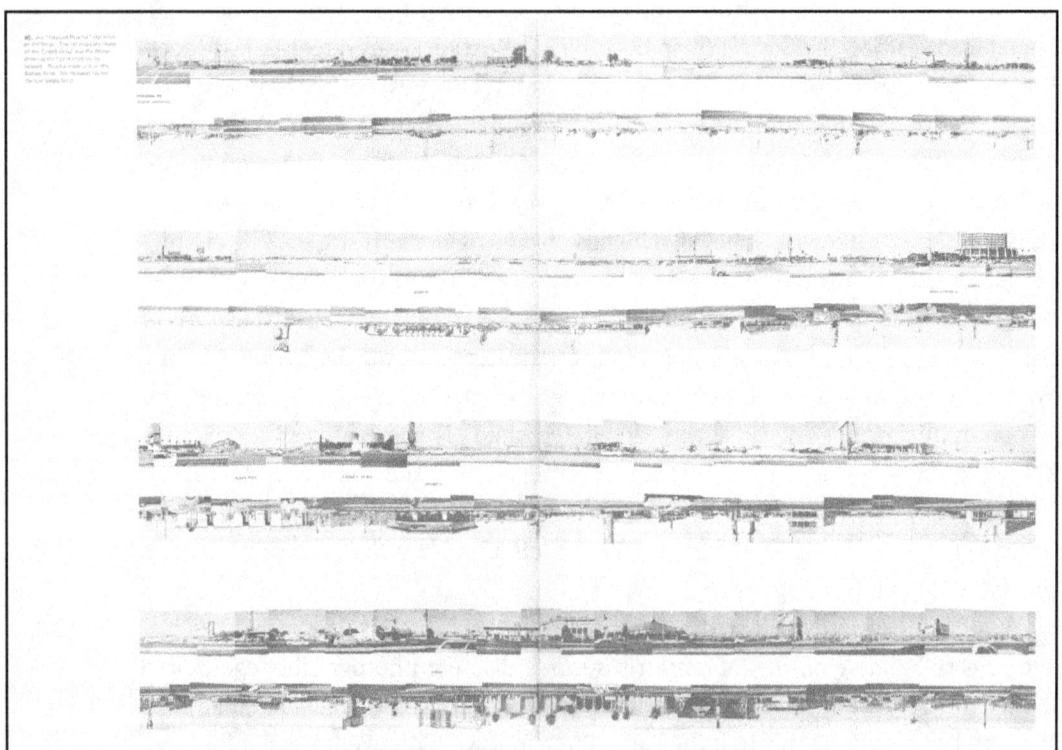

Figure 5.3. An "Edward Ruscha" elevation of the Strip (Venturi, Scott Brown, and Izenour, *Learning from Las Vegas*, 26–27. Courtesy of Venturi, Scott Brown and Associates, Inc.)

front hood of the car to capture the forward-moving view and also placed cameras in the side windows to document the roadside from a complementary angle. Scott Brown has identified this technique as "three-camera deadpan," a description that also ties their method to her early description of Ruscha's approach.[43]

Their "'Edward Ruscha' elevation of the Strip" consists of two two-page spreads and includes, as does Ruscha's example, photographs of both sides of the street separated by a white band and marked only with intermittent names identifying casinos and cross streets. The sequence along the street moves across both pages and down from left to right, top to bottom. The photographs' continuation across four pages emphasizes the significant expanse—"the unraveling of the famous Strip itself"—a horizontality reworked to conform to a conventional book format.[44] The vertical organization of the pages and the repetition of four sections of road within each spread combine to confirm the architects' exhaustive documentation of the roadside and to recreate the passage along the route, if not with the same phenomenological quality as Ruscha's original.

Likewise, "Piece of South Street 'Ruscha'" extends Ruscha's strip structure across a single two-page spread depicting "a commercial strip at the scale of Main Street."[45] Connected photographs in two bands again show both sides of the street and label cross streets whose names become more prominent graphic elements. This design also intersperses individual images of storefront displays. Thus this spread, clearly dependent on yet departing from Ruscha's precedent, has a divided focus. Looking across the street and into windows, with both distant and close-up views, highlights the pedestrian and vehicular perspectives on the street, even suggesting the possibility of a gaze that is both distracted and attentive. This composition attests, in a different way from the Las Vegas images, to a meaningful integration of static images and mobilized perspectives, as if bringing together aspects of the two modes of photography in Ruscha's thematic books; used by Venturi, Scott Brown, and Izenour's team; and integrated elsewhere in *Learning from Las Vegas*.

The photographs in *Every Building on the Sunset Strip* record the buildings along the street, and the book's unusual folded format recreates the experience of driving. The design allows the reader, if conceptually occupying the white area between the photographic bands—the middle of the road—to see both sides of the street at once as Ruscha restructures peripheral vision. The presentation of the Strip as an extended piece of paper also involves a sort of implied motion, analogizing the process of unfurling subsequent sections to traveling along the street. This effect of Ruscha's method is one that Venturi, Scott Brown, and Izenour likewise have perceived and recreated in their own representational methods and that Eleanor Antin first discussed in Ruscha's books from the early 1960s, like *Twentysix Gasoline Stations*. She suggests that the pictorial narrative here, which she charts from the artist's native Oklahoma City to Los Angeles, constitutes a road trip covering "1500 miles and sixty hours of life," connoting a journey in space and time.[46] While she emphasizes the same deadpan approach that Scott Brown does, Antin also provocatively suggests the possibility of a more subjective experience: "The work is very systematic. . . . Anyone who takes twenty-six photographs of the same subject and packages it as a complete work might be expected to have a point of view about the material. . . . His structure is deliberately sparse and casual and filled with holes, and it is here that actual experience resides. Suggestions are offered by the material he does give and spaces are left for us to enter. There is actually a good deal of information, but it's there as a kind of invitation."[47] Antin locates a linear narrative movement and represented motion in another of Ruscha's books called *Crackers* (1969), a series of photographs in which "minimally differentiated images are so leisurely and precise in the manner in which they record the action that the book turns into a movie. It's sort of a slow-motion flip-book."[48] While Ruscha has affirmed this intended flip-book effect in *Crackers*, he has also explicitly transformed *Twentysix Gasoline Stations*, after the fact, in his drawing *Flipping* (1973), which Antin's article reproduces.[49] In *Flipping*, the book becomes dynamic, held between hands turning pages from back to front. Ruscha seems to suggest that this physical manipulation and visual perception might together produce the effect of animation through apparent changes in the images from page to page. Here, then, the artist endows his earlier book of vernacular architecture with the same possibility of perceived motion that Antin describes in his other books. Ruscha's revision suggests that Venturi, Scott Brown, and Izenour follow a similar progression and take the intended effects of his photographic books to a logical culmination.[50]

In *Learning from Las Vegas*, the two-page spread of a "movie sequence traveling North on the Strip" (Figure 5.4) repeats multiple views from the car and presents images that frame the road and its signage in a succession that implies motion and incorporates specific dynamics from Ruscha's books. This layout contains a remarkable juxtaposition that contrasts the forward-looking sequence with selected, static glimpses of casinos on the roadside. Together, these two vantage points reiterate the similar confluence in a "Piece of South Street 'Ruscha,'" merging discrete views of selected buildings with a general sensation of moving along the Strip, as if both revealing the two different camera angles from the architects' mobile research and combining the photographs from Ruscha's thematic books with the perceptual dynamic of *Every Building on the Sunset Strip*, albeit again with several significant modifications. Here, the road's periphery is cleverly allocated to the margins, with the more central views showing the perspective down the middle of the road. This design then presents the architects' technique—multiple cameras strapped to the front and sides of the car—and offers simultaneous perspectives, as if from the driver's seat and out the passenger's window, forward-looking and peripheral, at once static and mobilized.

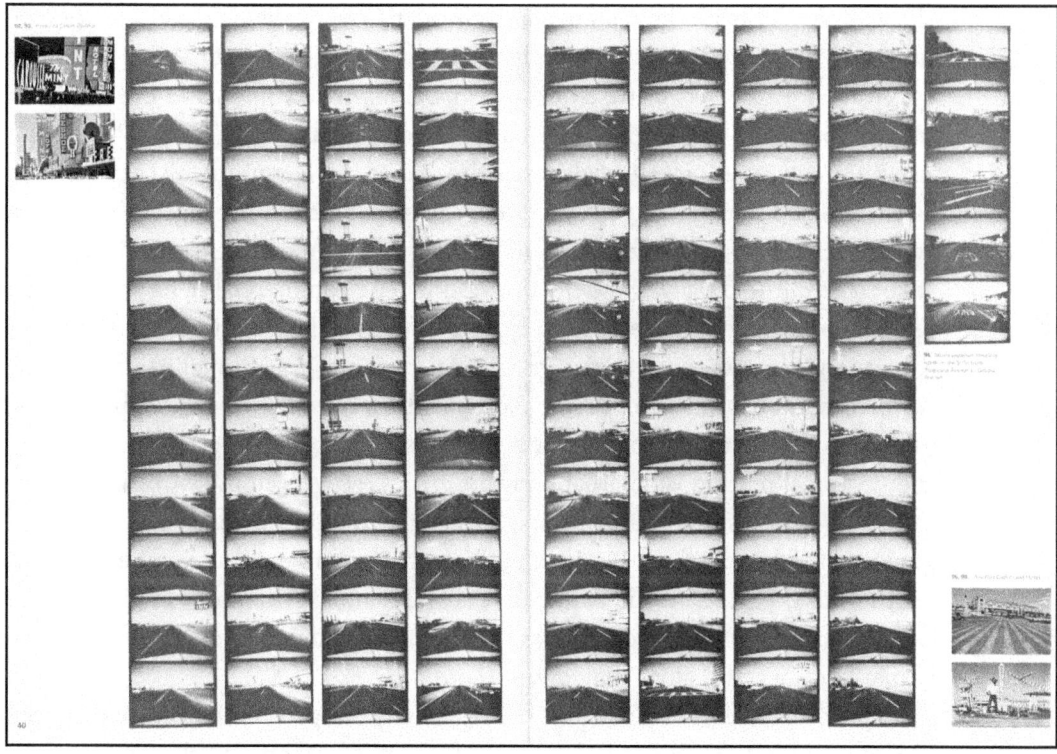

Figure 5.4. Fremont Street casinos; movie sequence traveling north on the Strip from Tropicana Avenue to Sahara Avenue; and Aladdin Casino and Hotel (Venturi, Scott Brown, and Izenour, *Learning from Las Vegas*, 40–41. Courtesy of Venturi, Scott Brown and Associates, Inc.)

The views through a car's windshield represent the automobile's forward motion through the sequential shifts in roadside signage. As the architects specify in this section of *Learning from Las Vegas*, "The emerging order of the Strip is a complex order.... It is not an order dominated by the expert and made easy for the eye. The *moving eye in the moving body* must work to pick out and interpret a variety of changing, juxtaposed orders, like the shifting configurations of a Victor Vasarely painting."[51] Vasarely's painting demonstrates these "shifting configurations" among the shapes within its grid. Printed in black and white, the painting is organized into squares of varying shades of black, white, and grey containing circles, ovals, and squares in the same palette. Within this limited range of shapes and colors, the viewer must "work to pick out" any pattern through a systematic study of the subtle differences, weighing consistency against variation. There is a system, with alterations within an otherwise ordered field, that produces steady yet varied rhythmic repetition and syncopated alternation of identical forms, enabling the coexistent and contradictory effects of distraction and attention.[52]

The grid format of repeated squares of Vasarely's painting makes the work an appropriate graphic counterpart to the architects' two-page layout of sequential images of the Strip. The rectangular frames and the triangular roadway are consistent geometric elements; the differences among adjoining squares of Vasarely's painting are restaged in the shifting signs along the strip. While the "complex order" of Vasarely's painting might also serve as a parallel iteration of the "paradoxical subtleties" of the highway addressed at the beginning of Learning from Las Vegas and illustrated by D'Arcangelo's arrowed print, D'Arcangelo's serial canvases are compositionally even more similar to the "movie sequence." Paintings like those entitled U.S. Highway 1 (1963) silhouette commercial signs prominently against otherwise uninflected landscapes and, like the architects' photographs, depict a view from the driver's seat while also connoting, through the systematic displacement of signs, a sense of travel along the highway.[53] This attempt to relate a lived understanding of particular environments through the graphic notation of perceptual motion is one that early art critics recognized in D'Arcangelo's canvases. As Dore Ashton has written, D'Arcangelo "is telling us that the sensation of space is fundamental . . . [and] something that enters into our total experience of the world."[54] As D'Arcangelo varies the scales and distributions of his signs, he conveys, like Venturi, Scott Brown, and Izenour's "movie sequence," the visual experience of travel along a highway.

Similarly, the "movie sequence" registers a kind of mobilized perception: when read top to bottom and left to right, the photographs put the viewer in the driver's seat and follow a legible, sequential journey. Here, as in Ruscha's Every Building on the Sunset Strip, visual shifts convey physical displacement as the reader's imaginary journey is played out by the steady rhythm of looking from frame to frame. As Appleyard has reiterated, "Travel through the city creates a sequence of experience. This sequence is a moving encounter with the environment, in which the traveler acts according to his own purposes, while the environment reciprocally shapes his experience. . . . A sequence may be enjoyed purely as a sensuous dialogue with the environment, or it may be used to glean information about the city, its structure and meaning. . . . The path experience, in this case, may be likened more to a novel or a film."[55]

Venturi and Scott Brown had already noted the differences between relative speeds on Main Street and the highway and described the sense of distraction with which one views the landscape from a moving vehicle. As they write, "on the highway the landscape becomes a series of events, more or less insistent, which swim into the driver's ken and rapidly out again to be succeeded by the next."[56] Furthermore, Scott Brown's "Learning from Pop" likewise calls for new ways of capturing the high-speed nature of the urban cityscape. As she writes, "New analytic techniques must use film and video tape to convey the dynamism of sign architecture and the sequential experience of vast landscapes."[57] By creating a kind of static graphic equivalent to a filmstrip, the architects reimagine the effect that Ruscha simulated in Every Building on the Sunset Strip. The caption for the illustration—"movie sequence traveling north"—makes clear this tension between photographic stasis and dynamic, narrative sequencing. In addition, the architects actualize a notion that surfaces in *Complexity and Contradiction*, in which Venturi sets out to articulate "the richness and ambiguity of modern experience, including that experience which is inherent in art."[58] The experience of the commercial strip was not only specifically tied to vehicular travel; it was also a guiding principle in the architects' research methods and representational strategies. Venturi's photograph of a typical main street from *Complexity and Contradiction*, the forerunner to Las Vegas's Strip, illustrates the clash between order in the tight geometry of the road and chaos in its seemingly collaged and visually dominant signage. As Venturi writes, "In the validly complex building or cityscape, the eye does not want to be too easily or too quickly satisfied in its search for unity within a whole."[59] As the architects restate this idea in *Learning from Las Vegas*, they suggest, as addressed above, that in the contemporary city, "the *moving eye in the moving body* must work to pick out and interpret a variety of changing, juxtaposed orders."[60] For Venturi and Scott Brown, just as vision is fundamentally corporeal, so too architecture as symbolic communication organizes and directs itself to the speed and contingencies of modern life and to bodies, usually in motion.

While Fried argues in "Art and Objecthood" that these two orders of experience—presentness to the eye and presence of the body—are mutually exclusive in the art of the 1960s, Oldenburg's sculpture and Ruscha's photography, as well as Venturi, Scott Brown, and Izenour's statements, contest such a conclusion. In fact, Fried's inclusion of Tony Smith's account of his drive on the uncompleted New Jersey Turnpike in 1966 highlights the significance of the kinetic perception of the highway environment. As Smith writes, "The experience on the road was something mapped out but not socially recognized. I thought to myself, it ought to be clear that's the end of art. Most painting looks pretty pictorial after that. There is no way you can frame it, you just have to experience it."[61] Smith's contends that this experience finds no expression in contemporary art—or as Fried interprets it, "There was, he seems to have felt, no way to 'frame' his experience on the road, that is, no way to make sense of it in terms of art, to make *art* of it, at least as art then was."[62] These perspectives speak to both the difficulty and the relevance of Ruscha's, and Venturi, Scott Brown, and Izenour's, search for innovative ways of looking at and representing this landscape in their respective studies. It is, therefore, significant that the architects studied and photographed Las Vegas, as Ruscha had Los Angeles, from a moving vehicle, thus recreating the characteristic vantage point from which commercial suburban environments are generally perceived and that they chose, by following Ruscha's depiction of similar environments, to recreate this everyday experience of the Las Vegas Strip by adopting his representational strategies.[63]

The impact of Ruscha's photography on *Learning from Las Vegas* is apparent. To a lesser degree, the compositions of his word paintings are evident in Venturi and Scott Brown's built projects and their representations, especially with respect to the BASCO Showroom and Warehouse (1979), which is paradigmatic of the decorated shed and is inspired by Las Vegas. This building is a simple box with a monochromatic blue façade dominated by the five thirty-four-foot, three-dimensional red letters—actually separated from one another and detached from the building itself—spelling out the company's name. This design effectively advertises the building's corporate identity within the commercial environment: from the road, the façade legibly reads as a continuous surface. While this solution seems not unrelated to Ruscha's monochromatic word paintings like *Ace* (1962) or *Talk About Space* (1963), the photographic compositions the architects created to document this building utilize techniques from both Ruscha's paintings and his photographs. The firm's photographs of the building show the various formats necessary to squeeze the long façade into a single image. One reflects the strong diagonal of paintings like *Standard Station, Amarillo, Texas* (1963), while another, taken in the parking lot at a distance from the building, utilizes joined photographs like *Every Building on the Sunset Strip*, connecting five different images—one for each letter—to form a complete view. These aesthetic choices reinforce the BASCO building's substantial length and horizontal orientation. Such compositions clearly imitate Ruscha's own and affirm the ways that the lessons learned from the artist and in Las Vegas resonate within the architects' design practice.

Organizing Signs of Life: Moving between Representation and Reality

Although *Learning from Las Vegas* introduced Venturi and Scott Brown's research to the architectural community, *Signs of Life: Symbols in the American City* (Figure 5.5) restaged their theories for the general public at an institution that was itself a symbolic center. Installed at the Smithsonian Institution during the nation's Bicentennial, this exhibition reconceived and redefined environments in a way that was typically American. The architects attempted to speak, not in dogmatic tones and universalizing principles, but instead through vernacular objects and individualized experiences.[64]

The exhibition documented three archetypal American environments: the private home, the suburban strip, and the main street. An entry hall with introductory material launched the exhibition and opened onto the first of the show's three thematic sections. "The Home" included façades and interiors of three houses, each representative of a common type: the Levittowner, the row house, and the colonial Williamsburg. Visitors viewed typical house fronts and model living

Figure 5.5. *Signs of Life: Symbols in the American City*, Renwick Gallery, Smithsonian Institution, Washington, D.C., 1976 (Photograph by Tom Bernard. Courtesy of Venturi, Scott Brown and Associates, Inc.)

rooms, while comic book–like speech balloons delineated the historical symbolism in the decorations and furnishings. Additional materials on the walls complemented the three-dimensional displays and provided further textual information and photographic documentation about domestic styling and symbolic communication. "The Strip" assembled salient elements of the commercial environment. Bracketed by entrance and exit signs from McDonald's, this corridor gallery displayed billboards, signage, and neon lights to reflect the composite atmosphere of the highway. The illumination in this room changed every few minutes to evoke the ambient differences between day and night. At the center of the room, a sort of billboard display, its form symbolically echoing those around it, reproduced photographs of roadside architecture and offered explications of urban symbolism. "The Street" included photographic displays and reproductions spanning popular culture and fine art, from contemporary magazine ads and actual commercial signage to nineteenth-century paintings, all accompanied by explanatory texts.

The exhibition's representations of familiar spaces and its inclusion of actual objects inevitably provoked comparisons to pop art. Reviews, for example, announce "Real Life: It's Art!"[65] and "Pop Art a hit in Washington."[66] Captions designate "'Signs of Life': [a] Pop encyclopedia,"[67] and descriptions assert that "the gaudy commercial lights and signs and visual jazz of 'Route 66' . . . [are] excitingly displayed at the Renwick and elevated to art,"[68] or "[t]he effect of this vibrant, abstract montage of color, light and motion, from McDonald's to Mobil, is quite startlingly beautiful in the perverse way of Pop Art. The Holiday Inn sign never looked so good."[69]

Because the architects have often explained that their discovery of this style led them "to reassess the role of symbolism and allusion in architecture and the use of traditional forms, decoration, and pattern in design,"[70] it is not surprising that they considered including a "Pop Art room" in *Signs of Life*.[71] While pop works did not make a literal appearance, the exhibition nonetheless retained traces of paradigmatic pop precedents. In "The Home," for example, the speech balloons recall Roy Lichtenstein's comics-inspired paintings, while domestic interiors resemble Oldenburg's *Bedroom* (1963). "The Strip," with its borrowed billboards and collected signage evokes Oldenburg's *Store* signs as well as James Rosenquist's and Robert Indiana's paintings.[72]

As the exhibition records demonstrate, when Venturi, Scott Brown, and Izenour pitched their ideas for the exhibition, they at first framed its installations through references to particular pop artists—Edward Kienholz and again Ruscha—who were chosen because their work involved environmental tableaux and suggested implied motion, respectively.[73] The architects embraced these pop precedents to activate the viewer's sensorial perception and to recreate the represented environments through an experiential aesthetic, inciting the effect that first appeared on the pages of *Learning from Las Vegas*.

The plan for *Signs of Life* (Figure 5.6) imagines ways that spectators would perceive individual installations through mobilized and embodied viewing. In their exhibition proposal, the architects explain their installations as simultaneously images and experiences. In the section dedicated to "The Home," viewers would take in domestic symbolism by walking through individual houses: entering front doors and passing through living rooms. The architects present their concept through a detailed description of the suburban house and an allusion to Kienholz's art: "The environment is like a Keinholtz [sic] sculpture, set for mowing the lawn and cooking on the barbeque or watching soap operas in the kitchen while waxing the floor with new 'Glo-Coat', except that only the objects that are symbolically important are here; everything else is abstracted."[74] In the architects' design, the viewers' movement through domestic spaces transports them from

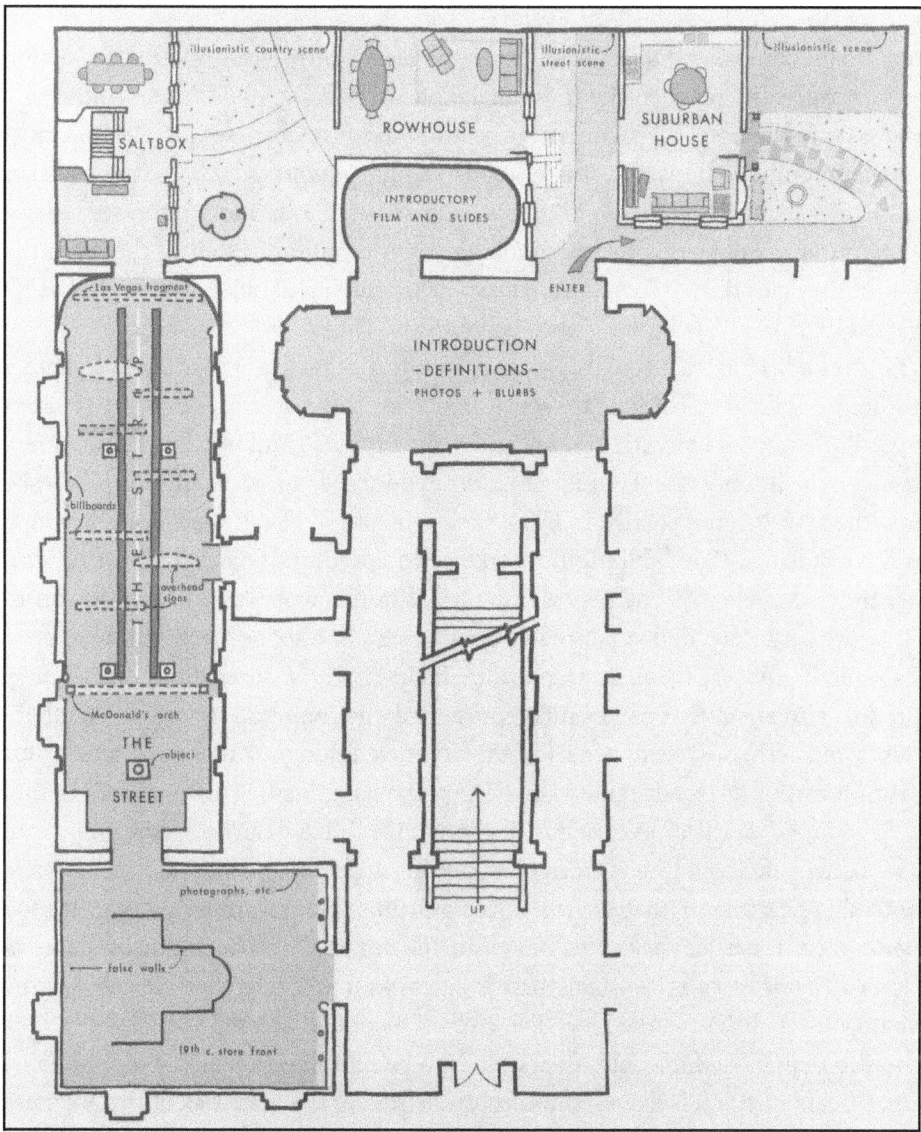

Figure 5.6. Exhibition plan for *Signs of Life: Symbols in the American City*, 1974 (Smithsonian Institution Archives, Record Unit 448, box 10, folder "Signs of Life: Symbols in the American City [33] February 27–September 26, 1974." Courtesy of Smithsonian Institution Archives.)

the realm of art literally into spaces of everyday life, emphasizing perception as a subjective process.

In works like *Roxy's* (1961) and *The Wait* (1964–65), Kienholz fabricates interiors into which viewers are invited; the settings are defined through arrangements of real objects. According to one reviewer, Kienholz's art "would have the viewer more involved, even physically, by requiring that doors be opened and closed by him and that materials be touched and prodded. . . . [O]ne is invited to participate. . . . One can sit on a sofa, smoke, browse through magazines, read letters, open compartments."[75] Another critic has acknowledged Kienholz's "ability to bestow reality on even the most trivial of surrounding objects: the coffee cup, the stain in the hotel foyer carpet, surge into the consciousness with the impact of reinvented phenomena. . . . It is his ability to make objects *real* . . . which makes his works such a revelation. . . . [Some] Pop artists . . . are more interested in objects purely as objects, [but] Kienholz is much more interested in them for the *stories* they can tell."[76] This narrative aspect of individual objects is similarly suggested in *Signs of Life* in the speech balloons in "The Home."

Kienholz constructs environmental sculptures that are accessible to a general audience, critical of reactionary social practices, and viscerally engaging to viewers, all of which align with Venturi and Scott Brown's thinking. Scott Brown recognized the intense effect of Kienholz's strategy of spectatorial inclusion when she saw the artist's retrospective in Los Angeles in 1966.[77] *The Beanery* (1966), which was included in that exhibition, reproduces a building: the artist's favorite local bar in Los Angeles. As one reviewer describes it, this work "assaults all the senses . . . with an intensified super-reality that demands response from all who enter its swinging doors."[78] Soliciting more than simply a visual reaction, *The Beanery* produces an effect that makes this represented environment, if not also its inhabitants and activities, seem as real as the original. Tellingly, Kienholz discusses his art in terms of its experiential value. The artist has stated, "I always thought that art should be an easier experience than what it is. Like I can't imagine going into The Louvre and standing in front of a painting and having a vicarious experience with this painting or that artist. It's too pristine; it's too properly hung; it's too perfect; . . . it isn't as easy as walking into *The Beanery*."[79] Robert Pincus's description of *The Beanery* as "a setting that is actual as much as archetypal" evokes the analogous qualities planned for "The Home" section of *Signs of Life*.[80]

Kienholz's *Eleventh Hour Final* (1968), a living room in which a disembodied head floats in the television-cum-tombstone listing the statistics of the Vietnam War, provides an especially provocative analogue for the suburban interior. Certainly, the *Signs of Life* version foregoes the sinister subject matter of Kienholz's room, but the real furniture and selected furnishings—carpet; sofa; coffee table with magazines, ashtray, and plastic flowers; side table with lamp; painting; and prominent television set—are similarly, almost identically, elaborated in each. The potential for the viewer's phenomenological inclusion in Kienholz's art occurs in the relationships created, or recreated, among individuals and objects, an interaction—physical, conceptual, even psychological—necessary for a lived understanding of architectural spaces.

In the exhibition proposal, "The Home" does not simply encourage imaginative projection but specifically necessitates the viewers' actual inclusion of themselves in, and passage through, the model rooms, experiences similar to those in Kienholz's environments. In the final installation at the Smithsonian, however, the façades and living rooms were adjacent, albeit physically separate, areas. Visitors walked around walls to peer into interiors. They could interact with the spaces conceptually, but because they could not actually enter them, physical engagement was thwarted. This resolution offered visitors the opportunity for comparative visual assessment—as the layout of the exhibition's brochure, which reproduces side-by-side images of the house façades and interiors, confirms—rather than distinct, embodied experiences.

As ultimately realized, "The Home" displaced the three-dimensional possibilities to a more two-dimensional effect, less akin to Kienholz's environmental sculpture and more related to the architects' documentary placards that catalogued California bungalows and Levittown houses, setting out numerous examples in grid formats that recall Ruscha's approach to detailing the architectural symbolism in his thematic books.[81] In displays like "Levittown," "The Row House," and "The Bungalow," photographs of individual homes appear side by side, encouraging viewers to compare the many examples and to discover, for instance, the different ways the house façades have been altered by their owners. Within each type, the viewpoint remains consistent, and most images are shot, like Ruscha's own, from across the street. In "The Row House" example, the architects also utilize Ruscha's suturing technique: the horizontal picture in the top right corner is composed of multiple shots joined together like the photographs in Ruscha's *Every Building on the Sunset Strip* to combine multiple examples and reproduce their context in a single image.

Ruscha's influence on Venturi, Scott Brown, and Izenour, already clear in *Learning from Las Vegas* and specific aspects of the *Signs of Life* installation, manifested even more significantly in the early proposal stages of the exhibition. The perceived motion implied on the pages of *Learning from Las Vegas* was also reenvisioned for *Signs of Life*. The installation planned for "The Strip" would have remade Ruscha's *Every Building on the Sunset Strip* as a moving installation. Venturi's earliest notes for *Signs of Life* suggest the potential use of Ruscha's method to incorporate in the exhibition "vi[s]ceral experience" and "animation."[82] In the exhibition proposal, the architects' explanation of "The Strip" brings this possibility to fruition and demonstrates the centrality of Ruscha's art for their design of the room dedicated to the highway environment.[83] As they write, "you experience one large, moving linear image of the strip. You walk the length of the room along a moving 'Edward Ruscha' elevation of a major strip." Positioned at eye level, two rear-illuminated screens measuring twelve to eighteen inches in height would have activated images of a commercial strip for forty to fifty feet along the center of the gallery. As the architects specify, "[i]ts movement in the opposite direction from the visitors' increases its speed of passing and simulates the experience of perception from an automobile."[84] Along this strip, and perpendicular to it, real signs would have hung from the ceiling or stood on the floor. Whether elevated or curbed, the signs would assume positions analogous to those along the highway.

In this technological intervention, the architects intended to activate the effect that Ruscha embedded in the structure of *Every Building on the Sunset Strip* and, in so doing, to actualize the implied motion of their *Learning from Las Vegas* "movie sequence." Furthermore, in an unpublished text for an exhibition catalogue, the architects excerpt the same phrase applied to Vasarely's picture in *Learning from Las Vegas*—"the moving eye in the moving body must work to pick out and interpret [a] variety of changing juxtaposed orders"—and use it as a caption for sequential images of the Strip, making the connection between vision and motion and observation and understanding in relation to the highway textually and graphically explicit.[85] Using *Every Building on the Sunset Strip*, which literally joins the images into a path whose planar, horizontality quality mimics that of the road, the architects theorized a more elaborate and three-dimensional version for *Signs of Life*. In its imagined form, this "moving 'Edward Ruscha' elevation" would have recast the various highway views in *Learning from Las Vegas* in a perceptual recreation of the viewer's mundane yet fully mobilized interaction with such spaces. Here the exhibition would have brought the two-page spreads in *Learning from Las Vegas* to a meaningful conclusion, representing for viewers the experience of driving down the highway by means of viewing a mobile landscape, like a film, exactly the direction in which architectural theorists like Appleyard, Lynch, and Myer were already moving, as had Venturi and Scott Brown. At the same time, creating this installation would have instantiated the experience of the car traveling along the highway in a way that matches contemporary accounts of the landscape and fulfills Walter Benjamin's assertion that "[r]eception in a state of distraction, which is increasing noticeably in all fields of art and is symptomatic of profound changes in apperception, finds in the film its true means of exercise."[86]

In the final installation of *Signs of Life*, the "moving 'Edward Ruscha' elevation" was replaced with a sort of billboard, its sides covered with information and images, many from the Las Vegas studio and subsequent publications, including the sequential photographs of the Strip. The signs that were to be situated either above or below the strip in an effort to imitate their original elevated or curbside locations, were instead distributed in a more random way throughout the gallery. Some viewers thus concentrated on the objects rather than their urban context. According to one review, "this presentation both glorifies and absolutely falsifies the strip. These signs are never seen like this, close up and close together. Here as never before they are beautiful objects."[87] Another declares, "The strip is full of enormous, brightly lit signs. . . . [T]hese magnificent pieces . . . are, in fact, lovely new forms of art."[88] Without the moving elevation as an organizing principle, the urban context and the viewer's embodied experience of it disintegrated, and the exhibition was, for some at least, overwhelmed by its institutional placement, as evidenced by its tendency to be read as pop art, absent any cohesive, three-dimensional experience.

Signs of Life did achieve plausibly kinetic episodes, as originally conceived by its designers; as one reviewer proclaimed, "Since this is a nation on wheels, walking through the exhibit is like driving across America."[89] According to another, "Today at the Renwick Gallery you can leave a quiet Williamsburg lane, turn—and abruptly face a neon lit runway, a conglomerate of enormous, garish signs and finally—only a few feet away, walk smack into the main street of Houston, Texas. . . . So real is it, in fact, that the neon runway, or strip, makes you practically taste hamburger as you pass the golden arches. A motel invites you to a comfortable night's rest, and you find yourself automatically looking for the price of gasoline as you pass the station."[90]

In the first months the exhibition was open, its popularity generated requests for a traveling version. The architects responded with ideas for a book and a movie, the latter of which, in their words, "will deal with the same ideas and images within the more realistic context of the moving driver and viewer and will instruct a student and lay audience in how to look at and interpret the American landscape."[91] In many ways, the movie itself sounds like an animated version of *Learning from Las Vegas*, but, like the parts of *Signs of Life* discussed above, this project never came to fruition. Nonetheless, its terms again reiterate the centrality of an active, mobile, and sentient perception within the architects' project, one that they have located within the legacy of pop art and through which they sought to shore up their research methodology and their own symbolic communication.

Notes

1. Robert Venturi, Denise Scott Brown, and Steven Izenour, *Learning from Las Vegas* (Cambridge, Mass.: MIT Press, 1972), 1.
2. Ibid., 2.
3. Ibid., 86. Individual comments on Roy Lichtenstein and Andy Warhol appear on pages 108 and 86, respectively. Those on Claes Oldenburg and Ed Ruscha will be discussed later in detail.
4. As they explain in *Learning from Las Vegas* (66), the double-hung windows in the Guild House exemplify a parallel to the vernacular symbolism in pop art: "Like the subject matter of Pop Art, they are commonplace elements made uncommon through distortion in shape (slight), change in scale (they are much bigger than normal double-hung windows), and change in context (double-hung windows in a perhaps high-fashion building)."
5. Ibid., 4.
6. Donald Appleyard, Kevin Lynch, and John R. Myer, *The View from the Road* (Cambridge, Mass.: MIT Press, 1964), 4.
7. Vincent Scully, introduction to *Complexity and Contradiction in Architecture*, 2nd ed., by Robert Venturi (New York: Museum of Modern Art, 1966; reprint 1996), 10.
8. Robert Venturi, *Complexity and Contradiction*, 104.
9. Denise Scott Brown, "On Pop Art, Permissiveness, and Planning," *Journal of the American Institute of Planners* 35 (May 1969): 186; italics in original.
10. Denise Scott Brown, "Learning from Pop," *Casabella*, December 1971, 15.
11. As Venturi has acknowledged, "Yes, Pop art was very important for its strong association with the ordinary. Denise knew this earlier than I did. She understood the relevance of Pop art before I did." Robert Venturi, "*Complexity and Contradiction* Twenty-five Years Later: An Interview with Robert Venturi," interview by Stuart Wrede, *Studies in Modern Art: American Art of the 1960s* (New York: Museum of Modern Art, 1991), 151.
12. Andy Warhol and Pat Hackett, *POPism: The Warhol '60s* (New York: Harcourt Brace Jovanovich, 1980), 39.
13. John Rublowsky, *Pop Art* (New York: Basic Books, 1965), 8–9. This statement seems to reference the art of Claes Oldenburg, Roy Lichtenstein, Andy Warhol, James Rosenquist, Tom Wesselmann, and Allan d'Arcangelo, respectively.
14. Peter Plagens, *The Sunshine Muse: Contemporary Art on the West Coast* (New York: Praeger, 1974), 139.
15. Venturi, Scott Brown, and Izenour, *Learning from Las Vegas*, 52.
16. See David Gebhard, introduction to *California Crazy: Roadside Vernacular Architecture*, by Jim Heimann and Rip Georges (San Francisco: Chronicle Books, 1980), 11–25.
17. Claes Oldenburg, *Notes* (Los Angeles: Gemini G.E.L., 1968), x. Oldenburg's comment refers to Los Angeles buildings like Barkies, the Pup Café, the Dog Café, and the Zep Diner. Several of Oldenburg's proposals for sculptures and buildings correspond to examples actually built in Los Angeles.
18. Claes Oldenburg, "The Poetry of Scale," interview by Paul Carroll, in *Claes Oldenburg: Proposals for Monuments and Buildings* (Chicago: Big Table Publishing Company, 1969), 25.
19. Venturi, Scott Brown, and Izenour, *Learning from Las Vegas*, 51.
20. Michael Fried, "Art and Objecthood," in *Minimal Art: A Critical Anthology*, ed. Gregory Battcock (New York: E. P. Dutton, 1968), 125; all italics in original.
21. Ibid., 127.
22. Ibid., 127–28.
23. Denise Scott Brown, "Remedial Housing for Architects Studio," in *Venturi, Scott Brown & Associates, On Houses and Housing*, ed. James Steele (New York: St. Martin's, 1992), 57. Elsewhere in the studio notes, the architects also reference Oldenburg: "Expand our classification system of ways in which attitudes are determined and comment on those which will be most useful to us in the studio. Make a bibliography of sources of information on attitudes towards housing and get as many of your sources into the Art and Architecture library as possible. To do this range widely from Madison Avenue to the School of Business to the Survey Research Center (University of Illinois) to local builders and their trade journals, to *Life, Time*, and the *New Yorker*, to TV, to Oldenburg and Keinholz" (54). "Remedial Housing

for Architects," also called "Learning from Levittown," studio was taught just after Oldenburg's retrospective exhibition at the Museum of Modern Art, New York. The catalogue for this exhibition, Barbara Rose, *Claes Oldenburg* (New York: Museum of Modern Art, 1969) and another recent publication, Claes Oldenburg, *Proposals for Monuments and Buildings, 1965–69* (Chicago: Big Table, 1969) are on the studio's bibliography. Robert Venturi and Denise Scott Brown, "Studio RHA: Bibliography," 26 January 1970, unnumbered box, The Architectural Archives, University of Pennsylvania by the gift of Robert Venturi and Denise Scott Brown (hereafter cited as Venturi Scott Brown Collection).

24. Venturi, Scott Brown, and Izenour, *Learning from Las Vegas*, 86.

25. Quoted in Stanislaus von Moos, *Venturi, Rauch & Scott Brown: Buildings and Projects* (New York: Rizzoli, 1987), 134; italics in original.

26. Quoted in Stanislaus von Moos, *Venturi, Scott Brown & Associates, 1986–1998* (New York: Monacelli Press, 1999), 188.

27. Robert Venturi, preface to *Learning from Las Vegas*, x.

28. See Venturi's comments on this subject: "Denise discovered Ed Ruscha when she taught at UCLA in the mid-1960s and we both had been learning from the Pop artists and their appreciation of the Everyday from the late 1950s on." Robert Venturi, "The Summit," in *The Magic Hour: The Convergence of Art and Las Vegas*, ed. Alex Farquharson (Weiz, Austria: Hatje Cantz, 2002), 48 (interview with Dave Hickey, Libby Lumpkin, Ralph Rugoff, Robert Venturi, Denise Scott Brown, and Steven Izenour).

29. Scott Brown, "On Pop Art," 184.

30. Ibid., 185–86.

31. Reyner Banham's remarks about Ruscha's photographs echo Scott Brown's comments: "There's no artist's touch there to confuse the issue. . . . The books offer no *verbal* clues as to how to look at the objects but that does not mean there are no clues as to how to look. The clear, non-verbal instruction that comes with, say, *Twenty-six Gasoline Stations* is 'These twenty-six gasoline stations are worth looking at.'" Reyner Banham, "Under the Hollywood Sign," in *Edward Ruscha: Prints and Publications 1962–74* (London: Arts Council of Great Britain, 1975), n.p.; italics in original.

32. Quoted in Henri Man Barendse, "Ed Ruscha: An Interview," *Afterimage* 8 (February 1981): 9, 10.

33. Quoted in A. D. Coleman, "My Books End Up in the Trash," *New York Times*, August 27, 1972, D12.

34. Scott Brown, "Remedial Housing," 56. Ruscha's books are included in the studio's bibliography; see Venturi and Scott Brown, "Studio RHA: Bibliography," January 26, 1970, Venturi Scott Brown Collection.

35. On this subject, see also Deborah Fausch, "Ugly and Ordinary: The Representation of the Everyday," in *Architecture of the Everyday*, ed. Steven Harris and Deborah Burke (New York: Princeton Architectural Press, 1997), 96–98.

36. Venturi, Scott Brown, and Izenour, *Learning from Las Vegas*, 1.

37. David Bourdon, "Ruscha as Publisher (Or All Booked-Up)," *Art News* 71 (April 1972): 34.

38. *L.A. Suggested by the Art of Edward Ruscha*, video by Gary Conklin; transcribed in *Leave Any Information at the Signal: Writings, Interviews, Bits*, ed. Alexandra Schwartz (Cambridge, Mass.: MIT Press, 2002), 223–24.

39. Venturi, Scott Brown, and Izenour, *Learning from Las Vegas*, 12.

40. Jaleh Mansoor has recognized the ways that flatness operates in *Every Building on the Sunset Strip* as the combination of the car's movement, the individual photographs, and the book's unique format recasts the flatness central to modernist practice and redoubles the forms characteristic of strip architecture: "The empirical flatness of the support . . . begins here to signal flatness as an experiential condition of daily reality, recorded with the bland facticity implicit in Ruscha's singular approach to photography." Mansoor addresses the centrality of the car to Ruscha's practice and the artist's disposition for realistic recording, which endows his books with an experiential dimension when Ruscha positions the car as mediating structure, as I will also discuss later. See Jaleh Mansoor, "Ed Ruscha's One-Way Street," *October*, Winter 2005, 130–34, quotation 133.

41. In addition, in the précis for the Las Vegas studio, there is a summary of the topic of "Twin Phenomena" by Doug Southworth: "This topic started as an investigation of the Strip from the notion of related opposites (e.g., 'dense-sparse', 'public-private') and with a desire to see a 'Nolli' map of public and private spaces and solids in Las Vegas. It continued however, on the theme of graphics, in the style of;

with an 'Edward Ruscha' panorama photograph of the Strip. Both map and panorama seem, in the end, to illustrate a topic names 'Pattern and order in the environment'; the concept of 'twin phenomena' is best used as a tool for form analysis when applied to a broadly repeated, pattern of elements." Robert Venturi and Denise Scott Brown, "Studio LLV: Learning from Las Vegas or Form Analysis as Design Research (The Great Proletariat Cultural Locomotive): Final Presentation," Yale University Studio, School of Architecture, Fall 1968, January 10, 1969, unnumbered box, Venturi Scott Brown Collection.

42. Quoted in Coleman, "My Books End Up in the Trash," 47.

43. Robert Venturi and Denise Scott Brown, recorded interview by the author, February 23, 2003. Of the films made during the "Learning from Las Vegas" studio, *Las Vegas Strip* (12 min.) and *Las Vegas Deadpan* (22 min.) are most related to the images discussed herein. Copies of both are in the Venturi Scott Brown Collection.

44. Venturi, Scott Brown, and Izenour, *Learning from Las Vegas*, 25.

45. Ibid., 126.

46. Eleanor Antin, "Reading Ruscha," *Art in America* 63 (November–December 1971): 67.

47. Ibid., 66.

48. Ibid., 67.

49. Ed Ruscha, "Interview with Edward Ruscha in his Western Avenue, Hollywood Studio," by Paul Karlstrom, in *Leave Any Information at the Signal*, 169.

50. See also Kevin Hatch, "'Something Else': Ed Ruscha's Photographic Books," *October* 111 (Winter 2005), 111–12, for a recent discussion of this tension between motion and stasis in *Twentysix Gasoline Stations*.

51. Venturi, Scott Brown, and Izenour, *Learning from Las Vegas*, 56; italics mine.

52. The structure and perceptual dynamics of Vasarely's painting also approximate Venturi, Scott Brown, and Izenour's description of the visual arrangement of the Strip and the effect of the road as an organizing principle, again reinforcing that travel along the strip is understood as a rhythmic passage in which "the constant rhythm [of the highway] contrasts effectively with the uneven rhythms of the signs. This counterpoint reinforces the contrast between two types of order on the Strip: the obvious visual order of the street elements and the difficult visual order of buildings and signs. . . . The system of the highway gives order to the sensitive functions or exit and entrance, as well as to the image of the Strip as a sequential whole." Venturi, Scott Brown, and Izenour, *Learning from Las Vegas*, 30–31. The series of seven images that illustrate this statement is a less elaborate version of those on the "movie sequence" spread. This shorter "sequence" of photographs, similarly taken from inside the car, with the steering wheel and rearview mirror apparent in the first few shots, likewise conveys the chaotic communication along the Strip and foregrounds the lived experience of the highway.

53. One of D'Arcangelo's serial paintings, *U.S. Route [Highway] 1* [#2] was included in *The Highway* exhibition, and a reproduction of this work appeared in the catalogue at the end of Scott Brown and Venturi, "The Highway," in *The Highway* (Philadelphia: Institute of Contemporary Art, 1970), 17.

54. Dore Ashton, "Allan D'Arcangelo's American Landscape," in *The American Landscape Paintings by Allan D'Arcangelo* (Buffalo: Burchfield Center, State University of New York College at Buffalo, 1979), 11.

55. Donald Appleyard, "Motion, Sequence and the City," in *The Nature and Art of Motion*, ed. Gyorgy Kepes (Cambridge, Mass.: MIT Press, 1965), 182, 184.

56. Scott Brown and Venturi, "The Highway," 12.

57. Scott Brown, "Learning from Pop," 17.

58. Venturi, *Complexity and Contradiction*, 16.

59. Ibid., 104.

60. Venturi, Scott Brown, and Izenour, *Learning from Las Vegas*, 56.

61. Fried, "Art and Objecthood," 131.

62. Ibid. In her discussion of Robert Smithson's work, Ann Reynolds has similarly addressed the relevance of Smith's account and Fried's essay to contemporary discussions of the American landscape, including Venturi and Scott Brown's ideas about the order of the Las Vegas Strip, their imaging of this environment, and its implications for a new aesthetic experience in *Robert Smithson: Learning from New Jersey and Elsewhere* (Cambridge, Mass.: MIT Press, 2003), 86–91.

63. It is not insignificant that the drawings of the "decorated shed" and the "duck" in *Learning from Las Vegas* both contextualize the architectural types in analogous positions: in both, the highway is labeled and the car is present, underscoring the importance of both as perceptual mechanisms guiding the understanding of the represented forms. Furthermore, this position of the car emulates the one in the photograph from Peter Blake's *God's Own* Junkyard (New York: Holt, Rinehart and Winston, 1964), fig. 101, reproduced on the same page. Venturi, Scott Brown, *Learning from Las Vegas*, 65.

64. This design approach aligned with the Smithsonian's vision for the exhibition. As Joshua Taylor, Director of the National Collection of Fine Arts, Smithsonian Institution, insisted during the exhibition's planning stages, "The emphasis of the show should be sensual; make people think about what it means to live in a city through the use of objects not primarily through photographs and long explanatory labels. . . . let people live in different situations not just read about them." Minutes of the Meeting on the Bicentennial Exhibition on City, 6 March 1974, "Renwick Gallery," VSB box 144, Venturi, Scott Brown Collection. See also Fausch, who identifies the architects' straightforward presentation of objects and information in the exhibition, with little intervening analysis, as an exemplary instance of their general, nonjudgmental approach and a primary component of their theorization of "the everyday." "Ugly and Ordinary," 76–106.

65. Beverly Russell, "Real Life: It's Art," *House and Garden*, 148 (August 1976): 79.

66. Mary Tuthill, "Pop Art a Hit in Washington," *Saginaw (Michigan) News*, March 7, 1976, E5.

67. Bill Marvel, "On Reading the American Cityscape," *National Observer*, April 24, 1976, 24.

68. Wolf Van Eckardt, "Signs of an Urban Vernacular," *Washington Post*, February 20, 1976, C3.

69. Ada Louise Huxtable, "The Pop World of the Strip and the Sprawl," *New York Times*, March 21, 1976, D28.

70. Denise Scott Brown, "Learning from Brutalism," in *The Independent Group: Postwar Britain and the Aesthetics of Plenty*, ed. David Robbins (Cambridge, Mass.: MIT Press, 1990), 205.

71. Robert Venturi, Notes, 31 July 1974, "Renwick," VSB box 144, Venturi Scott Brown Collection.

72. See also Stanislaus von Moos, "A Postscript on History, 'Architecture Parlante,' and Populism," *A+U* 12 (December 1981): 202.

73. Oldenburg's art, which was ultimately not included in the exhibition, also informed the planning stages of *Signs of Life*. Izenour's handwritten notes indicate the possibility of using Oldenburg's monuments in the exhibition, while the proposal for the exhibition lists Oldenburg among the "Photographs and People"—generally artists, critics, and scholars—whose work could contribute to their show. See Steven Izenour, Notes about *Signs of Life* exhibition, July 1974, "Renwick program," VSB box 99, Venturi Scott Brown Collection, and Venturi and Rauch, "Feasibility Study for a City Exhibition in the Renwick Gallery for the Bicentennial Celebration," August 31, 1974, "[no title] [feasibility study]," VSB box 144, Venturi Scott Brown Collection.

74. Venturi and Rauch, "Feasibility Study," August 31, 1974, Venturi Scott Brown Collection. The final draft for the project includes George Segal: "The experience should be like a Keinholtz environment, with dressed 'Segal' figures mowing the lawn, cooking on the barbacue [sic], a housewife watching soap operas in the kitchen while waxing the floor with 'new Glow Coat.'" Robert Venturi, Denise Scott Brown, and Steven Izenour, Draft of Renwick program, 16 July 1974, "Renwick drafts," VSB box 80, Venturi Scott Brown Collection. See also Steven Izenour, Notes on "Organization of Exhibit," "Renwick Program," VSB Box 80, Venturi Scott Brown Collection.

75. Maurice Tuchman, "Edward Kienholz," in *Edward Kienholz* (Los Angeles: Los Angeles County Museum of Art, 1967), 7, 10.

76. David Scott, "Edward Kienholz: An Introduction to the Works," in *Edward Kienholz, Tableaux 1961–1979* (Dublin: The Douglas Hyde Gallery, Trinity College, 1981), 5, 13; italics in original.

77. Denise Scott Brown, recorded interview by the author, February 2003.

78. *Edward Kienholz 1960–1970* (Dusseldorf: Städtische Kunsthalle, 1970), cat. 8.

79. Quoted in Robert L. Pincus, *On a Scale that Competes with the World: The Art of Edward and Nancy Reddin Kienholz* (Berkeley: University of California Press, 1990), 48.

80. Ibid., 45.

81. This kind of systematic documentation of particular types of architecture, clearly related to Ruscha's approach, also appears in the "schedules" of hotels, gas stations, motels, wedding chapels, and street furniture in *Learning from Las Vegas* on pages 38–39, 42–43.

82. Robert Venturi, sketches for *Signs of Life* exhibition, 31 July 1974, "Renwick," VSB box 144, Venturi Scott Brown Collection.

83. In his "conceptual diagram," a sketch for "The Strip," Izenour's inscription makes it clear that the two parallel lines, which appear in the exhibition plan of 1974, constitute the "Ruscha" elevation. See Steven Izenour, Sketch of "conceptual diagram" for The Strip in *Signs of Life*, 1974, "Renwick," VSB box 80, Venturi Scott Brown Collection.

84. Venturi and Rauch, "Feasibility Study," August 31, 1974, Venturi Scott Brown Collection. The asterisked note, which appears at the bottom of the same page to explicate the textual reference to Ruscha, reiterates the connections between the "moving 'Ruscha' elevation" and the images in *Every Building on the Sunset Strip and Learning from Las Vegas*: "Named for the artist Edward Ruscha who made one long photography of the entire Sunset Strip."

85. Robert Venturi, Denise Scott Brown, and Steven Izenour, Draft of Renwick catalogue, "[no title]," VSB box 80, Venturi Scott Brown Collection.

86. Walter Benjamin, "The Work of Art in the Age of Mechanical Reproduction," in *Illuminations*, ed. Hannah Arendt and trans. Harry Zohn (New York: Schoken Books, 1968), 240.

87. Patricia Krebs, "Psst . . . What is Your House Saying About You?" *The Charlotte Observer*, August 22, 1976, F1.

88. Benjamin Stein, "The Art Forms of Ever[y]day Life," *Wall Street Journal*, April 22, 1976, 20.

89. Benjamin Shore, "'Symbols of American City' a Monument to Bad Taste?" *St. Louis Missouri Globe-Democrat*, April 8, 1976, A14.

90. Jean Geddes, "Is Your House Crawling with Urban Symbolism?" *Forecast* (May 1976), 40, clipping in *Signs of Life* files, Record Unit 465, box 7, Smithsonian Institution Archives, Smithsonian Institution.

91. Robert Venturi, Denise Scott Brown, and Steven Izenour, "Proposal for a Book and Movie Version of 'Signs of Life: Symbols in the American City,'" "Signs of Life-Traveling," VSB box 179, Venturi Scott Brown Collection.

6

On Billboards and Other Signs around (*Learning from*) Las Vegas

JOHN McMORROUGH

> The sign is more important than the architecture.
> —ROBERT VENTURI, DENISE SCOTT BROWN, AND STEVEN IZENOUR,
> LEARNING FROM LAS VEGAS

> Familiar things seen in an unfamiliar context become perceptually new as well as old.
> —ROBERT VENTURI, COMPLEXITY AND CONTRADICTION IN ARCHITECTURE

Architecture as a discipline is founded on (or haunted by, depending on your view) the documents and insights of its previous generations, and *Learning from Las Vegas*[1] is one of those set pieces whose significance is as a defining marker, a touchstone of a moment in the discourse's development (Figure 6.1). When Robert Venturi, Denise Scott Brown, and Steven Izenour stated in *Learning from Las Vegas* that the new paradigm for architecture was "communication over space," it was both a literal description of the phenomenon of Las Vegas and its signage (the large marquees communicating over vast parking lots) and a polemic statement of the overturning of the modernist paradigm of space with a new one of sign (the efficiency of signs trumps the vastness of space). Depending on one's orientation, it indicates either architecture's reengagement with the city or the substantiation of architectural autonomy. In consideration of the phenomenon, the

Figure 6.1. Cover of revised edition of *Learning from Las Vegas* (Robert Venturi, Denise Scott Brown, and Steven Izenour, *Learning from Las Vegas* [Cambridge, Mass.: MIT Press, 1977]). Copyright 1977 Massachusetts Institute of Technology.

three terms that will occur with regularity are "Learning from Las Vegas," "sign," and "context."

Learning from Las Vegas is not a singular entity (nor a single publication), and it may be best understood as a convenient means for expressing various efforts, or a constellation and consolidation of elements: a set including not only the book in its original 1972 publication and its revised version in 1977 but also its incarnations as pieces published in *Architectural Forum* in 1968 and 1971[2] and references made to it in Venturi's and Scott Brown's subsequent writing, their initial trip together in 1967, and their studio given at Yale in 1968. *Learning from Las Vegas* the book cedes authority to "Learning from Las Vegas" the extended project.

As discussed by Venturi, Scott Brown, and Izenour in the book, of the meaning valences of the "sign," the primary version is that of the artifact, that is, literally, as a notice, direction, warning, or advertisement displayed or posted in public view (e.g., a traffic sign or the sign for a casino). The second sign is the sign as a conventional or arbitrary mark, figure, or symbol used to indicate the thing it represents. The sign operates not only as a recurrent figure but also as the thematic unity subsuming these various strands of thought. For the moment, let us assume that "sign" refers to actual signs—elements that indicate identity and direction—and that the meaning of these observations hinges on how signs operate, how they look, how they act, and how they are made.

Finally, "context," not only in form but also in ideas, comes out of Venturi's master's thesis on architectural context.[3] In the reading of signage as physical objects, the sign of (learning from) Las Vegas depends on the context in which it is read. Just as context is integral to the design of buildings (i.e., contextual clues allow for meaning to be understood), *Learning from Las Vegas* as an argument is framed by contexts such as location (as in Las Vegas and New Haven), discipline (as in architecture and graphic design), or time (as in its various publications and receptions from the 1960s to now).

In short, *Learning from Las Vegas* is a network of references (often to itself) combining to constitute its meaning, and this network has temporal, discursive, and geographic implications.[4] The book *Learning from Las Vegas* can be used as a sign to embody the greater idea of learning from Las Vegas, and the organization of the book itself provides a useful format. The book, in which even the notion of authorship is not without certain highly relevant issues of construction,[5] is itself divided into three parts. Although the first is a demonstration, the second is a proposition that attempts to generalize the effects of the sign, and the third is an application. What unites all sections is Venturi, Scott Brown, and Izenour's attention to graphics (or sign, symbol, image, etc.) rather than space.

This is a book that can be judged by its cover, which features a picture of a sign as image par excellence: the "Tanya" billboard on a highway just outside of Las Vegas. This image in particular is an example of the emerging commercial culture in which a new highway sensibility forms a legibility calibrated to the speed of the highway, but it is also an embodiment of those relationships. The perceiving subject is now the automobile, and the human figure (with its implications of anthropomorphism) occurs only as representation (as advertisement) in the reclining odalisque of the Tanya model.

Las Vegas is on the cover, and Las Vegas *is* a cover in the sense of an assumed identity that masks the real one.[6] Within this codification, it is itself fully present and absent at the same time. Las Vegas is a notation intended to designate the new condition of the highway strip, the intensification of an automobile-centered urbanism. In Venturi and Scott Brown's subsequent studio, it was Levittown as signifier of suburban development that was to be "learned from." In fact, the "learning from" formula as a case study format would evolve into one of the more recognizable brands of architectural argumentation.[7]

"Learning from Las Vegas" operates through a series of changes in context depending on its setting. This book about signs becomes itself a sign—a touchstone in debates ranging from semiotics, to populism, to postmodernism, and more. In resetting those contexts implied by learning from Las Vegas, it is possible to track those trajectories to understand the particular status of the sign implied by the extended project of learning from Las Vegas.[8]

What follows is an attempt to determine how the sign functions in this constellation of material surrounding *Learning from Las Vegas*—part symbol and part literal manifestation. The attributes representing differing trajectories come together as a new whole wrought from the extended learning from Las Vegas project.

Now we can describe the signs around Las Vegas as actual signs in the subject of the study, with the idea of context changing the meanings of the signs and arguments associated with them. These sign types are three in number: the marquee (pop art and populism), the graphic (and the influence of New Haven and its graphical bias), and the billboard (as Venturi's privileged expression of "sign" and its relation to the question of architectural form at the time), all of which propose a final question on the particular "sign-ness" of *Learning from Las Vegas* itself.

On Marquees

Tom Wolfe's essay "Las Vegas (What?) Las Vegas (Can't Hear You! Too Noisy) Las Vegas!!!" in which Las Vegas was presented as a city unlike any other, one made legible by its signs above all, turned Venturi's and Scott Brown's attention to Las Vegas. Venturi and Scott Brown led their Yale studio to Las Vegas in a moment concurrent with Wolfe's follow-up publication "Electro-graphic Architecture," which focused not only on the effects of the new sign but also on the new practices of the sign (Figure 6.2).[9] The appeal of this new architecture was its directness; as Wolfe states, "[In] the Young Electric Sign Co. era signs have become the architecture of Las Vegas, and the most whimsical, Yale-seminar-frenzied devices of the two late geniuses of Baroque Modern, Frank Lloyd Wright and Eero Saarinen, seem rather stuffy business, like a jest at a faculty meeting, compared to it."[10]

The framework that allowed for the appreciation of this new setting was facilitated by pop art, though the appearance of pop artists in *Learning from Las Vegas* is rather limited—the Andy Warhol quote about "boring things," the Allan D'Arcangelo painting, and the "quotation" of Edward Ruscha in the elevation of the strip—but their significance is profound: one gives an attitude, one is a territory, and one is a technique. Venturi follows pop art's lead in "extending esthetic attention to the mass media and in absorbing mass media material within the context of fine arts."[11] As Dan Graham notes, "What Venturi appropriates from the Pop artists is the understanding that not only can the internal structure of the architectural work be seen in terms of a relation of signs, but that the entire built (cultural) environment with which the building is inflected is constructed of signs. Pop art acknowledges a common code of schematic signs, conventionalized

Figure 6.2. Caesar's Palace sign (Venturi, Scott Brown, and Izenour, *Learning from Las Vegas* [rev. ed.], 59.)

meanings and symbols which link vernacular, environmental signs, to artistic/architectural signs."[12]

Although they make reference to some semiotic work, Venturi and Scott Brown's work is more empirically minded and performance-oriented in their interest in the sign (Figure 6.3). Of particular note is their usage of Alan Colquhoun's "Typology and Design Method," which has as its focus, not the dilemma of signification the semiotic project implies, but rather the necessity of models in the construction of design solutions, which is a more pragmatic interest than the semiotic dilemma.[13] In the midst of discussions of structuralist sign and semiological sign, Venturi, Scott Brown, and Izenour are interested not so much in an abstract version of the sign as in the material of the sign itself as a technological application and as an artistic model.

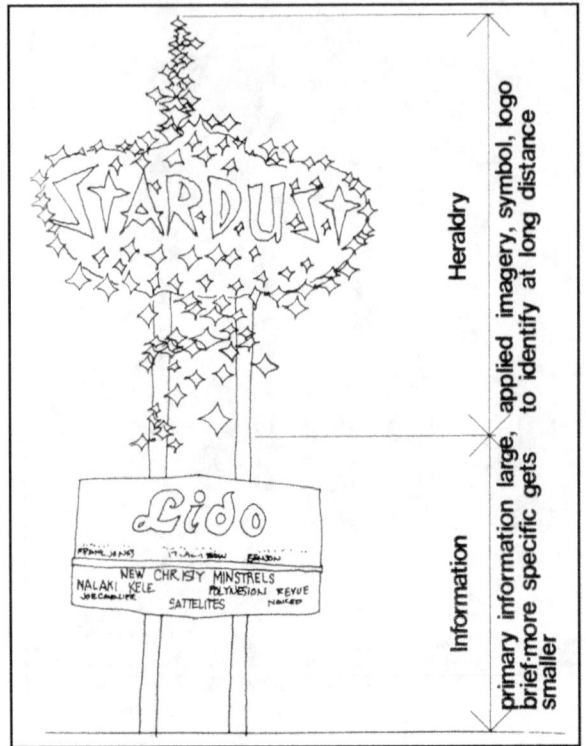

Figure 6.3. Physiognomy of a typical casino sign (Venturi, Scott Brown, and Izenour, *Learning from Las Vegas* [rev. ed.], 67.)

On Graphics

The second section of *Learning from Las Vegas* is not about Las Vegas in any real sense; it is about architectural style versus architectural ethics. The context of *Learning from Las Vegas* is not only its eponymous city but also the origins of the study as a studio offered at Yale in the fall of 1968. Most interpretations of the Yale influence on Venturi and Scott Brown have been by way of their affiliation with longtime Yale architectural historian Vincent Scully; however, there are other influences at play, and one can understand Venturi and Scott Brown's project in relation to other currents at Yale and within architectural education in general at the time.[14]

Part II of *Learning from Las Vegas* explores the difference between the implications of the "duck versus the decorated shed" as architectural models. The distinction is made by Scott Brown and Venturi in their essay "On Duck and Decoration."[15] Here the duck and shed comparison follows from the comparison of Paul Rudolph's Crawford Manor and the Guild House.[16] In each case the comparison of the duck and the shed represents a privileging of certain semantic efficiencies of the sign (as literal sign) over the supposed misleading posture of the duck (where the modeling of form becomes manifest as a non sequitur).[17] Mark Treib, following Venturi and Scott Brown's lead, comes to similar conclusions: "the eye-konic building is usually a prime design overkill: a design approach that treats every element of the building in an overstatement from its massing and profile to the cuff links worn by the waitresses."[18]

Charles Moore makes a similar observation, seeing a potential in "electric architecture" in regard to the dilemma of the function of "architectural place-makers": "In an electronic world where space and location has so little functional meaning there seems little point in defining cities spatially."[19] The Yale school of architecture, then under the deanship of Moore, was characterized by an extremely divergent architectural culture, including, concurrent with the Las Vegas studio, another studio offered by Barbara Stauffacher, the graphic designer of Moore's bathhouse at Sea Ranch.[20] Throughout the semester, Stauffacher's students made installations in the Yale Art and Architecture building elevator,[21] exposing faculty (Venturi and Scott Brown included) and students alike to an unavoidable super-graphic environment. Yale was a hotbed of supergraphics, but it would soon be featured in many urban and interior settings and deployed to a number of ends.[22]

A distinct graphic attitude appears in the pages of *Learning from Las Vegas*, typified by the following passage: "Symbol dominates space. Architecture is not enough. Because the spatial relationships are made by symbols more than forms, architecture in this landscape becomes symbol in space rather than form in space. Architecture defines very little: The big sign and the little building is the rule of Route 66."[23] The question remains what to make of the big, low space of the casino interiors, the foil to the large-scale sign of the exterior (Figure 6.4). The sign functions not only at the scale of overall identity, as implied by the decorated shed, but also at the micro scale of the orientation of the building's interiority (Figure 6.5). Here signs take on a different role: to overcome difficulties of orientation. This explicitly compensatory role of signage was seen as a failure of design, and illustrating this attitude, Venturi and Scott Brown relate, "Architects object to signs in buildings: 'If the plan is clear, you can see where to go.' But complex programs and settings require complex combinations of media beyond the purer architectural triad of structure, form, and light at the service of space. They suggest an architecture of bold communication rather than one of subtle expression."[24] The distinction between the boldness of supergraphic expression and the bold communication of Venturi and Scott Brown is a key.

These issues were addressed directly in the fall of 1967—the year before the Las Vegas effort—in a studio given by Venturi, Bruce Adams, and Scott Brown. The subject of that studio was an investigation of the spaces within the New York subway system, which at first glance might appear to be the opposite of the conditions of the vast expanse of Las Vegas, but it concerns a similar set

Figure 6.4. Fremont Street (Venturi, Scott Brown, and Izenour, *Learning from Las Vegas* [rev. ed.], 32.)

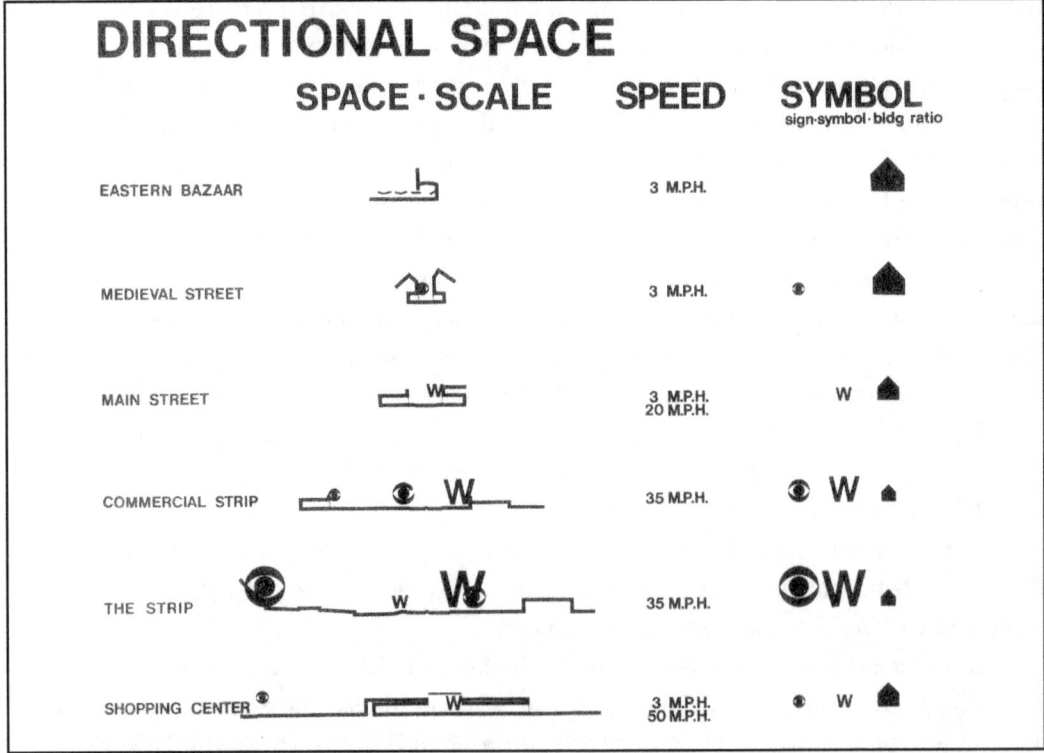

Figure 6.5. A comparative analysis of directional spaces (Venturi, Scott Brown, and Izenour, *Learning from Las Vegas* [rev. ed.], 11.)

of issues—rather than "communication and interaction over big spaces along the highway" in Las Vegas, it was "pedestrian signage and communication and its relation to circulation" in New York. The contribution of signs here is to a system of orientation in an otherwise unknowable space, that is, a space unmappable according to traditional forms of architectural orientation. Again, it is the function of signs to address an architectural lack (the lack of architecture's ability to address a particular situation): "The architect has limited control in the first place of the shapes of the subway spaces, which are formed by the streets above, the basements of the buildings and underground utilities. Where the architect can work is with lighting and the words and symbols of advertising as well as the assemblage of conventional subway elements such as gum machines."[25]

On Billboards

Until now we have discussed the sign of Venturi and Scott Brown and their contemporaries in a relatively social manner, but there is a formal component implied throughout. Venturi and Scott Brown's theoretical maneuvers have always been in the service of explicating the architecture. In *Learning from Las Vegas*, buildings follow the theory as an appendix ("Essays in the Ugly and Ordinary: Some Decorated Sheds"). The criteria of formalism act not as stable references, but as ones undergoing constant revision. If the dominant means of explaining formal relations at a pre-*Learning from Las Vegas* juncture were centered around questions of space, the formalism here is a question of communication. It is the transition from one kind of formalism into another, as influenced by the concept of media, as opposed to Venturi's *Complexity and Contradiction in Architecture*,[26] which argues for a formal accommodation of multiple forces, *Learning from Las Vegas* displaces the multiple forces in favor of more taut arguments regarding the relation of more singular elements. These relations have a distinct clarity: the double functioning element is now discrete, not a collection of integrated elements.

Much of the power of Venturi and Scott Brown's arguments has always rested in their well-crafted bon mots—encapsulations of complex ideas with (deceptively) simple turns of phrase (or images)—and it is this ability to instill insight telegraphically that has so marked their discursive style. Well-known examples in their writing include a critique of modernist (or specifically Miesian) simplification, which is summarily dispatched with "less is a bore," and an affirmation of the qualities of the American roadside, invoked with the revelation that Main Street is almost all right. In this case it is the billboard that acts as an architectural bon mot (Figure 6.6). In selecting the billboard as the model for architectural development, it is as if Venturi and Scott Brown take Alison and Peter Smithson's observations about the changing nature of architecture's source material from industry to media (in the essay "But Today We Collect Ads,"[27] the next step is "but today we

Figure 6.6. Stardust Casino and Hotel, Las Vegas, circa 1968 (Venturi, Scott Brown, and Izenour, *Learning from Las Vegas* [rev. ed.], 10.)

build ads!"), appropriating the format as a form of legitimization for the buildings and legibility for the practice.[28]

The privileging of the billboard is not entirely unprecedented; its revelatory power is preceded by the recurrent planarity of their earlier work. As far back as Venturi's Mother's House, we see elevations as a kind of billboard, with the image of a house as if drawn by a child providing an advertisement of domesticity. On the usage of the billboard as a privileged model, it is necessary to consider two ways in which the choice is significant: on one hand as a political/cultural device, and on the other as a formal device. Signage was, according to the dictate of modernism, seen as superfluous, to be minimized, if not avoided all together.[29] The billboard shares many of the qualities of large scale supergraphics, but its direct placement within the frame renders it closer to modernist conceptions of the correct relation between structure and support.[30]

The selection of the billboard as the privileged expression of a sign-based architecture is not entirely innocent either. The very existence of the billboard was a subject of debate at the time, and its use is a provocation as much as anything. As C. Ray Smith notes, "when Washington finally got involved in cleaning up our highways, ridding them of 500,000 billboards by means of the Highway Beautification Act of 1965, Robert Venturi was off lecturing around the country on behalf of bigger billboards. As he said in Oklahoma, 'Billboards, if anything, should be larger. Out here with your vast spaces, the great scale of your signs and billboards is a virtue and should be used for public purposes as well as commercial.'"[31]

Yet, as described by Paul Goldberger in 1971, "the Venturis' love affair with the billboard is secure enough to allow them an occasional moment of self-mockery." He cites an earlier press release by Venturi to announce the formation of a Society to Preserve Our Billboards, with Venturi himself acting as chairman. Among those not in on the joke was Philadelphia city planning commissioner Edmund Bacon, who excoriated Venturi for betraying his "responsibility as an architect" and acquiescing to "the crassest motives in our society."[32]

One project that utterly implied the assertion that the billboard is an adequate premise on which to build an architecture is the Football Hall of Fame "bill-ding-board," an entirely literal application of the decorated shed. Done in the same year as the Las Vegas studio, it expands the idea of the static billboard surface, approximating the effects of television and acting as a kind of giant screen for demonstrating famous plays in the diagrammatic language of Xs and Os. The interior of the billboard project makes more use of the idea of kinetic electrographics with neon, projected movies, and other forms of signage and light. Although the formal model for the differentiation between the sign and the shed is derived from an argument about representational honesty, it is based on the logic of efficiency and the balancing of budgetary limits of square footage devoted to the program versus the desired grandeur of the institution. As Venturi describes it, the building was "big in size, but small in cubage."[33] Again and again it is a logic not of representational fidelity but of efficiency that is implied in the discussion of such sign projects.

In the pursuit of a literal application of the billboard model to architecture, the "Recommendation for a Monument" represents the reductio ad absurdum of the argument. It is in many respects a modernist structure, an intended symbolic function (of pure modernist intention following a strict form-follows-function separation of sign from program and form), with a simply articulated architectural framework that firmly asserts the billboard sign as part of high architecture (Figure 6.7).[34] The argument, once uttered, is both propositional and prophetic, as the developments of Venturi and Scott Brown's work shows. In an era of diminishing control, the billboard is a zone of control condensed and retained. What is of note is that the message is as much about the architecture as the function. For the building to state "I am a monument" is of a different order than "Firecrackers" or "FUNCTION"; it is an assertion of a claim to architecture present, and it is a pictorial-verbal construction on the order of René Magritte's "*Ceci n'est pas une pipe*" (in the painting *La trahison des images* [*The Treachery of Image*]). But rather than disprove the connection between language and objects, in the case of Venturi

Figure 6.7. Recommendation for a monument (Venturi, Scott Brown, and Izenour, *Learning from Las Vegas* [rev. ed.], 156.)

and Scott Brown it seems to assert the adequacy of the claims of language to designate identity.

This consolidation of the complex and contradictory to the ugly and boring was not without its critics, some of whom include earlier supporters,[35] and it was in the pursuit of ordinariness that changes were made to the second edition of the book. The section that describes the work was dropped, and a subtitle was added: "The Forgotten Symbolism of Architectural Form."[36]

Afterimage

Finally, we return to where we began: Las Vegas was the site, and its signifying practice was suggestive of the tangents that combine in Venturi and Scott Brown's thought on pop art and populism, on the powers of graphics to trump form, all of which combine in the image of the billboard as the metonymic embodiment of the emerging consumer and media culture.

Learning from Las Vegas is a site that has had significant influence not only on architectural cultures generally but also on Venturi and Scott Brown themselves. Architects write to justify a specific project, a new vocabulary, or even (especially) an entire worldview of media and commercialism. More than thirty-five years after the fact, *Learning from Las Vegas*'s hold on the architectural imagination continues, but as with any pop art signifier, like Warhol and his soup cans, Venturi and his billboard marks a specific moment. How do we understand a figure like *Learning from Las Vegas* when the meaning associated with it is under so many layers of sediment? After looking at signs too long, the afterimage stays burned in our collective retina, its meaning fixed in its historical moment. The afterimage of the learning from Las Vegas project continues to act even after its initiating events no longer exist (one could speculate on the degree to which they ever did).[37]

To reread this material is an opportunity to reevaluate Venturi and Scott Brown's contribution in relation to their long-standing interest in the means by which their work (and architectural culture in general) faces contemporary conditions. But first one needs to discuss one of the intervening contexts between the late '60s and early '70s origin of the work and its reception today. In the second publication of *Learning from Las Vegas* (1977), the book was subject to changes not only of layout and meaning but also of the terms of the culture into which it was received: a culture with a postmodern slant and a setting in which *Learning from Las Vegas* was taken as an illustration for the development of postmodernism.[38] The promise of pop architecture was its aggressive commitment to the present.[39] In the solidification of the image, the work of Venturi and Scott Brown seems trapped within its set of references—Las Vegas, circa 1968. Typical of this attitude is Hal Foster's discussion of this work: "Pop worked to explore—if not critically, at least ambivalently—this new regime of social inscription. The postmodernism prepared by the Venturis was placed largely in its service—in effect, to design its appropriate byways."[40]

In the case of Venturi and Scott Brown, this alleged progeny is vehemently denied. The record they seem most intent on setting straight is the relation of their work to (historical-revival) postmodernism, which in their estimation may have been inspired by their example but misses the "more dour and dire origins" of their work, which is colored more, they feel, by "the social and civil right events of the 1960s."[41] Take note, though, of an oft-quoted remark from Scott Brown, who stated that they are not postmodernist, and neither was Freud a Freudian.[42]

One way to understand their claims to modernist credentials is in the sense that they are truly looking for a modern conception of signifying practices. The thinness of the appliqué is useful insofar as it accommodates the function of amelioration (whether as decoration or communication) within a material minimum. As they write, "Baroque architecture needs a depth of one yard to do its decoration, Renaissance architecture needs perhaps a foot, Rococo one centimeter and Art Deco could suggest seven or eight overlaid surfaces with the Deco low relief, but when you think about what that means for us today, we realize that our decorative surface should be two-dimensional—for many reasons, including cost."[43] But this reading of the functional capacity implied in the various contexts from which the work is drawn is not fully sufficient; there is a representational component that underscores Venturi and Scott Brown's interests, and it is one of a representation of architecture itself.

In "Las Vegas after Its Classic Age," Venturi and Scott Brown describe the following evolutions: from strip to boulevard, from urban sprawl to urban density, from parking lot to landscaped front yard, from asphalt plain to Romantic garden, from decorated shed to "duck," from electric to electronic, from neon to pixel, from electrographic to scenographic, from iconography to scenography, from Vaughan Cannon to Walt Disney, from pop culture to gentrification, from pop taste to good taste, from perception as a driver to perception as a walker, from strip to mall, from mall to edge city, and from vulgar to *dramatique*.[44]

The representational limit is reinscribed in the later reading of Las Vegas as skeptical of its new reliance on the scenographic. As Venturi states, "To simplify, the main thing is that it went from the archetype of strip and sprawl to the scenography of Disneyland. Scenography is not necessarily bad—the Place des Vosges is scenographic, and architecture, in a sense, does involve making scenes. The danger is that it becomes an exotic theater rather than an actual place."[45] Ultimately, the flatness of the billboard is seen by Venturi and Scott Brown as a most valid form of expression for reasons similar to those argued by Clement Greenberg in his description in "Modernist Painting."[46]

The signs of Las Vegas seen in the multiple contexts of *Learning from Las Vegas* appear to be much less indebted to the models of image that would put the meaning in terms of its relative profundity and seem rather more related to a wider range of practices, a network of projects (currently mislabeled as postmodernism), or as escaping definition (and legibility) altogether, all of which in one way or another attempt to exploit literal signs and communication technologies that play a formative and compensatory role within the built environment and that take the sign from the dilemma of signification and place it into the realm of the instrumental.

The renewed interest of late in representation seems to fall into the following positions: an architecture that can (or cannot) communicate to society at large (a position seemingly circumscribed by the inheritance of the postmodern period's linguistic fascinations) and an image to facilitate client communication, which somehow seems to be presented as truly a surplus to the serious matter of architecture's disciplinary concerns, even by those who argue the position.[47]

In their pursuit of understanding and utilizing the media logic of the time, Venturi and Scott Brown's effect is not only in their arguments in regard to architectural form but also in the form of architectural arguments.[48] The specific signs

Figure 6.8. Tanya billboard on the Strip, circa 1968 (Venturi, Scott Brown, and Izenour, *Learning from Las Vegas* [rev.ed.], 12.)

of Las Vegas (circa 1968) may be of limited continuing value, but as a form of research, "learning from" may be its most lasting conceptual legacy (Figure 6.8).

What is the significance of this work in the current moment and in the current disciplinary context? Why now? Architecture has the ambition to embody culture, and representation has historically been one of the means by which it enacts this mission. Architecture is also subject to the exigencies of the specifics at hand, using materials and techniques of expedient means—quick fixes to get the job done. Here again representation is one such application; it is a convenient way to achieve ends that surpass the limits of material and configuration, to tell what cannot be shown. The work of Venturi and Scott Brown is illuminating in both regards because "no architecture is not the answer to too much architecture."[49]

Notes

1. Robert Venturi, Denise Scott Brown, and Steven Izenour, *Learning from Las Vegas* (Cambridge, Mass.: MIT Press, 1977), xv.

2. Robert Venturi and Denise Scott Brown, "A Significance for A&P Parking Lots, or *Learning from Las Vegas*," *Architectural Forum*, March 1968, 37–43, and "Ugly and Ordinary Architecture of the Decorated Shed," *Architectural Forum*, November 1971, 64–53.

3. Robert Venturi, "Context in Architectural Composition: M.F.A. Thesis, Princeton University" [1950], in *Iconography and Electronics upon a Generic Architecture: A View from the Drafting Room* (Cambridge, Mass.: MIT Press, 1996): 335–74.

4. "That's the trouble with the Las Vegas crowd; they are so careful not to offend anybody, especially each other. They have two pages at the beginning explaining who does what, and their *proper names*, and how all of them are indispensable, and there are those thousands of footnotes, all of them accurate, and a lengthy list of acknowledgements. Have we left anyone out? Jesus Christ, I (I mean 'we') hope not!" Martin Pawley, "Miraculous Expanding Tits versus Lacquered Nipples," *Architectural Design*, February 1973, 80.

5. The concept of "Robert Venturi" is in some ways a media construction. As described by Venturi himself, "I have for some time wanted to make clear that the name 'Robert Venturi' when used to describe the written and architectural output of the firm Venturi and Rauch, as in 'Robert Venturi has designed his building thus and so' or 'Robert Venturi is developing his theory of architecture in such a manner,' is unfair to the people who have added their thought and creativity to our office, especially to the three other partners." Robert Venturi, "Note on Authorship and Attribution," *Learning from Las Vegas* (Cambridge, Mass.: MIT Press, 1971), xii.

6. "I use Rome to stand for urban tradition—Medieval and Baroque—and Las Vegas to stand for urban sprawl in general." Robert Venturi, "A Definition of Architecture as Shelter with Decoration on It, and Another Appeal for a Symbolism of the Ordinary in Architecture" [1978], in *A View from the Campidoglio: Selected Essays: 1953–1984* (New York: Harper & Row, 1984), 62.

7. The "Learning from" formulation has not only been applied to Las Vegas and Levittown, as mentioned, but also includes numerous occurrences in the work of Venturi and Scott Brown and their commentators (the present volume included). A partial listing would include "Learning from" the Beaux-Arts, Lutyens, Michelangelo, Art Nouveau, Shingle Style, pop, Aalto, and Tokyo and Kyoto, as well as chopsticks, doodles, and Mr. Bean.

8. The expanded project of *Learning from Las Vegas* cannot be explained simply in relation to Venturi's and Scott Brown's assignment of meaning or the content to their source material, nor can it be explained by the interpretation of their critics; rather, it exists as the messy totality of all at once.

9. Tom Wolfe, "Electro-Graphic Architecture," *Architecture Canada*, October 1968, 41–47.

10. Tom Wolfe, "Las Vegas (What?) Las Vegas (Can't Hear You! Too Noisy) Las Vegas!!!" in *The Kandy-Kolored Tangerine-Flake Streamline Baby* (New York: Noonday Press, 1965), 9. Given that Wolfe makes this statement before the *Learning from Las Vegas* studio in 1966, we can assume that Wolfe is not making reference to Venturi and Scott Brown in the evocation of the "Yale-seminar-frenzied devices," especially as Wolfe holds a doctorate from Yale in American studies. Wolfe does make positive references to the Learning from Las Vegas studio in a late version of the "Electro-Graphic Architecture" essay: "Robert Venturi is one of the few serious American architects to comprehend the possibilities of electric sign technology and to conceive of full-scale electro-graphic architecture. In fact this month (October) he has taken his third-year studio class at Yale to Nevada to study the electro-graphic landscape of Las Vegas with the same objective and scholarly thoroughness that might be applied to Athens or Pompeii." Tom Wolfe, "Electrographic Architecture," *Architectural Design* (July 1969): 382.

11. Lawrence Alloway, "POP ART: The Words" [1962], in *Topics in American Art since 1945* (New York: W. W. Norton & Company, Inc. 1975), 119.

12. Dan Graham, "Art in Relation to Architecture/Architecture in Relation to Art" *Artforum* 17, no. 6 (February 1979): 22–29. Venturi is also featured prominently in the other two articles of this series. See Dan Graham, "Signs," *Artforum* 19, no. 9 (April 1981): 38–43, and "Not Post-Modernism: History as Against Historicism, European Archetypal Vernacular in Relation to American Commercial Vernacular, and the City and Opposed to the Individual Building," *Artforum* 20, no. 4 (December 1981): 50–58.

13. Alan Colquhoun, "Typology and Design Method," in *Meaning and Architecture*, ed. Charles Jencks and George Baird (New York: George Braziller, 1969), 267–78.

14. It was longtime Yale architectural historian Vincent Scully who made the infamous statement that Robert Venturi's first book, *Complexity and Contradiction*, was "probably the most important writing on the making of architecture since Le Corbusier's *Vers une Architecture*." Vincent Scully, introduction to *Complexity and Contradiction in Architecture* (New York: Museum of Modern Art, 1966), 9.

15. Denise Scott Brown and Robert Venturi, "On Duck and Decoration," *Architecture Canada*, October 1968, 48.

16. It should be noted that in addition to being located in New Haven, Crawford Manor was designed while Rudolph was the dean at the Yale School of Architecture, further enforcing the degree to which New Haven was the implicit foil for Las Vegas.

17. Venturi and Scott Brown, "Ugly and Ordinary Architecture, or the Decorated Shed," Part I," *Architectural Forum*, November 1971, 64–67.

18. Mark Treib, "Eye-Konism (Part II): Sign as Building as Sign," *Print*, May 1973, 58.

19. Charles Moore, "Plug It In, Rameses, and See If It Lights Up: Because We Aren't Going to Keep It Unless It Works," in *[Re] Reading Perspecta: The First Fifty Years of the Yale Architecture Journal*, ed. Robert A. M. Stern, Alan Plattus, Peggy Deamer (Cambridge, Mass.: MIT Press, 2004), 242–45. Originally published in *Perspecta* 11 (1967): 243.

20. C. Ray Smith, "Bathhouse Graphics . . . 'Make it happy, kid'," *Progressive Architecture*, March 1967, 156–61. The original design of the Sea Ranch bathhouse, before the addition of the interior graphics, can be found in the Thirteenth Annual P/A Design awards in the January 1966 issue of *Progressive Architecture*. Smith was an active proponent of the supergraphic scene coming out of Yale. For more on his reportage of the phenomenon, see my own article, "Blowing the Lid Off Paint: The Architectural Coverage of Supergraphics," *Hunch 11: Representation*, January 2007, 68–77.

21. While they were tangentially aware of the supergraphics studio, Robert Venturi, when questioned on the matter, did not recall any direct connection or influence on their work or on that of the Learning from Las Vegas studio. Mentioned in conversation with author, Columbus, Ohio, April 15, 2006.

22. One of the more notable instances of community activism through supergraphics was New York's City Walls project (founded by artist Allan D'Arcangelo). For more information, see "Special Report: Supergraphics," *Approach* (Japan), Spring 1971, 12–39.

23. Venturi, Scott Brown, and Izenour, *Learning from Las Vegas*, 13.

24. Ibid., 9.

25. Robert Venturi and Denise Scott Brown (in conjunction with Bruce Adams), "Mass Communications on the People Freeway, or, Piranesi is Too Easy," *Perspecta* 12 (1969): 56.

26. Robert Venturi, *Complexity and Contradiction in Architecture*, 2nd ed. (New York: Museum of Modern Art, 1977), 43.

27. Alison and Peter Smithson, "But Today We Collect Ads," *Ark* 18 (November 1956): 48–50.

28. The importance of Las Vegas as a framework was grasped early, as demonstrated in the 1968 exhibition of Venturi and Rauch's work at the Philadelphia Art Alliance, "From Rome to Las Vegas exhibition," where large projected images of both cites were superimposed over projects and large pink letters were stenciled on the wall. The billboard motif also was featured prominently in Venturi's and Scott Brown's exhibition of their own work at the Whitney Museum of American Art in 1971 and their staging of the "Signs of Life: Symbols of the American City" exhibition at the Renwick Gallery in 1976.

29. Typical of this sentiment, as well as its codification, are remarks like, "If architecture is not to resemble billboards, color should be both technical and psychologically permanent," from Henry-Russell Hitchcock and Philip Johnson's *The International Style* (New York: W. W. Norton & Company, 1995), 87.

30. "Mural painting should not break the wall surface unnecessarily. Yet it should remain an independent entity without the addition of borders or paneling to fuse it to the architecture." Ibid., 85.

31. C. Ray Smith, *Supermannerism: New Attitudes in Post-Modern Architecture* (New York: E. P. Dutton, 1977), 188.

32. Paul Goldberger, "Less is More—Mies van der Rohe, Less is a Bore—Robert Venturi," *The New York Times*, October 17, 1971.

33. Robert Venturi, "A Bill-Ding-Board Involves Movies, Relics, and Space," *Architectural Forum*, April 1968, 74–79.

34. Kester Rattenbury, "Iconic Pictures: Recommendation for a Monument," in *This Is Not Architecture: Media Constructions* (London: Routledge, 2002), 73.

35. As Vincent Scully relates of the effect of the boring and ugly rhetoric, "Words like that alienate a lot of people. The Venturis impishly carry on about being boring and ugly. I understand why they do it, but it isn't true. Bob Venturi is very much a traditional designer, he's extremely esthetic." Goldberger, "Less is More – Mies van der Rohe; Less is a Bore – Robert Venturi," *New York Times*, Sunday Magazine Section (October 17, 1971): 34.

36. "Stripped and newly clothed, the analyses of Part I and the theories of Part II should appear more clearly what we intended them to be: a treatise on symbolism in architecture. Las Vegas is not the subject of our book. The symbolism of architectural form is." Venturi, Scott Brown, and Izenour, *Learning from Las Vegas*, xv.

37. Even as they are conducting the study on Las Vegas, Venturi and Scott Brown are concerned that in the name of beautification the qualities of the strip they admire will be lost.

38. 1977 also saw the publication of Charles Jencks's *The Language of Post-Modern Architecture* (New York: Rizzoli, 1977) and C. Ray Smith's *Supermannerism*.

39. Patricia Phillips, "Why Is Pop So Unpopular?" in *Modern Dreams: The Rise and Fall and Rise of Pop* (New York: Institute for Contemporary Art, 1988), 122.

40. Hal Foster, "Image Building," special issue: This Is Today: Pop After Pop, *Artforum*, October 2004, 273.

41. Venturi and Scott Brown have been quite vocal in their disdain for the label of postmodernism, almost from the inception of the term, while at the same time remaining adamant in their credit for the conceptualization of many of its constituent points. A relatively recent manifestation of this disavowal/accreditation would include Robert Venturi and Denise Scott Brown's *Architecture as Signs and Systems for a Mannerist Time* (Cambridge, Mass.: Belknap Press of Harvard University Press, 2004), in which they again elaborate on their disdain.

42. Quoted in Sam Jacob, "We Didn't Do It: Meet Robert Venturi and Denise Scott Brown, the Unwilling Godparents of Postmodernism," *Modern Painters* 17, no. 4 (December 2004–January 2005): 44.

43. Ibid, 43.

44. Robert Venturi and Denise Scott Brown, "Las Vegas after Its Golden Age," in *Iconography and Electronics Upon a Generic Architecture: A View from the Drafting Room* (Cambridge, Mass.: MIT Press, 1996): 123–28. Originally published in *Neon* [Nevada State Council of the Arts] (Winter 1995–96): 2–5.

45. Hans Ulrich Obrist and Rem Koolhaas, "Relearning from Las Vegas: An Interview with Denise Scott Brown and Robert Venturi," in *Harvard Design School Guide to Shopping* (Taschen: Köln, 2002), 616–17.

46. Clement Greenberg, "Modernist Painting" [1960], in *Clement Greenberg: The Collected Essays and Criticism; Volume 4: Modernism with a Vengeance, 1957–1969*, ed. John O'Brian (London: The University of Chicago Press, 1993): 85–93.

47. For an example of representation as a form of acquiescence to client pressure or a facilitator of communication between client and architect, see Alejandro Zaero-Polo, "The Hokusai Wave," *Perspecta* 37 (2005): 78–85.

48. As Rem Koolhaas has noted, *Learning from Las Vegas* was the first of a trend of architectural books after the manifestos that are "books about cities that imply manifestos." Obrist and Koolhaas, "Relearning from Las Vegas," 593.

49. Venturi, Scott Brown, and Izenour, *Learning from Las Vegas*, 145.

7

Signs Taken for Wonders

DELL UPTON

To look back at *Learning from Las Vegas* after thirty years evokes complex reactions. Unlike many other books of similar age, this one has never really left us. Its vigorous defense of architectural ornament, its equation of architecture with communication, and its evocative labels "duck" and "decorated shed" all remain current. At the same time, to reduce the book to these familiar elements is to miss much of its richness and complexity. This brief text contains a first-rate study of urban morphology written in the context of mid-twentieth-century discussions of urban community and "imageability," an analysis of the role of ornament and symbolism in architecture, and, building on these, a treatise on contemporary design.

Learning from Las Vegas was a milepost on two divergent roads—one leading to a populist celebration of architecture as it was and the other leading toward a highly theorized view of architecture as it ought to be. I vividly remember the excitement that greeted its publication (particularly of the widely disseminated, revised paperback edition) among those interested in the everyday landscape. In the climate of the 1970s, the work was welcomed as a telling polemic against cultural hierarchies, an affirmation of popular culture, and a Whitmanian (or Ginsbergian) celebration of the energy and messiness of American life and landscape. It is still known and read outside the discipline of architecture on these terms.

Yet although *Learning from Las Vegas* seems to celebrate popular tastes, particularly in its angry defense of the culture of the "silent white majority," its message is not that straightforward. Remember that Las Vegas was only "*almost* all right" (a phrase Robert Venturi first used in *Complexity and Contradiction in Architecture* in the same way he used it in *Learning from Las Vegas*).[1] Venturi, Denise Scott Brown, and Steven Izenour never intended to cast aside cultural hierarchies, only to remodel them. Just before the first edition of *Learning from Las Vegas* was published, Scott Brown took pains to emphasize "the agony in our acceptance of pop," declaring that "we are part of a high art, not a folk or popular art, tradition."[2] In *Learning from Las Vegas*, Venturi, Scott Brown, and Izenour claimed high-art status through an intricate, even convoluted, polemical game built around outsider and insider positions. They attacked modernists' insider aesthetics by appealing to outsiders' tastes, while their own declared immersion in popular aesthetics positioned them as the true insiders and their modernist targets as clueless outsiders. Thus they seized the high ground of high-art architecture by a surprise attack along the low road, using their pop-culture raw materials skeptically, instrumentally, and ironically to define a new path for high art as the pop artists whom they admired had done.[3]

The ambivalence at the heart of the book—Scott Brown's "agony"—is encapsulated in the famous categorization of commercial buildings as *ducks*, in which "the architectural systems of space, structure, and program are submerged and distorted by the overall symbolic form," or *decorated sheds*, in which "systems of space and structure are directly at the service of program, and ornament is applied independently of them." Ducks, Venturi tells us, were named after the Long Island Duckling, a roadside food stand illustrated in Peter Blake's *God's Own Junkyard*.[4] Many readers remember *Learning from Las Vegas* as a celebration of such buildings, which were the improvised, whimsical, one-off products of small businesspeople. However, the large-scale signs of the Las Vegas Strip that Venturi, Scott Brown, and Izenour studied were not those kinds of buildings, but better-financed, more carefully calculated commercial structures produced by a firm that had been designing and building signs since the 1920s. Thus two aspects of popular culture—the idiosyncratic creations of the self-dramatizing entrepreneur and professionally designed and fabricated corporate advertising—were conflated under the heading of "pop" as examples of nonelite taste.

But *Learning from Las Vegas* is not a study of roadside architecture per se. It was embedded in a particular midcentury architectural discussion, as architects and historians reassessed prewar modernism. Venturi and his colleagues used the labels "duck" and "decorated shed" to enter into an attack on "orthodox Modern architecture" that had been going on since the early 1950s.[5] In fact, the first work seriously to confront the modernist assumptions that *Learning from Las Vegas* questioned so acerbically was not found along American commercial strips but in Marseilles, at Chandigarh, and at Ronchamp. Le Corbusier's work played a central role as object lesson and case study in the debate to which Venturi, Scott Brown, and Izenour contributed. It is remarkable how often Ronchamp, in particular, figures, directly or by implication, in the literature that they cite.[6] The Swiss architect hovers over *Learning from Las Vegas*, coming clearly into view only in the brief set piece on the descendants of La Tourette. Yet the chapel of Notre Dame du Haut at Ronchamp haunts the pages of *Learning from Las Vegas* as a kind of ghostly presence, manifest by implication whenever the "heroic and original" is invoked. As I will suggest later in this chapter, our understanding of the implications and limitations of Venturi, Scott Brown, and Izenour's particular vision for architecture, which blended 1960s cultural pluralism with ideas borrowed from linguistics and semiotics that were beginning to transform many humanistic disciplines in the 1960s and 1970s, can benefit by bringing the visceral architecture of Ronchamp into full view as an alternative to *Learning from Las Vegas*'s sign-saturated polemic. Notre Dame du Haut stands as the quintessential duck next to Venturi, Scott Brown, and Izenour's decorated sheds. The ambivalence about ducks and decorated sheds—the fondness for ducks along the road but their rejection as high architecture—is one of many that structure and fracture *Learning from Las Vegas*. The book is ironic in the technical sense that its narrative repeatedly starts down one path then turns away from it; raises one set of issues, then lays them aside; and makes an observation, then ignores it.[7] These turnings and turnings back are a sign of the "agony" but also, frankly, attempts to preempt all possible lines of criticism. Thus the first half of *Learning from Las Vegas*, the study of urban morphology, explores many facets of the experience of the Strip, from signage to light levels to relationships between parking lots and buildings, night and day, interior and exterior, and desert heat and air conditioning. The dazzling multiplicity of the city is evident in the large-format first edition, with its plethora of charts, graphs, maps, and colored photographs that in some senses mimic the city's sensory profusion. But these are laid aside in the second half and even suppressed in the monochrome revised edition, with its new subtitle, "The Forgotten Symbolism of Architectural Form."[8] After all, as the authors explain, "Las Vegas is not the subject of our book. . . . [It is] a treatise on symbolism in architecture."[9]

Still, Las Vegas refuses to go away, for although Venturi, Scott Brown, and Izenour began to develop the theoretical ideas put forth in *Learning from Las Vegas* and in many other venues years before the Las Vegas studio, the choice of the Strip as a laboratory colored the argument in critical ways, as Karsten Harries has observed.[10] According to Venturi, Scott Brown, and Izenour, modernist architects deny architecture's symbolic function while seeking meaning in an unacknowledged way, through their "heroic and original" expressivist massing. But they find such abstract architecture barren because they believe it rejects architecture's rich heritage of symbolically charged conventional forms (meaning applied visual elements) that tap into deeply rooted social and cultural references and associations.[11]

To the modernists' strained efforts to achieve individual expression through dramatic massing, Venturi, Scott Brown, and Izenour offer Las Vegas as a counterexample of a legible architecture that works through the familiar and the obvious. The Strip is a commercial landscape. Its big signs strive, in the authors' words, for "bold communication rather than . . . subtle expression."[12] In fact, the entire Strip is "an architecture of communication over space."[13] Venturi, Scott Brown and Izenour refined this statement a few pages later, describing the Strip as "symbol in space rather than form in space."[14]

While the Las Vegas of Part I was a dizzying cacophony of messages competing for the driver's attention, it was not chaotic. Rather, it was a "difficult" multiple order, unlike the oversimplified, single order of the modernist city. Individual parts might clash, but they all worked according to some fairly straightforward principles. So the Strip (and their own agenda) seduced the authors and their colleagues and students into thinking that, like a sign, architecture has a relatively clear message to convey, one that can be transmitted most easily and most cheaply by words on signs rather than by "deformed" buildings—by a sign proclaiming "I AM A MONUMENT" standing on an ordinary building rather than by a monumental or heroic and original building.[15] Architecture is text.

The passing years have turned what might originally have been a strategic observation into a central conviction. Venturi now calls for "a generic architecture of surface" whose "electronic surfaces can be defined as sources of light . . . acknowledging a 24-hour architecture of now."[16] After thirty years of claiming that Las Vegas was merely a formal case study, Venturi now envisions it as our permanent condition. Architecture is television.

Venturi, Scott Brown, and Izenour modified their initial, overly simple description of architectural symbolism in the course of the famous comparison of Venturi and Rauch, Cope and Lippincott's Guild House with Paul Rudolph's Crawford Manor. There they parsed architecture's communicative properties in now-familiar terms borrowed from semiotics, stressing the paired qualities of denotation, which "indicates specific meaning" (such as the casino sign's fundamental message "Stop here" or "Spend your money here") and connotation, which "suggests general meanings" that are embedded in the forms of the signs.[17] These general meanings are "associative," based on past experience and social consensus, and set the social tone of the actions to be held under its banner or the context in which the primary message is to be understood. Architecture is language.

While it might seem odd at first glance that the prophets of complexity and contradiction should reduce architecture to such a straightforward communicative function—to what Harries calls "literary architecture" or "architecture as text"—it appears less strange if we understand that much of their celebration of complexity is devoted to architecture's visual qualities, or what used to be called formal analysis, and not to its signification.[18] In this respect, *Complexity and Contradiction* is more complex and contradictory than *Learning from Las Vegas*, in which the communicative or "symbolic" function of architecture is treated as a relatively simple matter. Was the 1960s Strip a purely visual, message-conveying environment? Is architecture a text? What message did it convey? In what manner? Is architecture a language? The emphasis on "conventional" decoration throughout *Learning from Las Vegas* and the choice of an explicitly commercial setting as a laboratory allow the reader to overlook these questions because the answers seem so obvious. For a work subtitled *The Forgotten Symbolism of Architectural Form*, *Learning from Las Vegas* offers remarkably little analysis of "symbolism" or of the ways in which "form" symbolizes. The semiotic theories to which it alludes assume that signs are arbitrary and conventional vehicles for communicating "meaning."[19] Meaning floats free of any particular relationship to objects, denoting and connoting whatever we agree that it will. So conventional meanings only become conventional in a social setting, and they only "mean" when employed in other social settings. This inherently social quality of signs makes it difficult to sustain the asocial, purely technical analysis of signs or symbols that the authors vehemently insist on undertaking.

As so often occurs in this work, however, insights that are mentioned but not pursued offer the possibility of other views of architecture's symbolic functions. In one such passage, Venturi remarks that

> The Strip shows the value of symbolism and allusion in an architecture of vast space and speed and proves that people, even architects, have fun with architecture that reminds them of something else, perhaps of harems or the Wild West in Las Vegas, perhaps of the nation's New England forebears in New Jersey.[20]

The Las Vegas that Venturi, Scott Brown, and Izenour describe so eloquently and accurately "reminds [visitors] of something else," offering, then drawing back, the possibility that one might visit harems, the Wild West, or the palaces of the Caesars. Here they allude to a fundamental process of modern life: the creation of consumer desire. Feeling a void that cannot be described, we seek an intangible palliative that cannot exist, but we settle for a tangible surrogate that *can* be bought. With each new acquisition, the intangible takes another step back and another purchase is necessary.[21]

This view of the signs is very different from the relatively monodirectional communication process that *Learning from Las Vegas* so often presents as it addresses the architects who must create decorated sheds. Here, "subtle expression"—even tact and delicacy—rather than "bold communication" is essential. The link between the desired but intangible—a new identity as the cure for one's felt inadequacy—and the tangible but available—a new setting or new possessions—must be implied rather than stated. Consumers are too sophisticated to believe that a real harem, Virginia City saloon, or Roman triclinium lie behind the casino's doors. They understand that no such direct exchange is possible. The ironic disruptions—the continual oscillation of the discourse from intangible to tangible, from fantasy to transaction—make it possible for the game to continue. Its terms are conveyed by the physical and visual qualities of Las Vegas's signs: their distortions of scale, "improper" use of classical detail, and contextual discord tell us that Caesar's Palace is *and* is not Caesar's palace.[22]

The art historian David Summers labels this process of being/not being *substitution*, a game in which all the players agree that the thing at hand will stand for a desired but absent object.[23] The substitute—the Strip's classical portico or miniature Eiffel Tower—is useful only to the extent that it is manifestly not that for which it stands. The difference between original and substitute cues our understanding of the present situation in a way that is even richer than if the original itself were present.[24] In this kind of "communication," interpretation is at least as important as initial assertion. "Symbolism" is transaction rather than representation, and a sign reading "I am a monument" does not necessarily communicate any less ambiguously than a heroic and original building. Is an architectural theory that takes the signs of the Strip as models satisfactory, then? If the kind of applied symbolism exemplified by signs and decorated sheds creates the most accessible kind of architecture and best represents the taste of the "silent white majority," why is it that ducks appear to capture the popular imagination?[25] Tellingly, the recent transformation and taming of the Strip, now renamed Las Vegas Boulevard, de-emphasized pure signs in favor of miniature Eiffel Towers, overblown Sphinxes, glass pyramids, and compressed Grand Canals—corporate reinterpretations of roadside ducks—as Venturi and Scott Brown themselves observed in a perceptive essay that chronicled a return visit to Las Vegas in the 1990s.[26] The reworking of the Strip demands a reexamination of the claims set out in *Learning from Las Vegas*. Does an "architecture of meaning" always include a message?[27] And is architecture's significance so easily divorced from its materiality? The duck says, "No!"

Here we might turn back to the heroic and original modernist architecture that *Learning from Las Vegas* denounces. Recall that the authors dismiss "orthodox Modern architecture" as lacking in content as a result of its overly personal formal vocabulary. Let us start with the most dramatic example of such heroic and original architecture: Le Corbusier's Chapel of Notre Dame du Haut (1951–53) at Ronchamp, France.

Le Corbusier was severely chastised for his challenge to modernist orthodoxy two decades before *Learning from Las Vegas* appeared. The architect James Stirling famously saw the chapel as a symptom of "the crisis of rationalism," while the critic Giulio Argan and the architect Ernesto Rogers debated whether Le Corbusier was attempting to "go 'beyond the rational'" or to plunge directly into the irrational at

Ronchamp.[28] The renowned historian Nikolaus Pevsner labeled Ronchamp as "the most discussed monument of the new irrationalism" and bitterly denounced Le Corbusier's "revolt from reason" for the "mid-century irresponsibility" and frivolity evident in architecture such as that of the Brazilian modernist Oscar Niemeyer.[29] Yet in their polemic, Venturi, Scott Brown, and Izenour conflate the kind of rationalist functionalism that Stirling defended and Alan Colquhoun criticized with its expressivist antithesis at Ronchamp. Together they were the "heroic and original" "orthodox Modern architecture," with its paucity of conventional imagery or "symbolism" that Venturi set out to demolish.

The testimony of its architect and of critics and visitors, however, casts Notre Dame du Haut in a very different light. Le Corbusier and his assistants reported that they envisioned the roof as a crab shell, a boat, a ski jump, a water sluice, and an aircraft wing.[30] Based on this testimony, Danièle Pauly depicted Le Corbusier's design process as one that dredged these images from conscious and unconscious memory and worked them into sculptural, architectural form—into an "architectural symphony."[31] Far from being irrational or lacking "content" in its abstraction, Notre Dame du Haut overflows with concrete, everyday images. These have nothing obvious to do with the function or denotative meanings of the building, but they were ways for Le Corbusier and his staff to use their experience in the world to think through the project at hand.[32]

The contemporary architect Frank Gehry describes his working method in similar terms. Gehry, who is known for creating dramatic sculptural buildings that would certainly earn Venturi's label "heroic and original," says that he begins by "looking for the image" through sketching and that he frequently works from everyday objects such as bottles, snakes, fishes, boats, and horses' heads.[33] Even in the Guggenheim Museum at Bilbao, Spain—a work comparable in expressivist abstraction to the chapel at Ronchamp—the architect and his assistants described elements of the design as "bootlike" and "sail-like." One corner was a "ship's bow," while the crowning element was the "flower."[34]

In both cases, of course, the concrete images were thoroughly transformed, even dissolved, in the course of the design process as they were subjected to the distinctly unsymbolic operations necessary to create usable, buildable structures. Gehry's poetic and metaphoric images become standing buildings thanks to sophisticated computers and their expert programmers.[35] Similarly, Robin Evans detailed the particular contribution of the engineering-drawing technique of ruled surfaces to the development of the final design of Le Corbusier's chapel.[36] The results were not ducks in the roadside sense, whatever their starting points. Nevertheless, whether or not the architects' accounts of their design processes are "true" or complete, their resort to such visual images is significant. The architects "see" a variety of ordinary objects even in the most abstract buildings.

Just as architects may begin with iconic images, viewers often seek such images in an unfamiliar building, although they may or may not see the same images that its architects cite. The aesthetician John Alford, an early analyst of Ronchamp, explicitly acknowledged his search for such icons: "In order to make the building and its aesthetic more intelligible to myself I found myself looking for analogies with other monuments, architectural or sculptural." He thought Ronchamp's resemblance to a Neolithic dolmen (tomb) and to a ship particularly compelling, but he assumed that these were part of Le Corbusier's intent—to fuse a "symbolic fortress and tomb" with the "Ship of Life or of the Soul."[37] This would make them connotative symbols in the Venturian sense. Most visitors are less driven to find theological messages in Ronchamp's appearance. They have compared the chapel's towers to thumbs, pots, "an industrialized farm silo, or a nautical vent duct" and the whole building to "men holding up a boat," Noah's Ark, "'bits of broken china thrown on top of the hill,'" a dove, a sitting duck, a monk's hood, a nun's cowl, praying hands, and, as Alford did, a ship.[38] Some of these connote modernity or function, but others (the sitting duck, the broken china) are metaphors of absurdity or of absent meaning.

In the light of such analogies, we may take issue with Venturi's claim that "allusion and comment, on the past or present or on our great commonplaces or old clichés, and inclusion of the *everyday* in the environment, sacred and profane . . . are lacking in present-day Modern architecture."[39] Architects and viewers do find such allusions in modern buildings, but they rarely see them (pace Alford) as denotative statements and not always as connotative ones. So we might ask, particularly of the meaningless images, whether they have "symbolic content" even if they do not communicate Venturian messages.

One way to think about this question would be to turn from the sober world of high architecture at Ronchamp and Bilbao to the lighthearted and irreverent landscape defined by the nicknames that lay people give to specific buildings. These constitute a kind of visual-verbal play that ranges through a wide variety of buildings of many ages and many types. For the most part, this play is free of the pervasive publicity and journalistic canonization that colors our reactions to instant monuments such as Ronchamp or Bilbao.[40]

Of a highly unscientific sample of over two hundred such names, two-thirds pun or otherwise play on the physical aspects of the building.[41] They append a concrete visual image such as those we have encountered at Ronchamp and Bilbao to a building's abstract architectural form, metaphorically moving the nicknamed building into a new context, often to the building's disadvantage.[42] The greatest number of nicknames compared a building to another object—almost always a smaller, more mundane object—based on the shape, color, or materials of the structure. Thus the shape of the office building at 885 Third Avenue in New York prompted the nickname Lipstick Building. It is complemented by the Lipstick and

Compact Case (or Lipstick and Powder Puff), the 1961 additions to the ruined Kaiser-Wilhelm-Gedachtsnis-Kirche in Berlin. The Fernsehturm, a broadcasting tower in Berlin, is Tele-spargel (Tele-asparagus) or the Toothpick. Another asparagus is Shanghai's Jin Mao Tower, intended by its architects to resemble a pagoda. A housing project in Sydney and Jerome L. Greene Hall at Columbia University in New York are both known as the Toaster. A roof that looks like a partly opened shell earned the Haus der Kulturen der Welt in Berlin the label Schwangere Auster (Pregnant Oyster). The Monument to Vittorio Emmanuele II in Rome is variously known as the Torta Nunziale (Wedding Cake), the Macchina da Scrivere (Typewriter), and the Dentures. Montreal's Olympic Stadium is the Giant Toilet Bowl, while Norman Foster's Swiss Re Tower in London was dubbed the Erotic Gherkin long before it was completed.

The most striking nicknames compare buildings to ordinary household appliances (St. Mary Maytag, the Lemon Squeezer, the Washing Machine, the Sponge[43]) or to foods (Tortenstück/the Slice of Cake, the Corncobs, the Golden Cabbage, the Durian, the Space Strudel[44]). All these names reimagine monumental buildings as everyday items that are normally used or consumed by people. They transform the human-architectural scale relationship into a distorted human-object relationship.

Human scale is evoked even more directly when nicknames compare buildings to human beings or parts of human beings. The tall antennae atop the AT&T (formerly South Central Bell and BellSouth) Building in Nashville distinguish it as the Batman Building. The linked, distorted towers of Gehry's Nationale-Nederlanden Building in Prague are thought to resemble Fred Astaire clutching Ginger Rogers, hence the Fred and Ginger Building. Der lange Eugen, a nickname for a twenty-nine-story parliamentary office building in Bonn, refers to Eugen Gerenmaier, the president of the Bundestag at the time the building was constructed and a man of short stature. Bowman's Erection for the Cathedral of Learning at the University of Pittsburgh, the Prick on the Plains for Bertram Goodhue's Nebraska State Capitol in Lincoln, Hoover's Last Erection for the Hoover Tower at Stanford University, and the Gentalia for the juxtaposition of the Sky Dome and the CN Tower in Toronto all use phallic metaphors to comment on the ambitions of architects and patrons.[45]

Building nicknames recontextualize through substitution. While Le Corbusier and Gehry subordinated images to the final product, viewers of those buildings projected their own images onto them to understand and "tame" (or dismiss) these idiosyncratic buildings. Nicknames aim to destabilize architecture by what seventeenth-century English poets called a metaphysical conceit (or image), one that links two unlikely things in a way that casts at least one of them into an unexpected light. As one informant wrote of two particularly striking nicknames, "Now try ridding your mind" of them when viewing the buildings.[46]

Architectural nicknaming is a metaphorical gesture that is grounded in architecture's materiality, specificity, and place-rootedness. Building on the Greek root of "metaphor," which means to transfer something from one place to another, Summers has stressed the relationality and spatiality inherent in visual (including architectural) metaphors. They are "real metaphors" whose significance derives from substitutions within the realm of mass and extension that we occupy and, just as importantly, from the context within which substitution is made. In his words, "Substitutes are effective in the space in which they are put because they are only 'real' in that space . . . we cannot interpret them without giving equal attention to their correlative spaces."[47] Summers's real metaphors are serious and sincere, whereas building nicknames are playful and ironic. His substitutions turn pumpkins into coaches, but building nicknames turn coaches into pumpkins.

Architectural nicknames are irreverent but rarely angry or demeaning. Even the many that are disparaging usually have a good-humored tone about them. Their playfully subversive substitution of images carries us back to the roadside ducks that *Learning from Las Vegas* named so memorably and that the authors equated with heroic and original architecture. A duck is a building intentionally shaped like another object or group of objects: no imaginative projection is necessary. Most often the image represents a mundane object of daily use—a clam box, a milk bottle, a coffee pot, a miner's hat, an automobile tire—or something edible—a chicken, an artichoke, a hot dog, a doughnut. Occasionally the building resembles a human being. In other words, ducks are explicit representations of the same kinds of objects that the nicknames project onto noniconic buildings.

Ducks, inhabitable sculptures, are one subcategory of the large body of colossi (and miniatures), ranging from civic monuments to roadside attractions, that populate the landscape.[48] In civic monuments, this scale shift often has a connotative intent. The adjacent Jefferson and Franklin D. Roosevelt memorials in Washington, D.C., are a case in point. The colossal statue of Jefferson, raised on a high pedestal, and the near-life-size, pedestal-less figures of FDR imply very different relationships between the great men and ordinary viewers. A roadside duck is intended to attract motorists' attention and to suggest the goods and services offered but presumably not to imply that humans are mere pipsqueaks compared to a barnyard animal. Yet in the cases of both the memorials and the commercial structures, the viewer is invited to experience the dislocation and disorientation that arises from finding oneself, like Alice in Wonderland, in an unfamiliar relationship to familiar things. Building nicknames offer the same defamiliarization, suggesting that the city itself has become a kind of funhouse (which is not necessarily a bad thing).The incorporation of concrete images into the processes of designing and experiencing Le Corbusier's and Gehry's buildings, the nicknaming of a Batman Building or a Durian, and a roadside entrepreneur's construction of a giant duck or doughnut are linked as playful exercises that manipulate the relationship between self and environment symbolically. In some cases Venturian communication enters into the process. When Alford read theological content into Ronchamp, he attributed both connotative and denotative messages to it. And architectural nicknames surely connote one's attitude toward a particular structure.

In framing architectural symbolism under the rubric of language, however, Venturi, Scott Brown, and Izenour are among those who, Pierre Bourdieu argues, fall so thoroughly under the spell of the language they use that they would reduce all cultural acts to propositions and messages: "Language spontaneously becomes the accomplice of this hermeneutic philosophy which leads one to conceive action as something to be deciphered, when it leads one to say, for example, that a gesture or ritual *expresses* something, rather than saying quite simply, that it is 'sensible' (*sensé*) or, as in English, that it 'makes' sense."[49] For Bourdieu, there is a sense of "rightness," of being in tune, involved in such actions that is partly somatic and that cannot be reduced to a denotative or connotative proposition.

Instead, it might be more appropriate to cast language into the realm of architecture, of the material, of what George Lakoff and Mark Johnson call "embodied realism." According to Lakoff and Johnson, we succeed in the world by sorting things into categories, simplifying differences and lumping our experience as much as possible into "basic-level categories," a kind of categorical least common denominator. They go on to argue that as the products of embodied minds actively and corporeally engaged in our surroundings, most of our basic-level categories are based on comparisons with and relationships to our bodies. Our figurative speech is rich with metaphors founded in these body-based, relational categories.[50]

An important aspect of architectural symbolism, then, lies in the metaphorical relationships that it proposes between bodies and buildings. Metaphor, wrote Donald Davidson, is the "dreamwork of language."[51] It has no hidden or other meaning—no message outside itself to which it points, no content that can be paraphrased.[52] The mundane iconic images and correspondences architects and viewers employed at Ronchamp and Bilbao helped to fit these "abstract" modern buildings into their own embodied frames of reference. They symbolized the buildings' relationships to the world as builders and viewers imagine it, a test that took the form of Summers's metaphorical substitution.

The anthropologist Dan Sperber, writing at about the time *Learning from Las Vegas* was published, denied that symbolism is "the semiotic minus language." According to Sperber, "Symbols are not signs. They are not paired with their interpretations in a code structure. Their interpretations are not meanings." The meaning of symbols is "absent meaning." Instead, symbolism represents knowledge about knowledge. It is a way of affirming what we think we know about what we know. That is, the power of symbolism lies not in its transmission of a message, but in its ritual, visual, or verbal enactment of relationships that we believe to be true, to be "right," or to "make sense," in Bourdieu's phrasing.[53]

It is not necessary, then, to discard language when we argue that architecture is neither a language nor a text. We simply need to acknowledge that even our verbal encounters with architecture depend on fundamental, embodied engagement with our material surroundings, an engagement based not simply on looking at signs but on immersion in a multidimensional landscape.[54]

So space cannot be discounted as easily as Venturi and his colleagues think. Even the automobile traveler along the Las Vegas Strip of thirty years ago was immersed in a large-scale, changing environment in which his or her relationship to objects constantly shifted as signs loomed and streamed by, one after the other.[55] Venturi's term "automobile scale" obscures the fact that such giant signs and giant architectural objects were part of the world long before the automobile came onto the scene because they were toys in a more important and more pervasive game than selling, one that *symbolizes* human being in the world.[56] This is why ducks are so popular, and it may be why they are replacing decorated sheds in modern Las Vegas as corporate-sponsored architects strive to emulate the kind of visual and spatial play that freelance roadside merchants practiced so energetically seventy years ago. *Learning from Las Vegas* is a monument in the history and theory of American architecture, but it is also a sign marking a curious turning point for the field. The expressive buildings produced by architects such as Le Corbusier, Niemeyer, Rudolph, and Eero Saarinen in the 1950s and 1960s explored the embodied relationships between people and their environments, their dramatic gestural forms eliciting a kind of somatic empathy from the viewer. In rejecting this kind of heroic and original architecture (for some very good reasons) and in using the results of their own field research so selectively, Venturi, Scott Brown, and Izenour set architecture on a road away from the material toward the cerebral. *Learning from Las Vegas*, along with *Complexity and Contradiction* (both issued in revised editions in 1977), inaugurated the period of high theory in architecture. *Complexity and Contradiction*'s reliance on modes of literary criticism and the communications model employed in *Learning from Las Vegas* helped deliver American architectural theory into the linguistic bondage from which it has yet to be liberated. Although Venturi and Scott Brown dislike being connected with their postmodern successors, the arbitrariness of "conventional" form that they championed undeniably opened the door for an architecture in which a billboard proclaiming "I am a monument" attached to a box could be perfectly acceptable, and they opened another door to the wordiness and immateriality of contemporary theory. Since the 1960s, exploration of architecture's materiality has been left to artists such as Dan Flavin, Gordon Matta-Clark, Dan Graham, and Rachel Whiteread.

To reexamine *Learning from Las Vegas* through the lens of the architecture that Venturi, Scott Brown, and Izenour rejected is not to call for a return to the heroic and original or to ignore the (unspecified) constraints that they claim make such an architecture impractical or inappropriate to our times. Rather, it is to turn the authors' call to learn from the entire landscape back on them. The lesson of the heroic modernists, the smart-aleck building namers, and the duck builders is that architectural meaning encompasses more than a one-way process of "communicating" and "symbolizing." Architecture is not language. Architecture is not a text. Architecture is not television.

Notes

Thanks to Paul Groth, Karen Kevorkian, Zeynep Kezer, and especially the editors, Michael Golec and Aron Vinegar, for comments on an earlier version of this essay. I have borrowed my title for this chapter from Franco Moretti's 1983 book on the sociology of literary forms.

1. Robert Venturi, *Complexity and Contradiction in Architecture* (New York: Museum of Modern Art, 1966), 102. Emphasis added.
2. Denise Scott Brown, "Pop Off: Reply to Kenneth Frampton," in *A View from the Campidoglio: Selected Essays, 1953–1984*, ed. Peter Arnell, Ted Bickford, and Catherine Bergart (New York: Harper & Row, 1971), 34, 37.
3. Robert Venturi, *Complexity and Contradiction in Architecture*, 2nd ed. (New York: Museum of Modern Art, 1977), 44; Robert Venturi, Denise Scott Brown, and Steven Izenour, *Learning from Las Vegas: The Forgotten Symbolism of Architectural Form*, rev. ed. (Cambridge, Mass.: MIT Press, 1977), 100, 105, 130; Scott Brown, "Pop Off," 37; Robert Venturi, "A Definition of Architecture as Shelter with Decoration on It, and Another Plea for a Symbolism of the Ordinary in Architecture," in *A View from the Campidoglio*, 63.
4. Venturi, Scott Brown, and Izenour, *Learning from Las Vegas*, 87.
5. Ibid., 137. Other aspects of *Learning from Las Vegas* are indebted to the discussion of urban form and meaning centered around the work of Kevin Lynch. Scott Brown's early essay "The Meaningful City" is important for understanding the place of *Learning from Las Vegas* in urbanist debates. Denise Scott Brown, "The Meaningful City," *AIA Journal* 43, no. 1 (1965): 27–32.
6. For example, see Alan Colquhoun's essay "Typology and Design Method," which Scott Brown acknowledged several times and which prefigures some of the important arguments about architectural symbolism that find their way into *Learning from Las Vegas*. Alan Colquhoun, "Typology and Design Method," in *Meaning in Architecture*, ed. Charles Jencks and George Baird (New York: George Braziller, 1967), 266–77.
7. Paul De Man, "The Concept of Irony," in *Aesthetic Ideology*, ed. Andrzej Warminski (Minneapolis: University of Minnesota Press, 1996), 178–82. Thanks to Aron Vinegar for directing me to this essay.
8. I am indebted to Michael Golec for this insight.
9. Denise Scott Brown, "Preface to the Revised Edition," in *Learning from Las Vegas*, xv.
10. Karsten Harries, *The Ethical Function of Architecture* (Cambridge, Mass.: MIT Press, 1997), 78, 81.
11. Venturi, Scott Brown, and Izenour, *Learning from Las Vegas*, 7, 101. The claim of impoverishment derives from Ernst Gombrich by way of Alan Colquhoun. Colquhoun, "Typology and Design Method," 274.
12. Venturi, Scott Brown, and Izenour, *Learning from Las Vegas*, 9.
13. Ibid., 8.
14. Ibid., 13.
15. Ibid., 149.
16. Robert Venturi, *Iconography and Electronics upon a Generic Architecture: A View from the Drafting Room* (Cambridge, Mass.: MIT Press, 1996), 55, 13.
17. Venturi, Scott Brown, and Izenour, *Learning from Las Vegas*, 100–101.
18. Harries, *Ethical Function*, 70, 78. Harries makes a similar point in arguing that Venturi mentions the role of architecture in the "articulation of space" but not in setting the tone for social action. Harries, *Ethical Function*, 81.
19. These assumptions are founded in the work of Fernand de Saussure. For a discussion of their impact on the plastic and visual arts, see James Elkins, *The Domain of Images* (Ithaca, N.Y.: Cornell University Press, 1999), 55; David Summers, "Conditions and Conventions: On the Disanalogy of Art and Language," in *The Language of Art History*, ed. Salim Kemal and Ivan Gaskell (Cambridge: Cambridge University Press, 1991), 185–90, 194–96.
20. Venturi, Scott Brown, and Izenour, *Learning from Las Vegas*, 53.
21. Henri Lefebvre, *Everyday Life in the Modern World* (New Brunswick, N.J.: Transaction Publishers, 1984), 90; Dell Upton, *Architecture in the United States* (Oxford: Oxford University Press, 1998), 33–35, which builds on Colin Campbell, *The Romantic Ethic and the Spirit of Modern Consumption* (Oxford: Blackwell, 1987); and Daniel Miller, *Material Culture and Mass Consumption* (Oxford: Blackwell, 1987).

22. Arthur C. Danto has commented on Las Vegas's dazzling layers of authenticity and inauthenticity. Arthur C. Danto, "Degas in Vegas," in *The Madonna of the Future: Essays in Pluralistic Art World* (Berkeley: University of California Press, 2001), 351–59.

23. David Summers, "Real Metaphor: Towards a Redefinition of the 'Conceptual' Image," in *Visual Theory: Painting and Interpretation*, ed. Norman Bryson, Michael Ann Holly, and Keith Moxey (New York: HarperCollins, 1991), 241, 243, 245.

24. Summers, "Conditions and Conventions," 204–5; italics in the original.

25. Venturi, Scott Brown, and Izenour, *Learning from Las Vegas*, 153; Denise Scott Brown, "Learning from Pop," in *A View from the Campidoglio*, 26–27; Scott Brown, "Pop Off," 35.

26. Robert Venturi and Denise Scott Brown, "Las Vegas after Its Classic Age," in *Iconography and Electronics*, 126. Something like the classic Venturian Strip survives in Las Vegas along the Boulder Strip, now a downscale residential and commercial district for Latino workers.

27. Robert Venturi and Denise Scott Brown, "Learning from Lutyens: Reply to Alison and Peter Smithson," in *A View from the Campidoglio*, 20.

28. James Stirling, "Ronchamp: Le Corbusier's Chapel and the Crisis of Rationalism," *Architectural Review* 119 (1956): 160–61; Alexander Tzonis, *Le Corbusier: The Poetics of Machine and Metaphor* (New York: Universe, 2001), 176.

29. Nikolaus Pevsner, *An Outline of European Architecture*, 7th ed., rev. (Harmondsworth: Penguin, 1970), 426–29.

30. Tzonis, *Le Corbusier*, 181; William J. R. Curtis, *Le Corbusier: Ideas and Forms* (New York: Phaidon, 1986), 179–80; Robin Evans, *The Projective Cast: Architecture and Its Three Geometries* (Cambridge, Mass.: MIT Press, 1995), 305.

31. Danièle Pauly, "The Chapel of Ronchamp as an Example of Le Corbusier's Creative Process," in *Le Corbusier*, ed. H. Allen Brooks (Princeton, N.J.: Princeton University Press, 1987), 132–34. The quote is from Danièle Pauly, *Le Corbusier: La Chapelle de Ronchamp/The Chapel at Ronchamp* (Paris: Fondation Le Corbusier; Basel: Birkhäuser, 1997), 122.

32. They may also have had a connotative function in that by naming the images, Le Corbusier and his assistants established the modern context in which they wanted this religious structure to be understood.

33. Bruce Lindsey, *Digital Gehry: Material Resistance/Digital Construction* (Basel: Birkhäuser, 2001), 7, 23, 82; Coosje van Bruggen, *Frank O. Gehry: Guggenheim Museum Bilbao*) (New York: Guggenheim Museum Publications, 1999), 40, 42.

34. van Bruggen, *Frank O. Gehry*, 36, 52.

35. Lindsey, *Digital Gehry*, 48–89.

36. Evans, *Projective Cast*, 293, 306–8.

37. John Alford, "Creativity and Intelligibility in Le Corbusier's Chapel at Ronchamp," *Journal of Aesthetics and Art Criticism* 16, no. 3 (1958): 302–4.

38. Stirling, "Ronchamp," 155; Tzonis, *Le Corbusier*, 181; Charles Jencks, *Le Corbusier and the Tragic View of Architecture* (Cambridge, Mass.: Harvard University Press, 1973), 152. The quotes are from Evans, *Projective Cast*, 305–6, 317.

39. Venturi, Scott Brown, and Izenour, *Learning from Las Vegas*, 53.

40. For example, Herbert Muschamp, "The Miracle at Bilbao," *New York Times Magazine*, September 7, 1997, 56–59, 72, 82.

41. Most of these nicknames were collected by way of a call for contributions on the e-lists of the Consortium of Art and Architectural Historians and the Society of Architectural Historians. The project garnered 185 different nicknames (discounting minor variations) for 143 different nineteenth- and twentieth-century European, North and South American, and Australian buildings. Others were collected from personal encounters, verbal reports from acquaintances, and library and Internet research. Interestingly, there were no African buildings and only a few Asian ones submitted. Slightly fewer than one-third of the nicknames were based on wordplay, meaning that people punned or otherwise manipulated the name of the building or building owner or the function of the building, as in "the Orifice" for The Oracle shopping mall in Reading, England.

42. Seventy of the nicknames were *clearly* derogatory (many others probably were), while only two were clearly admiring.

43. These are the names for St. Mary's Cathedral, San Francisco; St. Engelbert's Church, Cologne; the Calakmul Building, Mexico City; and Simmons Hall, MIT, respectively.

44. These are the names for the Museum of Modern Art, Frankfurt; Marina City, Chicago; the Secession Building, Vienna; the Esplanade—Theaters on the Bay, Singapore; and the Austrian Cultural Forum, New York, respectively.

45. John G. Bowman was the University of Pittsburgh chancellor who promoted the construction of the Cathedral of Learning. Surprisingly few nicknames employ sexual innuendoes as these do.

46. Benjamin Harvey, personal communication, Aug. 22, 2002.

47. Summers, "Real Metaphor," 245–46; Summers, "Conditions and Conventions," 184.

48. See Karal Ann Marling, *The Colossus of Roads: Myth and Symbol along the American Highway* (Minneapolis: University of Minnesota Press, 1984).

49. Pierre Bourdieu, *The Logic of Practice* (Stanford, Calif.: Stanford University Press, 1990), 36–37.

50. George Lakoff and Mark Johnson, *Philosophy in the Flesh: The Embodied Mind and Its Challenge to Western Thought* (New York: Basic Books, 1999), 17–18, 27, 30–38.

51. Donald Davidson, "What Metaphors Mean," in *On Metaphor*, ed. Sheldon Sacks (Chicago: University of Chicago Press, 1978), 29.

52. Davidson, "What Metaphors Mean," 43. Noël Carroll makes the same point with respect to visual metaphors. Noël Carroll, "Visual Metaphor," in *Beyond Aesthetics: Philosophical Essays* (Cambridge: Cambridge University Press, 2001), 355, 365.

53. The quote is from Dan Sperber, *Rethinking Symbolism* (Cambridge: Cambridge University Press, 1975), 1, 51–85.

54. On the verbal component of visual metaphors, see Carroll, "Visual Metaphor," 359.

55. It seems to me that, as they so often do, Venturi and his colleagues acknowledge this in Part I of *Learning from Las Vegas* and ignore it in Part II.

56. David Henkin, *City Reading: Written Words and Public Spaces in Antebellum New York* (New York: Columbia University Press, 1998), explores the ways in which antebellum New York was a city inscribed with texts at all scales, while Barbara Rubin, "Aesthetic Ideology and Urban Design," *Annals of the Association of American Geographers* 69 (1979): 339–61, discusses ducks before the automobile.

8

The Melodrama of Expression and Inexpression in the Duck and Decorated Shed

ARON VINEGAR

> I am convinced that I cannot exaggerate enough even to lay the foundation of a true expression.
> —THOREAU, *WALDEN*

The Modernist Drive for Expressive Transparency

One of the primary critiques of modernism that *Learning from Las Vegas* was engaged in was the dialectic between inside and outside and the assumption that the outside expressed the interior.[1] As Rem Koolhaas put it in his book *Delirious New York*, "In Western architecture there has been the humanistic assumption that it is desirable to establish a moral relationship between the two, whereby the exterior makes certain revelations about the interior that the interior corroborates."[2] Let's call this the modernist drive for "expressive transparency." In contrast, Robert Venturi, Denise Scott Brown, and Steven Izenour stress the contradiction between the inside and outside, drawing on examples from premodern eras, as well as American roadside architecture with its "false fronts," combination of styles (with "Moorish in front and Tudor behind"), and the diremption of the big sign from the boxlike generic building behind it. What *Learning from Las Vegas* seems to have in its sights is how to make sense of and to go on from a situation in which a certain modernist legacy of architecture was breaking down: where the drive for expressive transparency had contorted itself to the point in which the "expressive aim [had] distorted the whole."[3]

The drive for expressive transparency in modern architecture, and *Learning from Las Vegas*' response to it, is intimately related to the skeptical problem of knowing "other minds," a problem that is deeply involved with the relationship between the inner and outer, transparency and opacity, expression and inexpression. As the philosopher Stanley Cavell has put it, "at some stage the skeptic is going to be impressed by the fact that my knowledge of others depends upon their *expressing themselves*, in word and conduct."[4] That is to say, expression and action depend on some calibration of inner meanings and outward signs. If skepticism about other minds, our ability to "know" the other, depends on an interaction between the inner and outer—on the expressive capacities of a body and our willingness to acknowledge or avoid those capacities—then architecture's deeply rooted investment in the metaphorics of the body and its preoccupation with the relationship between the interior and exterior would suggest that it is one of the privileged domains in which skepticism about other minds is dramatized.

For Cavell, skepticism is not fundamentally triggered by our perceived lack of knowledge of the world, as it has been traditionally cast. Rather, it is about our responses and responsibility in relation to the world. Cavell's key term for this thought is "acknowledgment," a word that is meant not as an alternative to knowledge but rather as an interpretation of it;[5] that is to say, the world and others in it make claims on us that we can either acknowledge or avoid. Thus skepticism is not so much a discovery about the world but rather a particular relationship to it; it manifests itself less as ignorance of that world (a failure to know) than in our modes of ignoring or acting on what we already know.[6] The "ordinary" in Cavell's work is precisely that region that requires acts of acknowledgment and acceptance. Refusing to do so is always a possibility, but to do so just points to the fact that skepticism is a standing threat that is never overcome once and for all. And indeed, Cavell's major claim is that skepticism cannot be refuted, although we can—and, in fact, must—reconceive its truth.

A shorthand way of thinking about the dilemma of other minds—the mode of skepticism particularly at stake in this chapter—is roughly marked out by Walter Benjamin on the one hand and Venturi and Scott Brown on the other. In a well-known passage from his essay "Surrealism: The Last Snapshot of the European Intelligentsia," Benjamin advocates the transparency of the modernist building and its ability to express: "To live in a glass house is a revolutionary virtue par excellence. It is also an intoxication, a moral exhibitionism we badly need." Venturi and Scott Brown argue that internal to this logic of "moral exhibitionism" is the potential—already latent in Benjamin's passage—for architecture to twist itself into a full-blown *theatricality* in which the "expressive aim has distorted the whole."⁷ Thus, postwar modernism's theatricality was thwarting its own attempts to express.

Fantasies of Absolute Expression and Inexpression in the Duck and the Decorated Shed

The dialectic between expression and inexpression is taken up with a vengeance in the by-now infamous contrast—what Venturi and Scott Brown call an "indiscreet comparison"—between the Duck and Decorated Shed in *Learning from Las Vegas* (Figure 8.1). And it is this comparison that enacts the skeptical dilemma about knowing other minds. Venturi and Scott Brown's definition of both is worth quoting in full:

1. Where the architectural systems of space, structure, and program are submerged and distorted by an overall symbolic form. This kind of building-

Figure 8.1. Duck and Decorated Shed in *Learning from Las Vegas* (Robert Venturi, Denise Scott Brown, and Steven Izenour, *Learning from Las Vegas*, rev. ed. [Cambridge, Mass.: MIT Press, 1977], 88–89. Copyright 1977, Massachusetts Institute of Technology.)

becoming-sculpture we call the *duck* in honor of the duck-shaped drive-in, "The Long Island Duckling," illustrated in *God's Own Junkyard* by Peter Blake.

2. Where systems of space and structure are directly at the service of program, and ornament is applied independently of them. This we call the *decorated shed*.

As they note, "The duck is the special building that *is* a symbol; the decorated shed is the conventional shelter that *applies* symbols. . . . We think that the duck is seldom relevant today although it pervades Modern architecture."[8]

The two photographs reproduced from Blake's *God's Own Junkyard*, and the diagrams below them that illustrate the comparison, demonstrate that there is no hard-and-fast separation between the Duck and Decorated Shed. The "Long Island Duckling" is also "conventional" insofar as the photograph includes the adjacent "signs" that indicate that the Duckling sells game hens and turkeys as well as broiled roasted ducks. Moreover, we can see what look like two sheds behind the duck such that we could interpret the Duck as a conventional "sign" in its own right that is applied to the sheds in back.[9] Although the freestanding Duck is described as a "building-becoming-sculpture" at various points in *Learning from Las Vegas*, the authors also emphasize the sculptural qualities of the big neon signs in Las Vegas. Early images of the Duck and Decorated shed diagrams, appearing in articles before *Learning from Las Vegas*, are drawn at the same scale and with the same thickness of line (with the exception of the windows), as if to suggest that the curving, expressionistic lines of the Duck are the result of a twisted morphing of the Shed or vice versa (Figure 8.2). Further blurring the distinction, both the Duck and the Decorated Shed are concerned with the "function" of eating (a point to which I will return). Most importantly, both the Duck and the Decorated Shed are deeply concerned with issues of voice. In the diagrams the Duck and Decorated Shed have two window-eyes and a door-nose, but no mouth. The issue of voice and expression—giving expression to voice and voice to expression—are dominant concerns in this chapter.

What is even more telling of the skeptical dilemma is that the Duck and Decorated Shed diagrams, introduced directly beneath the photographs, render Both building types with a "face."[10] There could be no better testament that skepticism about other minds is central to these diagrams than the inclusion of eyes, the supposed "windows to the soul," and the canonical location and bearing of expressiveness in figural art and natural human interactions. This is reminiscent of a striking passage in *The World Viewed* in which Cavell talks about "a mood of nothing but eyes, dissociated from feeling."[11] Notice, however, that the dark, thicker line used to render the windows/eyes on the Duck makes

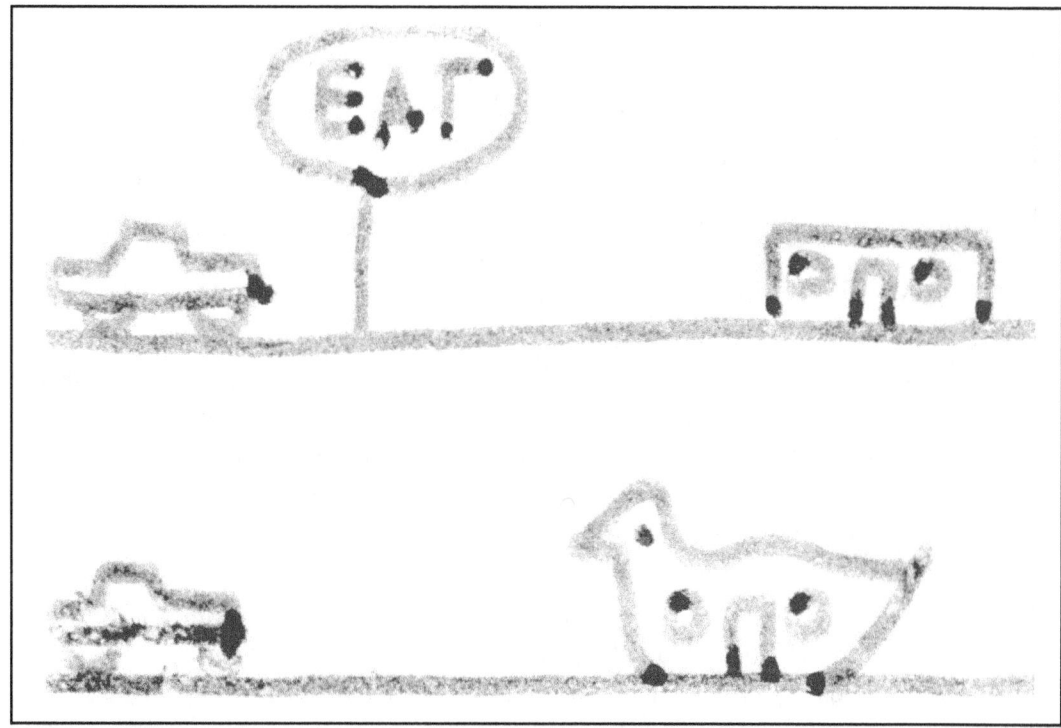

Figure 8.2. Duck and Decorated Shed from "A Significance for A&P Parking Lots, or Learning from Las Vegas." (Denise Scott Brown and Robert Venturi, "A Significance for A&P Parking Lots, or Learning from Las Vegas," *The Architectural Forum* [March 1968]: 41.)

them look more expressive than the ones on the Decorated Shed. And the overall "facedness" of both the Duck and the Decorated Shed is remarkably close to Cavell's claim that in skepticism, "the body . . . becomes a thing with senses, mostly eyes, disconnected from the motive power of the body."[12] It would seem that, despite their apparent opposition, both the Duck and Decorated Shed share an overarching proposition: if there is a "disconnection" between eyes, body, feeling, and voice, then perhaps we need to rethink that condition in order to see how we might reconfigure our *sense* of what architecture is and can be.

By beginning with the similarities between the Duck and the Decorated Shed instead of their differences—their indiscreteness one might say—I am suggesting that we are better served by understanding the comparison as voicing a certain *fantasy* of expression or inexpression. In calling it a fantasy, I mean an interpretation of reality, not simply a state separate from reality. As Cavell puts it, "fantasy is precisely what reality can be confused with. It is through fantasy that our conviction of the worth of reality is established; to forgo our fantasies would be to forgo our touch with the world."[13] This fantasy suggests a particular atmosphere, mood, or attitude in which the world is "colored" *as* Duck- or Decorated Shed-like. Rather than taking their comparison as simply a concrete discussion about discrete and stabilized ontologies "out there," we should see the Duck and the Decorated Shed as categories in terms of which a given response is evaluated.[14] If we approach the comparison from that angle, how we respond to architecture, how we permit it to count for us in specific ways, is inseparable from what architecture *is* at any given moment.

In other words, the Duck and the Decorated Shed are not "tired tropes"; they do not simply repeat the ontological categories of architecture involved in other well-known comparisons, such as Nikolaus Pevsner's famous opening line from *An Outline of European Architecture*: "A bicycle shed is a building; Lincoln Cathedral is a piece of architecture."[15] But neither do Venturi and Scott Brown abandon an interest in the "ontology" of architecture. Rather, they modify it with an attentiveness to the historical and affective dimensions that are perpetually redefining what it is and what it can do.[16] It is our mode of acknowledgment or avoidance of that acknowledgment—a certain category of *response*, perhaps a "confusion, an indifference, a callousness, an exhaustion, a coldness"[17]—that "inflicts" the status of "duckdom" on *any* building whatsoever. And *Learning from Las Vegas* makes it abundantly clear that many buildings throughout history should be seen as both Duck and Decorated Shed (though of course their sympathies are with the Decorated Shed for its relevancy *now*). It would appear that the Duck and the Decorated Shed operate as highly mobile, supple, and chiasmatically entwined terms—and at crucial points, each incorporates the other in order to survive.

Crawford Manor and Guild House: Plasticity and Flatness

In arguing against the "modernist" Duck's attempt to exude meaning independently of convention, Venturi and Scott Brown draw on the art historian Ernst Gombrich's argument about the "physiognomic fallacy"—primarily read through Alan Colquhoun's article "Typology and Design Method," published in 1967.[18] At the heart of this argument is the critique of any kind of direct expression that could bypass the use of conventional signs. In his essay "Expression and Communication," Gombrich tabulates a set of binary concepts to make this clear: on one side, expression, emotion, symptom, naturalness; and on the other, communication, information, code, convention.[19] Venturi and Scott Brown take up Gombrich's criticism of the claim that "shapes have physiognomic or expressive content which communicates itself to us directly" in order to question the supposed ideology of certain strands of modern architectural functionalism. Adhering pretty closely to Colquhoun's interpretation of Gombrich, they critique high modernism's "belief" that form is the logical expression of operational needs and techniques, which, in turn, is wedded to a mystical belief in the intuitive process. The result was, according to Colquhoun and Venturi and Scott Brown, a biological determinism inextricably linked with a permissive expressionism.[20]

Venturi and Scott Brown's characterization of the Duck as "a-building-becoming-sculpture" makes clear that issues of plasticity and modulation carry the weight of this hyperbolic expressionism. The words and phrases used to describe the Duck are revealing: overarticulated, dramatic, stridently distorted, overstated, twisted, violently heroic and original, and extraordinary.[21] The point is brought home through the comparison between Paul Rudolph's Crawford Manor in New Haven and Venturi and Rauch's Guild House in Philadelphia—both built as housing for the elderly—which are deployed as the contemporary examples of the Duck and the Decorated Shed (Figure 8.3).[22] Although the structure of Crawford Manor is really a "conventional" frame supporting masonry walls—consisting of poured-in-place concrete with concrete block faced with a striated pattern—it does not look it. It appears as if the supports are "made of a continuous plastic material reminiscent of *béton brut* with the striated marks of a violently heroic

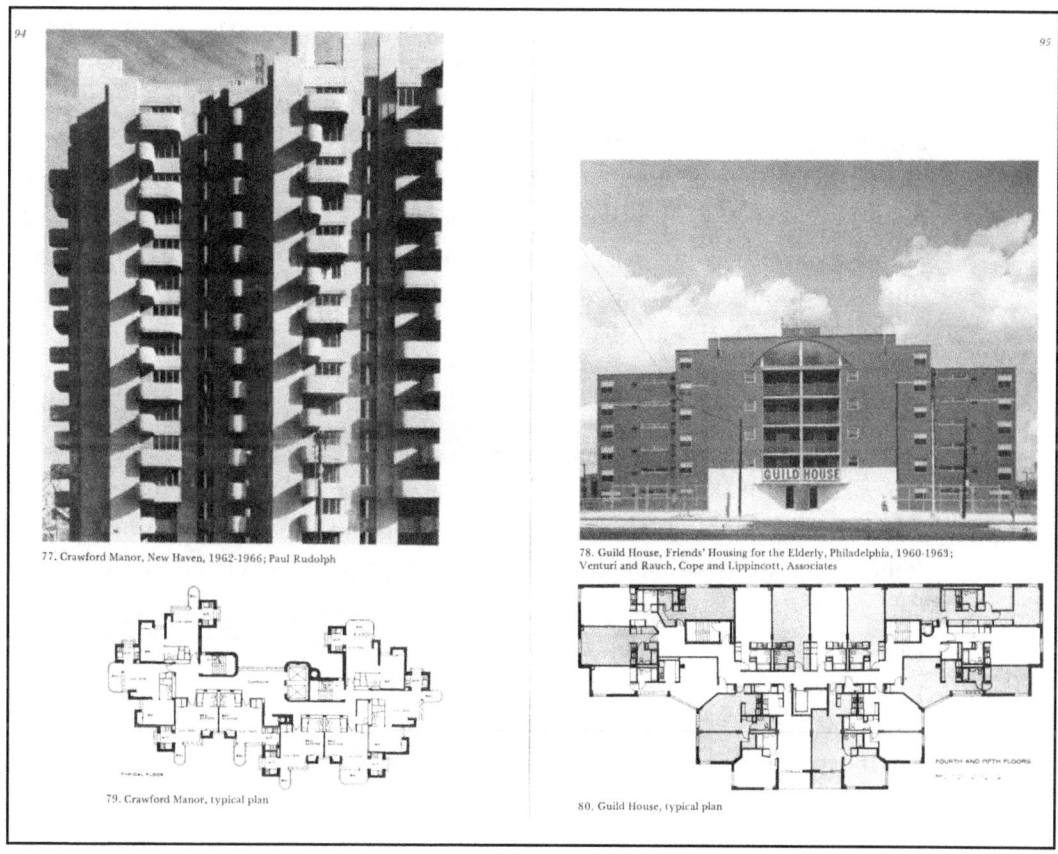

Figure 8.3. Comparison between Crawford Manor (*left*) and Guild House (*right*) (Venturi, Scott Brown, and Izenour, *Learning from Las Vegas* [rev. ed.], 94–95. Copyright 1977, Massachusetts Institute of Technology.)

construction embossed in their form." Further, "interior light is 'modulated' by the voids between the structure and the 'floating' cantilevered balconies." In contrast, the system of construction and program in the Guild House is ordinary and conventional and looks it. It is constructed of poured-in-place concrete plate, with curtain walls "pierced" by windows. The facing material is common brick, darker than usual to match the aged brick buildings in the surrounding neighborhood.

The flatness of the Guild House's cheap appliqué decoration on the façade is clearly meant to contrast with the plasticity of Rudolph's Crawford Manor. Its balcony railings recall patterns in "stamped" metal, and the double-hung conventional windows "puncture" the surface rather than "articulate" it and are explicitly symbolic rather than serving to "modulate" exterior light. The comparison is crowned by the description of the "unconnected, television antenna in gold anodized aluminum," an imitation of an "abstract Lippold sculpture," or "almost sculpture" (their words), that perches on the roof of Guild House and "ironically" refers to the sculptural Crawford Manor. As against the explicit, specific, and heraldic denotative sign that spells out "[I am] Guild House," Crawford Manor identifies itself through the "connotation implicit in the physiognomy of its pure architectural form, which is intended to express in some way housing for the elderly."[23]

This contrast between the expressionism of Crawford Manor and the deliberate damming of expression in the Guild House is dramatized by the frog's-eye view of the undulating, striated, and chiaroscuro-lit balconies of the former's "soaring tower" that makes a striking counterpart to the "deadpan" view of the tightly cropped and shadowless façade of the latter (Figure 8.4).[24] This engaging and carefully staged comparison—we might call it a "fantasy scene"—enacts the differences between the Duck and the Decorated Shed in the strongest possible terms.[25] But at times the comparison seems to take on a life of its own and suggests the symmetries as much as the asymmetries between the two positions. For example, what begins as a critique of Crawford Manor as a "sculptural duck" quickly transfigures into a statement about its "abstract expressionist" qualities, obviously bringing in another analogy to the abstract expressionist *painting* of Jackson Pollock.[26] But Pollock's "gesture" of dispersing painterly "expression" over the surface of the canvas—so that that expression achieves a certain degree of explicitness (let us call it the painting's "candor")—might be a lot closer to the "fantasy" of the deadpan Decorated Shed, and to the issues raised by pop art in general, than Venturi and Scott Brown are able to acknowledge.

It seems fairly obvious that in the critique of the Duck, Venturi and Scott Brown are arguing for the irrelevance of any contemporary version of architecture based on the premises of *architecture parlante*. As Detlef Mertens succinctly described this approach: "Eighteenth-century critiques of rhetoric, theatricality, and allegory sparked formal experiments in architecture that sought to eliminate the use of conventions or applied signs in favor of the direct expression of the inner

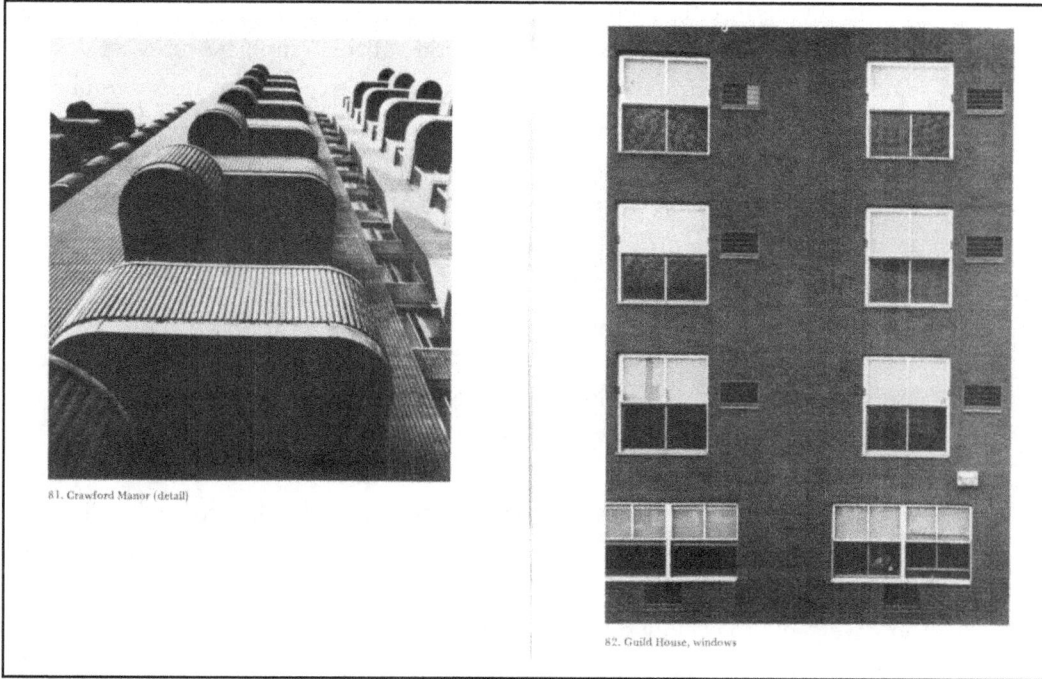

Figure 8.4. Frog's-eye view of Crawford Manor *(left)* and a deadpan view of Guild House *(right)* (Venturi, Scott Brown, and Izenour, *Learning from Las Vegas* [rev. ed.]. 96–97. Copyright 1977, Massachusetts Institute of Technology.)

nature of a building."[27] And as Karsten Harries has rightly pointed out, "[Claude-Nicolas] Ledoux's *architecture parlante* is an architecture of ducks."[28] It does not take much extrapolation to conclude that Venturi and Scott Brown are engaging in a critique of what one might call the "logocentrism" of postwar modern architecture; that is, in Paul de Man's definition, "the unmediated presence of the self to its own voice as opposed to the reflective distance that separates this self from the written word."[29] Although Venturi and Scott Brown's comparison of the Decorated shed with the Duck is, in a sense, such a critique, it does not deny the fact that we are nevertheless still tethered to our words and, more specifically, to our *voice* in those words.[30] Thus the issue of expression and inexpression and their relative "articulations" are at the heart of the comparison between the Duck and the Decorated Shed.

The Duck and the Melodrama of Expression

If melodrama is characterized as the site of "excessive expression"—the point at which, in the words of Venturi and Scott Brown, "expression has become expressionism"— then one might say that the Duck is the melodramatic figure in which a fantasy about absolute expressiveness is aired.[31] However, melodrama, as Cavell is quick to point out, is also the locus of the "emptiness of expression," a situation that resonates with *Learning from Las Vegas*'s critique of the "empty gestures" of postwar modernist architecture.³² One might say that the excessive expression embodied in the Duck is meant to suggest a symptom of our inability to mean what we say or do, as if we were required to force an idea of architecture to fit a circumstance that is no longer viable—what Venturi and Scott Brown call, at various points, architecture's "strident," "overstated," and "irrelevant "articulations." The Duck seems to stake out the region of a modernist drive for transparency pushed to its breaking point: the condition in which the modernist quest for purity, totality, and its version of absolute expression would seem to suffocate us rather than express our needs, wants, and ideals. Ludwig Wittgenstein explains the straits of this condition in the following way: "The ideal, as we think of it, is unshakeable. You can never get outside it; you must always turn back. There is no outside; outside you cannot breathe."³³ If this quest for purity and totality has created an absolute interior cut off from the world "out there," the "solution" is not simply to reach out to that world (where would you be reaching *to* or *from*?) but rather to reconsider how we came to occupy this condition in the first place. As Wittgenstein put it: "The *preconceived idea* of crystalline purity can only be removed by turning our whole examination around (One might say: the axis of reference of our examination must be rotated, but about the fixed point of our real need.)"³⁴ Wittgenstein's sentiment is echoed by Venturi and Scott Brown in one of their key statements: "meeting the architectural implications and the critical social issues of our era will require that we drop our *involuted* [my emphasis] architectural expressionism and our mistaken claim to building outside a formal language and find formal languages suited to our times."³⁵ I take it that the quest to "find formal languages suited to our times" is somewhat analogous to Wittgenstein's "real need"; that is, both voice a desire to locate the criteria for our real needs in the ordinary, rather than in the ideal and its quest for purity and transparency. If we bring these thoughts to bear on the Duck, then its version of absolute expression would also seem to disclose a fear of absolute inexpression.

What was once the modernist optimism that we might be able to link up the material with the mental, behavior with its expression, architecture with that behavior, and those conjunctions with political and social change now manifests itself as the suppression or suffocation of behavior, in which the modernist ideal has been twisted to such a degree that *what* was to be expressed is no longer even clear. Venturi and Scott Brown's critique of the Duck is based not, as they say, on its "dishonesty," but rather on its "irrelevancy."³⁶ In other words, the Duck is not meaningless; rather, it is pointless. The Duck marks the region in which the drive for expressive transparency begins to confront its unacknowledged aporia: a certain kind of opacity that is the condition of any communicability whatsoever. It is as if to say that that suppressed need had resulted in the twisting of architecture's "public face" into a thickened grimace or mask, in which "a certain theatricality [becomes] the sign of an inability to mean, to get our meaning across."[37] What this condition calls for is not less exposure in response to an overexposure, but rather more exposure, and of a different kind.

Dead Ducks and the Imagination of Stone

A certain strand of postwar modern architecture had been designing what *Learning from Las Vegas* specifically calls "dead ducks"—a phrase that is repeated in many variations throughout the book.[38] The word "dead" suggests a coldness that recalls a certain kind of response—or, more accurately, a lack of responsiveness—that would bring architecture to such a "frozen" region. If we keep to the spirit of the skeptical account I am pursuing here, the designing of dead ducks suggests that "there is a life and death of the world, dependent on what we make of it."[39] In Cavell's analysis of Shakespeare's plays *The Winter's Tale* and *Othello*, he recounts a "tragedy" of skepticism (or better, skepticism *as* tragedy) involved in the avoidance of the other—an inability to acknowledge the other—that is allegorized by the male protagonists in those plays, Leontes and Othello, turning their female partners, Hermione and Desdemona, into stone (the latter figuratively before literally killing). It is the men's coldness that turns the women to stone, and in Hermione's case, she is figured specifically as stone *sculpture*.[40] This draining of life is a mark of Leontes' and Othello's inability—or is it rather their unwillingness?—to acknowledge the limitations of knowledge, their respective partners' separateness from them, and thus the seam of their connection to them. What was closer than they could "know" is placed beyond the warmth of human life, love, and liberty. One might call it Leontes' and Othello's interpretation of "metaphysical finitude as an intellectual lack."[41] A situation that called for acknowledgment on their part, a particular interpretation of knowledge, was avoided.

The coldness that figures the woman as a stone sculpture in these accounts sounds remarkably like the "building-becoming-sculpture" that characterizes the Duck for Venturi and Scott Brown. To repeat, it is our mode of acknowledgment or avoidance of that acknowledgment—a certain category of *response*—that inflicts the status of duckdom on *any* building whatsoever. The explicitly gendered nature of Cavell's account of the tragedy of skepticism is even more poignant considering Scott Brown's early struggle with the architectural community's disavowal of her, and her contribution in the shared enterprise with Venturi, her partner and husband.[42] It was in fact Scott Brown's modification of her earlier work on the "physiognomic" and "heraldic dimensions" of architecture that resulted in the idea of the Duck and the Decorated Shed, and that came to exemplify their approach to architecture in *Learning from Las Vegas*. I would claim that the The Duck and the Decorated Shed figure her critique of the discipline's inability to acknowledge issues of separateness and limitation that are at the heart of any shared enterprise, be it public or private.

It is striking to note that Scott Brown makes an analysis similar to Cavell's in her influential essay, "Room at the Top? Sexism and the Star System in Architecture." At one point she uses the metaphor of a "lady . . . carved on the helm of the ship to help sailors cross the ocean" as a figure for the desire for guidance when faced with "unmeasurables."[43] This is clearly meant as an analogy to the "guru" system in architecture, as if to say that taking the "lead" or following the "star(s)" involved turning a woman to sculpture instead of acknowledging the unmeasurability of the difficulties and pleasures of shared life, labor, and "star power." This line in Scott Brown's essay also resonates with a sentence in Cavell's *The Claim of Reason*: "What I have wished to bring out [in the discussion of Othello and Desdemona] is . . . the way human sexuality is the field in which the fantasy of finitude, of its acceptance and its repetitious overcoming, is worked out."[44] Perhaps we could see the discipline of architecture that Scott Brown was critiquing as avoiding that "finitude." If architecture is involved in issues of acknowledgement of the other, then an *ignoring* of Scott Brown, a response that is not simply an *ignorance* but, more precisely, an avoidance, thrusts aside both her public and private life, one through the other. It denies Venturi and Scott Brown's *shared* life and work in and as "an exposure of finite singularities."[45] Thus the Duck emblematizes the frozen state of denial of the other, but when paired with the Decorated Shed, the two become entwined as a figure of attempting to overcome other minds skepticism.

Writ large, the Duck enacts a "melodrama of modernism"—at one point in *Learning from Las Vegas*, it is called "an architectural soap opera"—in which the entire building becomes a (sculptural) "ornament" to its own communicative impasse. Venturi and Scott Brown's understanding of the disavowal of ornament and its return as "one big ornament" (the entire distorted building or Duck) perhaps finds more of an echo in Gianni Vattimo's understanding of ornament and kitsch than in Clement Greenberg's. To Vattimo, "*Kitsch*, if it exists at all, is not what falls short of rigorous formal criteria and whose inauthentic presentation lacks a strong style. Rather, *Kitsch* is simply that which, in the age of plural ornamentation, still wishes to stand like a monument more lasting than bronze and still lays claim to the stability, definitive character and perfection of 'classic' art."[46] The condition of transparency and its ideals caught up in its own communicative impasse is clearly captured in an image from *Learning from Las Vegas* that equates the Duck with a "minimegastructure," rendered in much the same shape as the Duck but drawn with jagged, expressionistic lines (Figure 8.5). The equation is meant to imply that the totalizing, self-enclosed, overdesigned '70s megastructure is the Duck's "tautegorical" double. The issue of the megastructure and "total design" allegorizes

Figure 8.5. Equation of the minimegastructure with the Duck (Venturi, Scott Brown, and Izenour, *Learning from Las Vegas* [rev. ed.], 146. Copyright 1977, Massachusetts Institute of Technology.)

the inability to acknowledge "limitations" and issues of "separateness"—the fact that, in a particular light, (total) design might look like the point where reason has turned its attention to each social detail and personal relation, what Venturi and Scott Brown see as verging on "total control."[47] Is the Decorated Shed, with its "explicit" symbolism and "deadpan" façade, indeed the therapy for our "involuted, architectural expressionism"?

The Decorated Shed and the Melodrama of Inexpression

In contrast to the Duck, the Decorated Shed would seem to enact a certain hyperbolic inexpressiveness—what Cavell terms a "screened unknowingness." He characterizes this "melodrama of unknowingness" as "one of splitting the other, as between outside and inside."[48] Sometimes such divisions are necessary in the straights of what Venturi and Scott Brown call, drawing on Aldo Van Eyck's terminology, the "sickness of spatial continuity." And sometimes the therapy for such ills is drastic. In a different scenario, but drawing on the same logic, Koolhaas suggests the architectural equivalent of a lobotomy in the form of a radical separation between exterior and interior in the Manhattan skyscraper.[49] This solution indicates not just an attempt to abolish, "the dialectic of inside and outside," to use Jameson's phrase, but also the acknowledgment and acceptance of distinctions, limits, and separateness that the Duck would disavow. It is as if *Learning from Las Vegas* was calling for a good dose of *seduction*—to be separated from oneself, led outside oneself—in order to *expose* architecture to itself and others again in a different way,[50] as if distinctions and limitations had to be acknowledged over and over again daily (which does not necessarily mean "endlessly"). One might say that the Decorated Shed articulates an architecture of the *secret*, a word whose etymology and sense point toward a separation—a condition of "apartness," a necessary opacity—as a way of articulating our "shared" concerns. *Learning from Las Vegas*' "solution" is a simple "shed" *for* a secret, but it is a shed with no secret hidden *within* it.⁵¹ After all, if the Decorated Shed is exemplary of a *screened* unknowingness, its mode of illuminating that unknowingness is surely surface and *exposure*, not depth and interiority. The dilemma for architecture, then, might be to find the "perfect exteriority that only communicates itself" as a pharmakon against an advertising that "is a system of signals that signals itself."⁵² This would be a quest for a certain kind of expressiveness that no longer expresses an inner depth or core but rather that exposes its conditions of mediation in the act of manifesting itself.

If we take visibility in Jean-François Lyotard's sense to mean "an exteriority that discourse can't *interiorize* [my emphasis] in signification," then the food for thought that the "Eat" sign raises in the Decorated Shed diagrams is indigestible.⁵³ I take it that the speech balloon/large sign in the Decorated Dhed diagrams—the sign reading "Eat" that separates the car from the building—is crucial to working out the stakes involved in the issues of separateness, limitation, and distinction that are at the heart of skepticism about other minds. Although one has to wait until the end of the second part of *Learning from Las Vegas* to encounter speech balloons in their strict cartoon form in an image from the "Learning from Levittown" studio (Figure 8.6), they are strikingly evident as literal balloons in the image of the Decorated Shed (Figures 8.1 and 8.2).⁵⁴ In fact, in most versions of the Decorated Shed, the quivering line of the pole carrying the "Eat" sign looks more like a string attached to a balloon than a solid columnar structure supporting an elevated sign. In his book on comics, David Carrier suggests that speech balloons attempt to overcome the skepticism of other minds by revealing another (fictional) persons' thoughts displayed transparently to the reader "as if" we could literally read (look into) their minds.⁵⁵ But one could just as easily argue that sophisticated uses of speech balloons are another manifestation of the skeptical dilemma of other minds rather than a mere convention for its overcoming.

It is significant that in all the Decorated Shed diagrams, either the speech balloons are either literally untethered from their "source," the architecture itself, or the sign is conspicuously "applied" to the false facade of the shed; they are either placed slightly in front of or farther away from the shed-like structures. Carrier notes that it is paramount that the "things" or characters in the fictional cartoon scenes never acknowledge the speech balloons *as* speech balloons because that would call attention to the opacity that supposedly makes it difficult to register other minds.⁵⁶ But if I am not mistaken, the little pools of ink in the eye-like building windows of an earlier rendition of the Duck and the Decorated Shed look remarkably like tiny pupils looking up at the separation of language from its physical body (Figure 8.2).⁵⁷ In fact, owing to the dual register of the image in Figure 8.2, it actually appears as if the "Duck" is looking up at the "Eat" sign that the Decorated Shed is also "looking" at. How far is architecture separated from the words used to articulate itself or, more precisely, from its own "voice," in those

Figure 8.6. Precedents of suburban symbols from the Learning from Levittown Studio, Yale University, 1970 (Venturi, Scott Brown, and Izenour, *Learning from Las Vegas* [rev. ed.], 158. Copyright 1977, Massachusetts Institute of Technology.)

words? What voice, if any, does it have in speaking about itself at a crucial point in history in which the "meaning" of architecture seems to be either suffocating itself at the hands of its own ideals (to be locked in) or risking irrelevancy in the face of and in competition with an increasingly mediatized environment (to be locked out)?

Manfredo Tafuri's well-known response to this dilemma in regard to the increasing closure of capital and the capitalist city was to demonstrate a condition of architectural "muteness" on the part of some modernist architects that gave them a critical distance from those capitalist structures, but ultimately resulted in a condition of absolute alienation from the city as such. Jameson notes that Venturi and Scott Brown's Duck is perhaps a late capitalist version of Tafuri's account of the building's separation and isolation from its environment, now "celebrating its own disconnection as a message in its own right."[58] Venturi and Scott Brown, however, forge another response to this dilemma. In an act of architectural ventriloquism, the "voice" of architecture is separated from its body in the Decorated Shed.[59] But the analogy to ventriloquism is not quite accurate; it is, in fact, a disanalogy. The Decorated Shed is a ventriloquism gone awry, and thus the situation is more akin to a badly synchronized film, as Maurice Merleau-Ponty describes it in *Phenomenology of Perception*:

> When a breakdown of sound all at once cuts off the voice from a character who nevertheless goes on gesticulating on the screen, not only does the meaning of his speech suddenly escape me: the spectacle itself is changed. The face which was so recently alive thickens and freezes, and looks nonplussed, while the interruption of the sound invades the screen as a quasi-stupor.[60]

In the speech balloons of the Decorated Shed, we get a real sense of how our words and our voice in speaking them are achieved through fragile acts of barely achieved *composure*. The Decorated Shed calls attention to this fragility. In doing so, they imply that the ways we converse and exchange words and ideas about architecture—about anything—might not express or reveal the attitudes and connections that we are willing to give voice to.

This is all to say that the speech balloon in the Decorated Shed allegorizes the temptation of language to drive a wedge between us and other minds. But this is not a perspicuous way of putting things. After all, if our words drive a wedge between us, are we, in effect, saying that modern architecture has been "driven" to that same point, as if we were somehow in the thrall of a natural force that has pushed us outside our common "language games" and thus outside the social? It would be more accurate to say that if our words (on architecture) force a wedge between us, we are responsible for that condition, either because we have done the driving or because we do not have the will to undo it. [61] As Michel Foucault put it, "Man" may be a "vehicle for words which exist before him," but those words "are called back to life by the insistence of his words."[62] Calling architecture back to life might involve seeing how it can remotivate itself within a range of communicative possibilities that are never strictly idiomatic (private and opaque) nor entirely conventional (public, shared, and transparent).

The "Eat" Sign, Primitive Language, and the Search for Criteria

What then does the "Eat" sign signify about our appetite for architecture? Is that appetite mostly for "images," as Fredric Jameson argues in *Postmodernism, or, the Cultural Logic of Late Capitalism*?[63] Or is it our appetite for "signs," "texts," or "theory," as many would argue of *Learning from Las Vegas*? Considering the close connection between our appetite for books and architecture, we cannot help but wonder what kind of reader *Learning from Las Vegas* is trying to attract? Do Venturi and Scott Brown want a reader of primitive judgment, either swallowing (good) or spitting out (bad), as Sigmund Freud would have it? Or would they prefer a bovine reader, a "ruminator," as Friedrich Nietzsche would say? I take it that they want the latter, considering their critiques of the relationship between interior and exterior and their consistent demands for "delays in judgment." One thing is certain: the word "eat" is not *merely* a "sign." As Gertrude Stein once noted, "Americans can and do express everything . . . in words of one syllable made up of two letters or three and at most four."[64] It is hardly surprising, then, that one of the inspirations for *Learning from Las Vegas* was the Los Angeles–based artist Ed Ruscha. His obsession with monosyllabic words such as "no," "ok," "smash," and "oof," suggests that Americans are somewhat comic and definitely *primitive*.

I take the coupling of the schematic shed with the "Eat" sign less as an indication of *Learning from Las Vegas* initiating a linguistic turn in architectural theory than as an attempt to explore our primal needs and satisfactions: a taking stock of what we need from architecture, from life, in terms of what we are getting or not getting from it. To make a loose analogy, we might think of the Decorated Shed with its "Eat" sign as an updated version of Henry David Thoreau's declaration in *Walden* that "None of the brute creation requires more than Food and Shelter."[65] The first chapter of that book, "Economy," is taken up with a minute rendering of the monetary costs of materials and foodstuffs to provide for the author's nourishment and shelter for eight months. Thoreau's obsession with economics is his way of coming to terms with how "dear" things are to him, his attempt to account for how those sundry things might count. Are we so needy that we can only utter our needs, or register "signs of life," in monosyllabic words? One does not have to imagine what Theodor Adorno's reply would be: "the bread on which the culture industry feeds humanity, remains the stone of stereotype."[66] But we often mistake stones for bread, and we are liable to break both too soon.

Clearly the word "Eat" in the Decorated Shed is not merely a word. Here we might fruitfully recall the opening passage of Wittgenstein's *Philosophical Investigations*, where he asks us to conceive four spoken words—"block," "pillar," "slab," and "beam"—as a complete primitive language. He then queries, "is the call 'Slab!' . . . a sentence or a word?"[67] And if it is a sentence, is it a "complete" sentence or merely a degenerate, elliptical, or truncated one? As John Austin points out in *How to Do Things with Words*, "in primitive languages it would not yet be clear, it would not yet be possible to distinguish, which of the various things that . . . we might be doing we were in fact doing. For example 'Bull' or 'Thunder' in a primitive language of one-word utterances could be a warning, information, a prediction, etc."[68] Primitive language games are constitutively indeterminate, as Wittgenstein, Austin, and Cavell have shown us. When confronted with such an extreme erasure of context, we must consider some different (primal) scenes for these calls. We might surmise that the people speaking this language are incapable of speaking in sentences, "as if their words, hence their lives, were forever somehow truncated, stunted, confined, contracted," or we might imagine that these words are spoken calmly in a "deserted landscape" or perhaps in the context of a "noisy environment"—let us say in a construction site, or in the "cacaphonic context" of Las Vegas, or in any media saturated environment—in which they are uttered "not sluggishly or vacantly but in shouts."[69] In such situations we must, out of necessity, pay close attention to the illocutionary force of the word. As Austin put it, "Language as such and in its primitive stages is not precise, and it is also not, in our sense, explicit. . . . [E]xplicitness in our sense, makes clearer the *force of the utterance* or 'how . . . it is to be taken.'"[70] The deliberate lack of *context* (or explicitness, to use Austin's wording) in which the word "Eat" is exposed in the Decorated Shed is a provocation for the reader to acknowledge that it is up to us to locate the shared criteria—our attunement in ordinary words—and thus to figure out how the "eat" sign is to be taken.

Is the word "Eat" an imperative: "Eat damn it!"? Imagine the harsh paternal voice of the culture industry ramming something down our throats. Do we take it willingly? Or is that voice the soft and loving one of a parent figure serving up what Adorno calls "pre-digested pablum" for our childish consumption (two sides of the same coin)? Or is it the muttering of a starving man, woman, or child who can only muster a single word to express an urgent life-and-death need? Is it the pulsating, loud, shrill, and repetitive voice, "eat, eat, eat," that must scream to be heard in the din of Las Vegas (think of the title of Tom Wolfe's famous essay on Las Vegas or imagine the chanting accompanying an eating competition). Or is it the staging of a scene of reorigination in which we are again "in-fans," literally on the verge of language without yet being "in" it? How are we to tell? It is as if we are afflicted with a case of tonal agnosia, in which "the expressive qualities of the voice disappear—their tone, their timbre, their feeling, their entire character—while words . . . are perfectly understood."[71] This might be the appropriate time to turn to the role of the deadpan in relation to the fantasy of expression and inexpression that takes place through the Duck and Decorated Shed.[72]

Deadpan and the Absorption of Skepticism

Freud's evenhanded, nonjudgmental attitude toward psychic phenomena, which so inspired Scott Brown, can also be seen in Ruscha's approach to the ordinary environment we live in. In fact, it was this approach that most attracted Scott Brown to Ruscha's work. Ruscha's art books began to appear in 1962, and no doubt inspired Scott Brown's own photographic record of vernacular architecture in Los Angeles while she was a professor at UCLA in the mid-1960s.[73] It is hardly surprising, then, that Ruscha was subsequently invited to the Learning from Las Vegas studio at Yale (he never came); that the Yale studio group visited Ruscha's studio during their four days in Los Angeles before preceeding to Las Vegas; that two of the photographs of the Las Vegas Strip in *Learning from Las Vegas* are directly inspired by Ruscha's book *Every Building on the Sunset Strip* (1966); that they hired a helicopter in Las Vegas as Ruscha did to have photographs taken for *ThirtyFour Parking Lots*; that they produced a film called *Deadpan Las Vegas* (or *Three Projector Deadpan*); or that Scott Brown's article "Pop Art, Permissiveness, and Planning" is illustrated with three of Ruscha's photographs. For Scott Brown, Ruscha's photographic art books were the primary exemplification of a "deadpan," nonjudgmental approach to the environment.

She remarks on his books in the following way:

> His *Sunset Strip*, a long accordion fold-out, shows every building on each side of the strip, each carefully numbered but without comment. Deadpan, a scholarly monograph with a silver cover and slip-on box jacket, it could be on the piazzas of Florence, but it suggests a new vision of the very imminent world around us.[74]

And in her notes for the Levittown studio at Yale in the winter of 1970, Scott Brown asks,

> What new techniques are required to document new forms? We should aim to dead-pan the material so that it speaks for itself. Ruscha has pioneered this treatment in his monographs (*The Sunset Strip, Some Los Angeles Apartments*). It is a way to avoid being upstaged by our own subject matter.[75]

In another reference to Ruscha, she notes, "his *TwentySix Gasoline Stations* are photographed straight: no art except the art that hides art."[76] This passage in her essay "On Pop Art, Permissiveness, and Planning," echoes Ruscha's own claim that what he was after "was no style or a non-statement with a no-style" that would result in a "collection of facts."[77] The point is further echoed when Scott Brown, contrasts Ruscha's approach with the premature systematizing of some aspects of humanism and high modernism: "Where the facts and intangibles are many, a mystique or system—a philosophy of Man and the Universe or a CIAM grid—may substitute for the collection of facts or hard thought."[78] Later in the essay, she calls architects and urban designers "Johnnies-come-lately" on the scene who "can learn from others," such as Ruscha.[79] Although this passage refers to a specific instance of "learning from Ruscha," its lesson is better seen as a *transcendental* one: the first task of the architect and urban planner, she suggests, is a responsiveness that delays judgment in order to heighten sensitivity.[80] As Scott Brown puts it, "we are still outraged if an architect comes out for billboards or if a planner removes the *emotion* [my emphasis] from his voice when talking of urban sprawl."[81] Removing emotion from the voice should recall the issue of tonal agnosia in relation to the "Eat" sign, and alert us to the importance of the deadpan technique for Scott Brown and, ultimately, for the visual and rhetorical strategies in *Learning from Las Vegas*. There is no doubt that Venturi and Scott Brown's "aim to dead-pan the material so that it speaks for itself" contributed to their dissatisfaction with Muriel Cooper's "interesting Modern styling" of MIT's first edition of *Learning from Las Vegas* and their embrace of the newly "stripped" and "clothed" second edition, with its deadpan approach to design.[82]

Not surprisingly, it is the issue of "superficiality" that has exposed *Learning from Las Vegas* to the most criticism. Venturi, Scott Brown, and Izenour's interest in issues of image, surface, and flatness has been read reductively, with accusations of an "aesthetics of disappearance" à la Paul Virilio, Baudrillardian accounts of the simulacral condition of the American city, and critiques of postmodern "stage-set architecture" and its collusion with the "culture industry." I hope, instead, to try to come to grips with their *acknowledgment* of what the technique of deadpan flatness might mean in terms of their work.[83]

Deadpan is "literally" defined as a flat or emotionless face, the word "pan" being slang for "face" in nineteenth-century America. It is a mode of rhetorical delivery, used in speeches, public lecturing, and comedy, that is primarily associated with Anglo-American society. As a sociohistorical phenomenon, deadpan has been linked to nineteenth-century American literature, oratory, and popular forms of theatre, and it played a role in facilitating the movement between high and low culture and in negotiating issues of revelation and concealment within the shifting boundaries of the public and private in frontier America.[84] If deadpan originated in the work of writers, humorists, and storytellers such as Mark Twain, it flourished in popular theatre and subsequently in silent film. Its presence continues to resonate in the dry comedy of Bob Newhart, Bill Murray, and Rick Mercer and in the farce of deadpan: the droning voices and placid faces ubiquitous in television and radio advertising.

The great silent film actor and comedian Buster Keaton—popularly known as "old stone face"—is probably the most famous and striking example of deadpan humor in action. All of Keaton's movies feature his trademark deadpan visage that never flinches no matter what mishap befalls him (Figure 8.7). In three different stretches of writing, Cavell directly refers to the logic of Keaton's comedy as one that "absorbs skepticism." "[Keaton's] refinement is," as Cavell puts it, "to know everything skepticism can think of."[85] He suggests that Keaton's deadpan humor is an ideal attitude in the face of skepticism, a stance toward the world and others

Figure 8.7. Buster Keaton's deadpan visage, publicity still ca. 1924

in it that is an exemplary tarrying with skepticism that neither succumbs to it nor definitively overcomes it.[86] One might call it a comic acknowledgment of the world.

Cavell's account of Keaton centers around his particular countenance and the "Olympian resourcefulness of his body."[87] The lack of emotion in his face and his eternal agility are signs of Keaton's peculiar receptiveness to the world. His gaze allows an evenness or readiness in which any object might be as good or bad as any other.[88] Keaton, in other words, is ready for the best and worst that the world has to offer. Perhaps we might characterize it as Keaton's acknowledgment "that it is not a matter of knowing but accepting the world."[89] This should recall Scott Brown's suggestion, using Ruscha as the primary example, that we might cultivate a sensitivity to the world—heighten our responsiveness to it—by delaying judgment. She reminds us that it is a matter of our attunement or mood toward objects in the world—in her words, "an open-minded and nonjudgmental investigation" of it—that would enable us to do so.[90] We should hardly be surprised, then, to find that Cavell also talks about Keaton in terms of the "philosophical mood of his countenance" and his "human capacity for sight, or for sensuous awareness generally."[91]

The "mood" of deadpan suggests that it is precisely the opposite—perhaps separated by a hair's breadth—of what Martin Heidegger calls "the pallid lack of mood of indifference to everything."[92] In *Being and Time*, the mood of indifference is, at various points, described as a "muffling fog," "smooth," and the "gray everyday." These images conjure up an atmosphere in which everything is reduced to the same color, texture, and tone, and in which we are "in" the world but in it in a literally oppressive way, with no way of "voicing" that condition. That is to say, we have no way of acknowledging how or why we are "engulfed" by the world, yet we seem to withdraw from it, or it from us; such that it loses its hold. One might call it, for lack of a better word, a condition of apathy.

Heidegger specifies that "indifference, which can go along with busying oneself head over heels, is to be sharply distinguished from equanimity."[93] In another passage in *Being and Time*, Heidegger calls it "undisturbed equanimity."[94] Equanimity is thus characterized by a calm and even-tempered "resoluteness" that has a vision of "the possible situations of the potentiality-of-being-as-a whole."[95] The sense of "resoluteness" and "sober readiness" at the heart of equanimity is intimately related to Heidegger's understanding of what he calls the "*equiprimordial disclosedness of the world.*"[96] And for Heidegger, disclosure and attunement are closely linked: "*In attunement lies existentially a disclosive submission to world out of which things that matter to us can be encountered.*"[97] What is striking in this sentence is that Heidegger italicizes *every* word, as if each one might matter to us; all might bear equal weight of priority and expressiveness. This is, perhaps, the crucial difference between indifference and equanimity: indifference is a matter of not caring enough about anything, and equanimity is the openness to care about possibly everything in the right mood. Venturi puts it this way: "*Learning from Las Vegas*—and learning from Everything."[98]

It is "as if" the deadpan attitude exemplified by Keaton, Ruscha, and the Decorated Shed refuses to give us the "out" of being too quickly normative in our categorization of good, bad, best, or worst objects or people in the world. This is dramatized by Cavell's point that Keaton appears in his films to be *of a piece* with objects in the world (Heidegger might say "together with." To be of a piece with objects in the world does not necessarily mean to be at peace with them).[99] In "Pop Art, Permissiveness, and Planning," Scott Brown also notes, in relation to her ideas about delaying judgment in order to heighten sensitivity, that "architects and urban designers have been too quickly normative."[100] Here a sentence from

Freud's essay "Negation" comes to mind: "Judging is the intellectual action which decides the choice of motor action, which puts an end to the postponement due to thought and which leads over from thinking to acting."[101] In fact, Scott Brown has entitled one section of her and Venturi's most recent book, *Architecture as Signs and Systems in a Mannerist World*, "Think before You Judge."[102] If this delay in judgment might heighten our sensitivity to the world, then—as Cavell, Heidegger, Ruscha, and Scott Brown make clear—that would seem to involve a sense of openness, readiness, equanimity, and, at times, inexpression. How might we relate this to the (re)presentational strategies in *Learning from Las Vegas*?

Of course, the issue of flatness is operative throughout the text, with its emphasis on the false front, billboard-like architecture of Las Vegas, exemplified by the Decorated Shed with the big sign dominating the generic building behind. The signs that read or speak "I am a Monument"; "Fire Station No. 4"; or "Guild House" are the primary instantiation of a deadpan approach—a flat denotation— that would allow the architecture to "speak" in order to avoid upstaging itself. I would like to make the claim here that the desire not to be upstaged that the deadpan epitomizes is a way of acknowledging that our expressions, our needs, and our satisfactions should not be overwhelmed or denied by vehicles of expression that do not satisfy us. It voices a desire to avoid a mode of theatricality that might prevent us from getting our meaning across, or a desire to be receptive enough to enable "a submission to the world out of which things that matter to us can be encountered."[103] Deadpan takes the issue of voice, expression, and encounter down a notch to reimagine how and where they might *seam* together differently.

In terms of flatness, we also need to mention Venturi and Scott Brown's built work. One obvious example would be one of Venturi's early buildings, the Vanna Venturi House, built for his mother in 1962 (Figure 8.8). The clapboard front and back denoting "home" is merely a flat appliqué that provides a "sandwich" for the middle ground of the interior "lived" space. Or consider the façade of Guild House, which extends beyond the bulk of the shed at the front. [104] In *Learning from Las Vegas*, not only is Guild House photographed in an extreme close-up that serves to stupefy it beyond all expression, but also the flatness is accentuated by the fact that the windows in the second recessed plane are slightly larger than the ones on the front façade, thus counteracting any sense of recession in perspectival depth.[105] What is never noted is that we somehow needed Venturi and Scott Brown to point out these urban phenomena. After all, this kind of Decorated Shed has been ubiquitous in American culture for decades in fantasy and reality, not to mention *Learning from Las Vegas*' tracking of that genealogy back to Egyptian architecture. And the Duck, for that matter, is a phenomenon that was conceptualized, if not theorized, years earlier by Norman Bel Geddes as "Coney Island Architecture."[106]

Figure 8.8. Robert Venturi, Vanna Venturi House, 1962; by permission of VSBA, Inc.

Venturi and Scott Brown's insistence on the disruption of the smooth workings of the dialectic between interior and exterior in architecture calls attention to the world *as* obtrusive, opaque, and disrupted.[107] If media seems to saturate our environment in a "seamless" way, as we hear endlessly repeated, then Venturi and Scott Brown's operations find the seams, not exactly by "seaming" it actively, but *as if* they were allowing the world to reveal its seams to them. They seem to suggest that, with enough patience and resolve on our part, the seams might be rendered visible to us, and thus the world and our desires for the seams that we want might coincide. I see this attitude as informing an intriguing passage in *Walden*: "Look at a meeting house, or a court-house, or a jail, or a shop, or a dwelling-house, and say what that thing really is before a true gaze, and they would all go to pieces in your account of them."[108] This passage could easily be read as perpetuating the division between appearance and reality—the desperate "wish to read the reality behind the architectural mask," in the words of Bernard Tschumi[109]—but I would rather see it as something akin to Cavell's claim, in relation to Buster Keaton and Charlie Chaplin, that "No possibility, of fakery, simulation, or hallucination, goes beyond the actualities of their existence" or to Ruscha's observation that Los Angeles makes one aware that everything is ephemeral from the right angle.[110] After all, who has not had their world unseam itself along the lines out of which they have constructed it?

Although Venturi and Scott Brown do state, at times, that if we removed those façades there might be nothing left behind them, there *is* something behind

THE MELODRAMA OF EXPRESSION AND INEXPRESSION • 187

them—it may be the wasteland of a beer-can-strewn desert at the limits of the city or the comfy interior of Vanna Venturi's home. As Ruscha writes, sounding a lot like Venturi and Scott Brown, "there's *almost* . . . nothing behind the facades [my emphasis]."[111] It is not as if the false facades are "hiding" anything or acting as a screen to prevent us from seeing that there is nothing behind them. We *know* that the inside is different from the outside; it announces that fact in a very straightforward manner. And what would it be like to know all those possibilities and more? It would be, to repeat Cavell's characterization of Keaton, "to know everything that skepticism can think of." Is that refinement somehow beyond the actualities of our existence? Is that possibility only available to us in film? If it is only available in film, why does it always seem that *architecture* bears the burden of exemplifying living in the face of such a world? I am thinking of the well-known image of Keaton in *Steamboat Bill, Jr.*, in which the façade of a house collapses around Keaton, yet he emerges unscathed due to a well-placed open window (Figure 8.9). Or is that a well-placed Keaton? Timing is everything. Only someone with the right attitude and with a knack for the openness, receptivity, and awareness of

Figure 8.9. Buster Keaton's impeccable timing and undashable attitude, *Steamboat Bill, Jr.*, 1924.

a Keaton can prepare you for whatever fate befalls you. In Cavell's memorable phrase, Keaton is "undashable rather than dashing."[112]

The British artist Steve McQueen's short black-and-white video *Deadpan* (1997) draws many of these issues forward. It is a restaging of that famous scene in *Steamboat Bill, Jr.*, in which McQueen himself plays the role of Keaton. In the video, in contrast to the film, the façade does not fall once but perpetually, captured from different angles by the camera, as if to say that an acceptance of distinctions and limits is, if not exactly endless, at least an event that we must perpetually risk. To quote Ruscha, "It [the Hollywood sign] might as well fall down. That's more Hollywood—to have it fall down or be removed. But in the end, it's more Hollywood to put it back up, see? [Laughter.]"[113] Or perhaps it is more (Learning from) Las Vegas? At this point the "dialectic" between inside and outside is *beside* the point. What "befalls" us in such a mood is that architecture would no longer seem to be grounded in the traditional metaphorics of building as such, but rather would seem more concerned with our imaginative confrontation with the fragility and depths of surfaces, and the way they are posed, exposed, and deposed.

Ruscha once claimed that his first book, *Twentysix Gasoline Stations*, had "an inexplicable thing I was looking for, and that was a kind of a 'Huh.'" A few lines later he notes that, "One of them [his books] will kind of *almost* knock you on your ass."[114] That response seems to be what Scott Brown was looking for in the design of *Learning from Las Vegas*. Jean-Luc Nancy has posed the question: "Can we think of a triviality of sense—a quotidianness, a banality, *not* as the dull opposite of a scintillation, but as the grandeur of the simplicity in which sense exceeds itself?"[115] Perhaps we can. And perhaps that is the best lesson to take from *Learning from Las Vegas*: that in the end, in the face of Venturi and Scott Brown's explicit emphasis on communication, "learning from," and "signs," the book never shakes a sense that knowing is not enough. It acknowledges that flat-out.

Notes

1. Fredric Jameson, "Architecture and the Critique of Ideology," *The Ideologies of Theory: Essays, 1971–1986* (Minneapolis: University of Minnesota Press, 1987), 2–59.

2. Rem Koolhaas, *Delirious New York: A Retroactive Manifesto for Manhattan* (New York: Monacelli Press, 1994), 100. Koolhaas attributes the break from this model, toward the deliberate discrepancy between container and contained, to issues of "bigness" where "less and less surface has to represent more and more interior activity." This is worked out in more detail in his book *S, M, L, XL* (New York: Monacelli, 1996).

3. Robert Venturi and Denise Scott Brown, "On Ducks and Decoration," *Architecture Canada* 10 (1968): 48.

4. Stanley Cavell, "Knowing and Acknowledging," *Must We Mean What We Say?* (Cambridge: Cambridge University Press, 2002), 254.

5. On acknowledgment, see Cavell, "Knowing and Acknowledging," 238–66, and "Part Four: Between Acknowledgment and Avoidance," *The Claim of Reason: Wittgenstein, Skepticism, Morality, and Tragedy* (Oxford: Oxford University Press, 1979), 329–496.

6. Cavell's favorite way of characterizing the beginning of skepticism is "the conversio of metaphysical finitude into intellectual lack." See Cavell, Disowning Knowledge in Six Plays of Shakespeare (Cambridge: Cambridge University Press, 1987), 138; and Cavell, "Knowing and Acknowledging," 263.

7. Walter Benjamin, "Surrealism: The Last Snapshot of the European Intelligentsia," *Reflections: Essays, Aphorisms, Autobiographical Writings*, ed. Peter Demetz (New York: Schocken Books, 1986), 180. Venturi and Scott Brown, "On Ducks and Decoration," 48. To push this further, I suspect that architecture is one of the privileged sites that reveals the overlapping of the *two* fundamental yet asymmetrical aspects of the threat of skepticism: the uncertainty of knowing the world out there—what is commonly called external world skepticism (material)—and skepticism about other minds (mental). One way to think about this overlapping in architecture is to couple Benjamin's claim that architecture is a "kleine welt"—that it exemplifies, in a compressed and bounded way, the external world and our relationship to it *as such*—with Ludwig Wittgenstein's assertion about the impression one gets from good architecture: "that it expresses a thought. It makes one want to respond with a gesture." See Walter Benjamin, "Rigorous Study of Art," *October* 47 (Winter 1988): 84–90; and Ludwig Wittgenstein, *Culture and Value*, ed. G. H. Von Wright, trans. Peter Winch (Oxford: B. Blackwell, 1990), 22e.

8. Robert Venturi, Denise Scott Brown, and Steven Izenour, *Learning from Las Vegas* (Cambridge, Mass.: The MIT Press, 1977), 87.

9. These sheds are actually adjacent buildings, and not directly connected to the Duck.

10. The only images that I have found that deviate from this "facing" are the images of the Duck and Decorated Shed in Venturi and Scott Brown's early article "On Ducks and Decoration," (1968) in which the door/nose is placed next to the two windows/eyes.

11. Stanley Cavell, *The World Viewed: Reflections on the Ontology of Film* (New York: Viking Press, 1971), 129.

12. Stanley Cavell, "Reply to Four Chapters," in *Wittgenstein and Skepticism*, ed. Denis McManus (New York: Routledge, 2004), 286, and "The Quest of Traditional Epistemology: Closing," *The Claim of Reason*, 191–243.

13. Cavell, *The World Viewed*, 85.

14. Cavell, "Knowing and Acknowledging," 263–64.

15. See Joseph Masheck, "Tired Tropes: Cathedral versus Bicycle Shed; 'Duck' versus 'Decorated Shed,'" *Building Art: Modern Art Under Cultural Construction* (Cambridge: Cambridge University Press, 1993); and Nikolaus Pevsner, *An Outline of European Architecture* (London: Pelican Books, 1960), 1.

16. Stanley Cavell, *In Quest of the Ordinary: Lines of Skepticism and Romanticism* (Chicago: Chicago University Press, 1988), 67–69, and *The Claim of Reason*, 441–42. A good commentary on these passages can be found in Espen Hammer, *Stanley Cavell: Skepticism, Subjectivity, and the Ordinary* (London: Polity, 2002), 172–73.

17. Cavell, "Knowing and Acknowledging," 263–64.

18. Ernst Gombrich, "On Physiognomic Perception" and "Expression and Communication," in *Meditations on a Hobby Horse: And Other Essays on the History of Art* (New York: Phaidon, 1963), 45–69; and

Alan Colquhoun, "Typology and Design Method," *Arena* 83, no. 913 (June 1967): 11–14. Colquhoun's article was republished in George Baird and Charles Jencks's *Meaning in Architecture* (New York: G. Braziller 1970, c. 1969). Both Gombrich and Colquhoun are cited on page 132 of *Learning from Las Vegas*.

19. Gombrich, "Expression and Communication," 57.

20. Venturi, Scott Brown, and Izenour, *Learning from Las Vegas*, 131–34. I use the word "supposed" here to point out that this is their reading of the situation and not necessarily one I agree with.

21. All of these words and phrases are mobilized in *Learning from Las Vegas*.

22. Instead of quoting each particular passage on the Guild House and Crawford Manor in *Learning from Las Vegas*, all the following direct and indirect quotes can be found in Venturi, Scott Brown, and Izenour, *Learning from Las Vegas*, 90–103.

23. Ibid., 100. Venturi and Scott Brown acknowledge that Crawford Manor also has a sign, but it is modest and tasteful, not explicit.

24. Ibid., 135. Venturi and Scott Brown are well aware of the ability of viewpoint and cropping in photography to capture particular kinds of effects. In fact, they criticize the architects and theorists of the "Modern movement" for doing just that.

25. Due to the different layout of the revised edition, the comparison between Crawford Manor and Guild House is even more dramatic than it is in the first edition.

26. Venturi, Scott Brown, and Izenour, *Learning from Las Vegas*, 91, 93, and 104. The shopworn contrast in *Learning from Las Vegas* between pop art and its reaction against abstract expressionism is one of the duller moments in an otherwise exciting and exacting book.

27. Detlef Mertens, "The Shells of Architectural Thought," in *Hejduk's Chronotope*, ed. K. Michael Hays (Princeton, N.J.: Princeton Architectural, 1996), 32.

28. Karsten Harries, *The Ethical Function of Architecture* (Cambridge, Mass.: MIT Press, 1997), 73.

29. Paul de Man, "The Rhetoric of Blindness," *Blindness and Insight: Essays in the Rhetoric of Contemporary Criticism* (Minneapolis: University of Minnesota Press, 1983), 114.

30. The issue of tethering and abandonment to our words is key to Cavell's criticism of Derrida's reading of John Austin's *How to Do Things with Words* and a way of marking out an emphasis on his calling for or recalling of voice in contrast to Jacques Derrida's emphasis on the suppression of voice. See Stanley Cavell, "What Did Derrida Want of Austin?" *Philosophical Passages: Wittgenstein, Emerson, Austin, Derrida* (Oxford: Blackwell Publishers, 1995), 42–65.

31. See Stanley Cavell, *Contesting Tears: The Hollywood Drama of the Unknown Woman* (Chicago: The University of Chicago Press, 1996), 40 and 43; and Venturi, Scott Brown, and Izenour, *Learning from Las Vegas*, 139. Much of what follows entails an engagement with issues of melodrama, theatricality, unknowingness, and other minds explored in *Contesting Tears*.

32. Cavell, *Contesting Tears*, 40; and Venturi, Scott Brown, and Izenour, *Learning from Las Vegas*, 150.

33. Ludwig Wittgenstein, *Philosophical Investigations*, trans. G. E. M. Anscombe (Oxford: Basil Blackwell, 1976) §103.

34. Ibid., §108.

35. Venturi, Scott Brown, and Izenour, 161

36. Ibid., 101.

37. Cavell, *Contesting Tears*, 40. Wittgenstein's major example of knowing "other minds" in the *Philosophical Investigations* is raised through the issue of pain and our acknowledgment or avoidance of that pain. The language used to describe the Duck in *Learning from Las Vegas* resonates with those passages.

38. Venturi, Scott Brown, and Izenour, *Learning from Las Vegas*, 162.

39. Cavell, *In Quest of the Ordinary*, 68.

40. Cavell, *The Claim of Reason*, 481–96; and Cavell, "Othello and the Stake of the Other," and "Recounting Gains, Showing Losses: Reading *The Winter's Tale*," in *Disowning Knowledge in Six Plays of Shakespeare*, 125–42, 193–222.

41. Cavell, "Knowing and Acknowledging," 263, and *The Claim of Reason*, 493.

42. They were married on July 23, 1967, and Denise Scott Brown became a partner in the firm in 1969.

43. Denise Scott Brown, "Room at the Top? Sexism and the Star System in Architecture," in *Gender, Space, Architecture*, ed. Jane Rendell, Barbara Penner, and Iain Borden (New York and London: Routledge, 2000), 261.

44. Cavell, *The Claim of Reason*, 492.

45. Jean-Luc Nancy, *The Inoperative Community*, ed. Peter Connor, foreword by Christopher Fynsk (Minneapolis: University of Minnesota Press, 1991), 29. This is what Nancy calls "finitude compearing." For Nancy, this "compearance" implies not juxtaposition but "exposition." The connections between Nancy's understanding of "exposure" and Cavell's use of that same term in relation to acknowledgment in *The Claim of Reason* is well worth exploring. See Cavell, *The Claim of Reason*, 432–40.

46. Gianni Vattimo, *The Transparent Society*, trans. David Webb (Baltimore: John Hopkins University Press, 1992), 72.

47. A succinct account of these issues can be read in the section of *Learning from Las Vegas* entitled "Megastructures and Design Control," 148–50. My characterization (caricature?) of design draws on Cavell's brief discussion of it in *The World Viewed*, 91. His account seems to resonate with Vattimo's understanding of design as the bourgeois form of "utopia." See Vattimo, *The Transparent Society*, 62–64. These accounts come across as rather crude conceptions of design then and now.

48. Cavell, *Contesting Tears*, 90.

49. Koolhaas, *Delirious New York*, 100.

50. Jean-François Lyotard, "Gift of Organs," *Driftworks*, ed. Roger McKeon (New York: Semiotext(e), 1984), 89.

51. See Jacques Derrida, *The Gift of Death*, trans. David Wills (Chicago: University of Chicago Press, 1995), 20–21; Derrida and Maurizio Ferraris, *A Taste for the Secret*, trans. Giacomo Donis, ed. Giacomo Donis and David Webb (Cambridge: Polity Press, 2001), 57; and Gilles Deleuze and Felix Guattari, *A Thousand Plateaus*, trans. Brian Massumi (Minneapolis: University of Minnesota Press, 1987), 286–90. The secret also speaks directly to the issue of "bigness" in architecture, as that has been worked out by Koolhaas.

52. The first part of the quote is from Giorgio Agamben, *The Coming Community*, trans. Michael Hardt (Minneapolis: University of Minnesota Press, 1993), 64, and the second is from Theodor Adorno's essay "The Schema of Mass Culture," *The Culture Industry* (London: Routledge, 2002), 82.

53. Jean-François Lyotard, *Discours, Figure* (Paris: Klincksieck, 1974), 13. This is my translation.

54. Denise Scott Brown had written about the use of the comic strip form and speech balloons in her article "Little Magazines in Architecture and Urbanism," *AIP Journal*, July 1968, 228. The speech balloon continues to play a prominent role in Venturi and Scott Brown's subsequent exhibitions and articles.

55. David Carrier, *The Aesthetics of Comics* (University Park: Pennsylvania State University Press, 2000), 73–74.

56. Ibid., 29–30. Also see Wittgenstein, *Philosophical Investigations*, §427: "'While I was speaking to him I did not know what was going on in his head.' In saying this, one is not thinking of brain-processes, but of thought-processes. The picture should be taken seriously. We should really like to see into his head."

57. Here I am thinking of the duck and decorated shed image in Robert Venturi and Denise Scott Brown, "A Significance for A&P Parking Lots, or Learning from Las Vegas," *Architectural Forum*, March 1968, fig. 2, 39.

58. Jameson, "Architecture and the Critique of Ideology," 58–59.

59. For a history of ventriloquism, see Steven Connor, *Dumbstruck: A Cultural History of Ventriloquism* (Oxford: Oxford University Press, 2000), and more recently, David Goldblatt, *Art and Ventriloquism* (New York: Routledge, 2006).

60. Connor, *Dumbstruck*, 11.

61. Here I am drawing on Cavell's use of the word "driven" to suggest our "naturalizing" of the skeptical repudiation of our attunement with each other. For example, see Cavell, *In Quest of the Ordinary*, 48–49, 60.

62. Michel Foucault, "La Folie, l'absence d'oeuvre," in *Dits et écrits: 1954–69*, vol. 1, ed. Daniel Defert and François Ewald (Paris: Gallimard, 1994), 412–20.

63. Fredric Jameson, *Postmodernism, or, the Cultural Logic of Late Capitalism* (Durham, N.C.: Duke University Press, 1991), 97–101.

64. Gertrude Stein, *Gertrude Stein's America by Gertrude Stein*, ed. Gilbert A. Harrison (New York: Liveright, 1996), 94.

65. Henry David Thoreau, *Walden* (Oxford: Oxford University Press, 1999), 13.

66. Theodor Adorno, "The Culture Industry: Enlightenment as Mass Deception," *Dialectic of Enlightenment*, trans. Edmund Jephcott (Palo Alto, Calif.: Stanford University Press, 2002), 119.

67. Wittgenstein, *Philosophical Investigations*, §2 and §19.

68. John Austin, *How to Do Things with Words*, 2nd ed., ed., J. O. Urmson and Marina Sbisà (Cambridge, Mass.: Harvard University Press, 1975), 72.

69. Stanley Cavell, "Notes and Afterthoughts on the Opening of Wittgenstein's *Investigations*," *Philosophical Passages*, 158–59.

70. Austin, *How to Do Things with Words*, 73.

71. Oliver Sacks, *The Man Who Mistook His Wife for a Hat and Other Clinical Tales* (New York: Summit Books, 1985). This diremption of thought and emotion was exploited and formalized in the form of what Koolhaas calls the architectural equivalent of a lobotomy in relationship to the discrepancy between the container and the contained in the skyscraper: "the surgical severance of the connection between the frontal lobes and the rest of the brain to relieve some mental disorders by disconnecting though processes from emotions." See Koolhaas, *Delirious New York*, 100.

72. Also see Michael Golec's contribution to this book, "Format and Layout in *Learning from Las Vegas*." My own take on the design and layout of the first and revised editions is worked out in a chapter entitled "Reducks, 1972, 1977," in my book, *On Learning from Las Vegas: Skepticism and the Ordinary* (Cambridge, Mass.: The MIT Press, 2008), 111–71.

73. Scott Brown was photographing vernacular architecture for some time before this in South Africa and Philadelphia. For the ubiquitous references to Ruscha throughout Venturi and Scott Brown's early work, see Katherine Smith's essay.

74. Denise Scott Brown, "On Pop Art, Permissiveness, and Planning," *Journal of the American Institute of Planners*, May 1969, 185–86.

75. Denise Scott Brown, "Remedial Housing for Architects Studio," in *Venturi, Scott Brown & Associates: On Houses and Housing*, ed. James Steele (New York: St. Martin's, 1992), 56.

76. Scott Brown, "On Pop Art," 185

77. Interviews with Ed Ruscha in *Leave Any Information at the Signal: Writing, Interview, Bits, Pages*, ed. Alexandra Schwartz (Cambridge, Mass.: MIT Press, 2002), 217, 26.

78. Scott Brown, "On Pop Art," 186.

79. Ibid., 185.

80. I mean "transcendental" here in the Kantian sense of the condition of possibility of any particular experience.

81. Scott Brown, "On Pop Art," 185.

82. "Preface to the Revised Edition," *Learning from Las Vegas (1977)*, xv. For a detailed account of Cooper's design of the first edition of *Learning from Las Vegas* and Scott Brown's design of the revised edition see my "Chapter 5: Reducks, 1972, 1977," in *I AM A MONUMENT: On Learning from Las Vegas*, 111–71.

83. Jurgen Habermas uses this specific phrase ("stage-set architecture") in his brief discussion of *Learning from Las Vegas* in "Modern and Postmodern Architecture," in *Rethinking Architecture: A Reader in Cultural Theory*, ed. Neil Leach (London: Routledge, 1997), 234.

84. For instance, see Randal Knoper, "'Funny Personations': Theater and the Popularity of the Deadpan Style," in *Acting Naturally: Mark Twain in the Cultural of Performance* (Berkeley: University of California Press, 1995), 55–73.

85. The three instances I will be discussing occur in the following publications of Cavell: "What Becomes of Things on Film," *Themes Out of School: Effects and Causes* (Chicago: University of Chicago Press, 1988), 174–77; *The Claim of Reason*, 452; and *The World Viewed*, 36–37. The chapter entitled "The Dandy (55–59)," in *The World Viewed* is also relevant here. To be clear, Cavell never uses the word "deadpan" in his discussion of Buster Keaton.

86. This is neither the time nor the place to delve into the crucial role that "exemplarity" plays in Cavell's work, but I would be remiss if I didn't call brief attention to it. It is deeply indebted to issues of Kantian aesthetic judgment that are woven throughout Cavell's writings on ordinary language philosophy, criticism, modernism, skepticism, and Emersonian Perfectionism.

87. Cavell, *The World Viewed*, 37.

88. Cavell, *The Claim of Reason*, 452.

89. Cavell, "What Becomes of Things on Film," 174.

90. Venturi and Scott Brown, "Preface to the First Edition," in *Learning from Las Vegas*, xi.
91. Cavell, *The World Viewed*, 36–37.
92. Martin Heidegger, *Being and Time*, trans. Joan Stambaugh (Albany: State University of New York Press, 1996) §345.
93. Ibid., §345. As far as I know the term "equanimity" is used sparingly in *Being and Time*.
94. Ibid., §134
95. Ibid., §135.
96. Ibid., §137
97. Ibid.
98. Robert Venturi and Denise Scott Brown, *Architecture as Signs and Systems for a Mannerist Time* (Cambridge, Mass.: Belknap Press of Harvard University Press, 2004), 40.
99. One might say that Keaton's "pursuit of happiness" registers as an "ontological equality" between objects and human subjects. See Cavell, *The World Viewed*, 35–36, 72.
100. Scott Brown, "On Pop Art, Permisiveness, and Plannning," 185–86.
101. Sigmund Freud, "Negation (1925)," *Penguin Freud Library* (London: Penguin, 1991), 11:437–42.
102. Venturi and Scott Brown, *Architecture as Signs and Systems*, 109. Although I won't pursue it here, Scott Brown's discussion about delaying judgment, or as she so wonderfully puts it, "judgment with a sigh," exemplifies and acknowledges what is arguably the most important approach to architectural theory and practice in the last forty years: taking architecture production *as* a form of research. Witness Rem Koolhaas's *Delirious New York*, which he characterizes as a "manifesto with research," or his research-intensive design studios at Harvard, or the Dutch architectural firm MVRDV's projects, such as "Data City," that explore the relationship between the accumulation of information and issues of form.
103. Heidegger, Being and Time, § 137, 138.
104. Venturi, Scott Brown, and Izenour, *Learning from Las Vegas*, 100.
105. Cavell, *The World Viewed*, 132.
106. Venturi refers to Henry Russell Hitchcock rather than Bel Geddes in Venturi and Scott Brown, *Architecture as Signs and Systems*, 35. Norman Bel Geddes, *Horizon* (Boston: Little, Brown, and Company, 1932), 185.
107. Cavell makes references to Heidegger in relation to Buster Keaton in such a way. See Cavell, "What Becomes of Things on Film?, 174, 175: "Buster Keaton is the silent comic figure whose extraordinary works and whose extraordinary gaze . . . illuminate and are illuminated by the consequent concept of the worldhood of the world announcing itself."
108. Thoreau, *Walden*, 88.
109. Bernard Tschumi, "The Pleasure of Architecture," in *What is Architecture?*, ed. Andrew Ballantyne (New York: Routledge, 2002), 178.
110. Cavell, *The Claim of Reason*, 452; and Ruscha, *Leave Any Information at the Signal*, 245.
111. Ed Ruscha, "L.A. Suggested by the Art of Edward Ruscha," *Leave Any Information at the Signal*, 223.
112. Cavell, "What Becomes of Things on Film," *Themes Out of School*, 174.
113. Ruscha, "L.A. Suggested by the Art of Edward Ruscha," 222.
114. Willoughby Sharp, "'. . . A Kind of Huh?' An Interview with Edward Ruscha," *Leave Any Information at the Signal*, 65–66.
115. Jean-Luc Nancy, *The Sense of the World*, trans. Jeffrey S. Librett (Minneapolis: University of Minnesota Press, 1997), 18.

9

Learning from Las Vegas . . . and Los Angeles and Reyner Banham

NIGEL WHITELEY

The influential British architectural historian and theorist Reyner Banham (1922–88) belonged to the same generation as Robert Venturi (b. 1925) and Denise Scott Brown (b. 1931) and shared many of their architectural values. This chapter shows the great similarities of value and outlook in *Learning from Las Vegas* (1972) and Banham's almost contemporaneous *Los Angeles: the Architecture of Four Ecologies* (1971) (Figure 9.1). It then pinpoints areas of disagreement between Venturi, Scott Brown, and Izenour and Banham and moves to a discussion of the different authors' views on Las Vegas, drawing on other texts written by Banham around this time. It reveals that the Venturi, Scott Brown, and Izenour version of Las Vegas's significance was not the only one in currency in the period when *Learning from Las Vegas* appeared in its first and second editions and that the different interpretations of Las Vegas reveal contested architectural values during the period when modernist values were being challenged by postmodern ones.

Learning from Las Vegas has much in common with Banham's *Los Angeles: the Architecture of Four Ecologies*, and both reveal a permissive sensibility which is symptomatic of the time they were written. The first part of this paper looks at the shared values and parallels between the two books before moving on to significant differences of interpretation about the relationship of Pop and "high" culture. This is followed by Banham's own interpretation of Las Vegas which, while overlapping with much of Venturi, Scott Brown, and Izenour's, suggests some markedly different lessons.

Figure 9.1. Cover of Reyner Banham, *Los Angeles: The Architecture of Four Ecologies* (London: Pelican Books, 1973. Cover designed by Gerald Cinamon.)

Challenging Orthodoxies

The sort of orthodoxy Venturi, Scott Brown, and Izenour and Banham challenged was expressed by Nikolaus Pevsner in *An Outline of European Architecture*, first published in 1943 and receiving its sixth edition in 1960. "A bicycle shed is a building," the introduction commences, "Lincoln Cathedral is a piece of architecture." This distinction can be traced back to Ruskinian ideas about fundamental differences between architecture and building, but as a modernist Pevsner rejects John Ruskin's prioritization of ornament and decoration in order to codify a twentieth century, but supposedly transhistorical, aesthetic of architecture that has three aspects: "First, [aesthetic sensations] may be produced by the treatment of walls, proportions of windows, the relation of wall-space to window-space.... Secondly, the treatment of the exterior of a building as a whole is aesthetically significant, its contrasts of block against block. . . . Thirdly, there is the effect of our senses of the treatment of the interior, the sequence of rooms." Not only are the types of architectural aesthetics described as distinct categories, but they are hierarchical: it is only the third that is unique to architecture: "What distinguishes architecture from painting and sculpture is its spatial quality. In this, and only in this, no other artist can emulate the architect. Thus the history of architecture is primarily a history of man shaping space."[1]

The tendency to categorize hierarchically in order to define the supposed essentialism of a discipline was typical of other arts up to the 1960s. As regards painting, for example, Clement Greenberg, the great proponent of abstract expressionism and postpainterly abstraction, contemporaneously with Pevsner's sixth edition of his *Outline*, published his "Modernist Painting" essay, in which he proposed that the artist should seek "that which was unique and irreducible in each particular art." Painting, it followed, might be expected to concentrate on "the flat surface, the shape of the support, the properties of the pigment."[2] The reason for this way of thinking about the arts was not just a Victorian-like tendency for categorization or even a desire for the operation of a certain kind of logic; rather, it was because, as Greenberg argues, "it would, to be sure, narrow [a discipline's] area of competence, but at the same time it would make its possession of that area all the more certain."[3] That commitment to "certainty," with its quest for essentialism and purity, demanded an attitude and aesthetic of exclusiveness and rejected anything that espoused the more inclusive and immediate values of commercialism. Popular culture was summarily dismissed as "ersatz culture, kitsch, destined for those who [are] insensitive to the values of genuine culture."[4] Nor did Greenberg welcome the excitingly uncertain and insecure future of the time, open as it was to the "spirit of exploration and experiment," as the pioneer happenings artist Allan Kaprow put it.[5] In art in the 1960s, the challenge to orthodoxies included pop art, minimalism, conceptual art, land art, environments, happenings, and performances. In architecture, a parallel experimentation was at its most radical in projects emanating from Archigram, Cedric Price, Haus-Rucker-Co, Superstudio, Coop. Himmelblau, Eventstructures Research Group, Ant Farm, Archizoom, and Experiments in Art and Technology, among others. Not only was 1972 the year of the first edition of *Learning from Las Vegas*, it also witnessed the publication of the English language edition of Jim Burns's *Arthropods: New Urban Futures*, Gerald Woods, Philip Thompson, and John Williams's appropriately named *Art Without Boundaries*, and Harold Rosenberg's *De-Definition of Art*, all symptomatic of the mood of experimentation and challenge to orthodoxies.[6]

The change that was occurring in the arts in the 1960s was nothing less than a paradigm shift, and it is best summed up in Rosalind Krauss's phrase "the expanded field." Writing in 1979 in relation to sculpture, Krauss commented on the way that the category "sculpture" had been "kneaded and stretched and twisted" during the 1960s and '70s to the extent that it may "include just about anything"[7] from video installations, through earthworks, to minimally material concepts; it had become "a field in which there are other, differently structured possibilities."[8] Venturi, Scott Brown, and Izenour and Banham were doing something closely akin to this: challenging orthodoxies and thinking through differently structured possibilities so that the dualistic division into "cathedral or bicycle shed" could become, inter alia, cathedral *as* (decorated) bicycle shed (as may apply to Venturi, Scott Brown, and Izenour) or even cathedral *and* bicycle shed (as Banham might have argued). Banham's two most important books of the 1960s were *Theory and Design in the First Machine Age* (1960) and *The Architecture of the Well-tempered Environment* (1969). The former reassessed the contribution and importance of the expressionist wing of modernism that had been dismissed by historians like Pevsner in favor of the *sachlichkeit* (less is more), classical one. The latter examined the history, impact, and significance of mechanical services in relation to built form and the extent to which conventional assumptions about "architecture" might be superseded by the more inclusive concept of "fit environments for human activities."[9] Thus *Theory and Design* could, in effect, be thought of in terms of offering some alternative, radical cathedral designs from those that Pevsner had lauded, whereas *The Architecture of the Well-tempered Environment* would not necessarily exclude all cathedrals, but it was more likely to focus on the importance of bicycle sheds because (1) they had been dismissed by previous generations of historians as unworthy of appreciation and (2) they might be an intelligent and functional solution to a problem rather than one shaped by cultural habits, traditions, and customary practices.[10] Venturi was seriously challenging orthodoxies by the mid-1960s with, primarily, such essays as "Complexity and Contradiction in Architecture" and "Justification for a Pop Architecture." Scott Brown wrote "On Pop Art, Permissiveness and Planning" in 1969, following their original, controversial essay "Significance for A&P Parking Lots, or Learning from Las Vegas," published a year earlier.[11]

Learning from Las Vegas and *Los Angeles: the Architecture of Four Ecologies* challenged particular orthodoxies about what those cities represented. Las Vegas had been described by one eminent member of the design establishment as "among the most brutal, degrading, and corrupt [cities] that consumer society has ever created. . . . [It] shows just what depths of communicative poverty can be reached by a city left to its own arbitrary development, responsive only to the needs of . . . casino and motel owners, and to the needs of real estate speculators."[12] Los Angeles, according to one commentator, was "the noisiest, the smelliest, the most uncomfortable, and most uncivilised major city in the United States. In short a stinking sewer."[13] The conventional wisdom was that the only lesson that could be learned from either city was that both rudely demonstrated the dangers of permissiveness and popular culture without the conventional controls and planning provided by supposedly responsible professionals.

Openness and Inclusiveness

An attitude of openness and a commitment to inclusiveness are fundamental ingredients of both *Learning from Las Vegas* and *Los Angeles*. Both cities were characterized, according to their respective authors, by "inclusion." "The order of the Strip *includes*," wrote Venturi, Scott Brown, and Izenour, "it includes at all levels, from a mixture of seemingly incongruous land uses to the mixture of seemingly incongruous advertising media plus a system of neo-Organic or neo-Wrightian restaurant motifs in Walnut Formica. It is not an order dominated by the expert and made easy for the eye. The moving eye in the moving body must work to pick out and interpret a variety of changing, juxtaposed orders." The reward of this sort of environment was high: "vitality . . . may be achieved by an architecture of inclusion."[14] Diversity and pluralism were ends in themselves: "We think the more directions that architecture takes at this point, the better."[15] The alternative of a singular style, uniformity, and order—the conventional architectural habits of thought—often resulted in an overwhelming "deadness that results from too great a preoccupation with tastefulness and total design."[16] This meant that the architect and planner had to put aside their usual assumptions and even their professional taste culture. It was no good approaching Las Vegas with preconceived opinions: the architect had to suspend disbelief because, Venturi, Scott Brown, and Izenour argued, "withholding judgement may be used as a tool to make later judgement more sensitive. This is a way of learning from everything." One of the problems was that "architects [were] out of the habit of looking nonjudgmentally at the environment."[17] For all the professional's claimed open-mindedness, "there is a fine line between liberalism and old-fashioned class snobbery."[18]

That old-fashioned snobbery had also militated against Los Angeles being taken seriously by the architectural and planning professions. Books had tended to concentrate on the city's modernist monuments by the Greene brothers, Frank Lloyd Wright, Irving Gill, and Rudolf Schindler, thereby excluding the commercial vernacular of hamburger bars and other forms of pop architecture at one extreme and the freeway structures and other forms of civil engineering at the other. Both of these extremes, Banham argued, "are as crucial to the human ecologies and built environments of Los Angeles as are dated works in classified styles by named architects," for it is the "polymorphous architectures" that blend together to form the "comprehensible unity" that constitutes L.A.'s identity.[19] The inclusiveness may lack order and a clearly defined form and might even appear chaotic, but, like Venturi, Scott Brown, and Izenour on Las Vegas, Banham wanted the visitor to L.A. to suspend their disbelief, otherwise he or she would experience "confusion rather than variety . . . because the context [would escape] them."[20] A necessary part of understanding the context was the ability to cope with movement as "the language of design, architecture, and urbanism in Los Angeles is the language of movement. . . . [T]he city will never be fully understood by those who cannot move fluently through its diffuse urban texture, cannot go with the flow of its unprecedented life."[21] To do so—and admit its success—Banham argued, "threatens the intellectual repose and professional livelihood of many architects, artists, planners and environmentalists because it breaks the rules of urban design that they promulgate in works and writings and teach to their students."[22] Professionals, therefore, hated L.A. as much as they looked down at Las Vegas. However, Banham warned, "the common reflexes of hostility are not a defence of architectural values, but a negation of them, at least in so far as architecture has any part in the thoughts and aspirations of the human race beyond the little private world of the profession."[23] L.A. may have lacked conventional formal cohesion, but it undeniably offered a "sense of possibilities."[24]

High and Pop

Both Venturi, Scott Brown, and Izenour and Banham upheld a "both/and" acceptance of "high" and popular culture. *Learning from Las Vegas* was not an antimodernist diatribe; indeed, the authors clearly stated that "because we have criticized Modern architecture, it is proper here to state our intense admiration of its early period when its founders, sensitive to their own times, proclaimed the right revolution. Our argument lies mainly with the irrelevant and distorted prolongation of that old revolution today."[25] Banham had often expressed similar sentiments in his attempt to reform modernism and argue for a technologically oriented architecture in keeping with the second machine age, and in *Los Angeles* he devotes a chapter to "The Exiles"—principally Gill, Schindler, and Richard Neutra—and their achievement in the 1920s, which he rates alongside the achievements of the European masters. But an acceptance of modernism, however qualified, did not necessarily contradict a love of pop, and it is this for which both books are mostly remembered. Banham's chapter on California "Fantastic" architecture takes in such celebrated pop buildings as Grauman's Chinese Theatre, the Aztec Hotel, Tahitian Village and Brown Derby restaurants, Johnies diner, the Jack-in-the-Box hamburger stand, and Disneyland, as well as the folk monument of Watts Towers (Figure 9.2). The sources in *Learning from Las Vegas* are almost wholly pop and demonstrate "the validity of the commercial vernacular."[26] Both authors approvingly quote Tom Wolfe's writings about signs, electrographic architecture, and the shift within pop architecture to "whole structures designed primarily as pictures or representational sculpture."[27] However, this is the point at which Venturi, Scott Brown, and Izenour and Banham part company.

Figure 9.2. Simon Rodia, Watts Towers, 1921–54 (Photograph by author.)

Upward, Downward, Sideways

"Learning from popular culture," Venturi, Scott Brown, and Izenour explained, "does not remove the architect from his or her status in high culture. But it may alter high culture to make it more sympathetic to current needs and issues."[28] Furthermore, "we look backward at history and tradition to go forward; we can also look downward to go upward."[29] Venturi, Scott Brown, and Izenour liken this approach to pop artists like Roy Lichtenstein, who plundered popular culture such as the comic strip to rejuvenate fine art. Lichtenstein was still a fine artist making unique works, but the subject matter was popular in its source. This is the approach Venturi, Scott Brown, and Izenour wanted the architect to adopt because it could lead to a relevant and popular architecture that met suburbanites' aspirations and tastes. Banham saw it differently. He diagnosed a "sliding scale of commercial frugality versus cultural or aesthetic status"[30] on which the lower down the scales of financial substance and cultural pretensions one goes, the better sense it apparently makes ... to buy a plain standard building shell ... and add symbolic garnish to the front, top, or other parts that show. It makes even better sense, of course, to acquire an existing disused building and impose your commercial personality on it with symbolic garnishes. But even if you are a major commercial operator with a chain of outlets ... it still makes financial sense to put up relatively simple single-storey boxes, and then make them tall enough to attract attention by piling up symbols and graphic art on top.[31]

Banham was effectively describing the "decorated shed"; at the other extreme might be the "duck." Although Banham and Venturi, Scott Brown, and Izenour were diagnosing the same cultural phenomenon, they drew quite different lessons. Whereas Venturi, Scott Brown, and Izenour wanted to use the commercial decorated shed as the model for a renewed serious architecture, Banham saw it as an end in itself. It represented a type within diversity that made up the "polymorphous architectures" of Los Angeles. Each of the different architectures existed on a continuum: all were valid and equal, and no particular one should necessarily learn from another. They were successful when they grew out of and expressed their own sociocultural "ecology." Compared to this, with "high" drawing on "low," Venturi, Scott Brown, and Izenour's model is vertical. At the "cultural status" end of the continuum, Banham praises the Case Study houses by Charles and Ray Eames, Craig Ellwood, and Pierre Koenig that had grown out of the Miesian minimalist tradition but that could be seen as an expression of a geographical and sociocultural "ecology" of L.A. There may be some lessons that this type of architecture could learn from commercial pop, but they would be likely to be at the level of rethinking the home as a vehicle for a lifestyle rather than anything architecturally more radical or compromising. Fundamentally for Banham, architects' architecture should coexist with pop as parts of the greater whole.

Banham's "lesson" of Los Angeles, if it was a lesson, was the diversity and richness of the city's "polymorphous architectures" as part of the experience of its openness and inclusiveness. While Venturi, Scott Brown, and Izenour implore the reader to "learn" from Las Vegas—even if this necessitated a suspension of disbelief about enjoyment of the place—Banham, on one level, really asks no more of readers than to "enjoy" L.A.'s "splendours and miseries ... [and] graces and grotesqueries [because they] appear to [him] as unrepeatable as they are unprecedented." Forget about learning from L.A., he seems to be stating, because "it is immediately apparent that no city has ever been produced by such an extraordinary mixture of geography, climate, economics, demography, mechanics and culture; nor is it likely that an even remotely similar mixture will ever occur again."[32] But, of course, there is a lesson underneath the enjoyment, which is that Los Angeles fundamentally challenges a deeply established professional orthodoxy:

> Los Angeles emphatically suggests that there is no simple correlation between urban form and social form. Where it threatens the "human values"-oriented tradition of town planning inherited from Renaissance humanism it is in revealing how simple-mindedly mechanistic that supposedly humane tradition can be, how deeply attached to the mechanical fallacy that there is a necessary causal connexion between built form and human life, between the mechanisms of the city and the styles of architecture practised there.[33]

The lessons of Las Vegas were far more specific and transferable. *Learning from Las Vegas* was attempting nothing less than to "reassess the role of symbolism in architecture."[34] In that sense, "Las Vegas is not the subject of [their] book. The symbolism of architectural form is."[35] According to its authors, Las Vegas was no more—and no less—than "a vivid initial source for symbolism in architecture. We have described in the Las Vegas study the victory of symbols-in-space over forms-in-space."[36]

The difference between the lessons identified by Venturi, Scott Brown, and Izenour and those identified by Banham may be partly explained by the difference in audience for the books. Venturi, Scott Brown, and Izenour were writing as architects seeking "a new modesty in our designs and in our perception of our role as architects in society."[37] The reader is often assumed to be an architect for whom the lesson about architecture as symbol may transform her or his thinking about contemporary designing. *Los Angeles* was part of a series published by Pelican Books to "present the great architects, buildings and towns of the world in their social and cultural environments."[38] The readership was, therefore, wider than Venturi, Scott Brown, and Izenour's—it was professional *and* lay.

Las Vegas, Lesson 1: Enjoyment

Perhaps the different lessons can be explained by the character of the two places. Had Banham focused on Las Vegas rather than Los Angeles, he may have deduced the same lessons. Banham was not drawn to Las Vegas in the way he was to L.A. In *Los Angeles*, he is condescending about Las Vegas, claiming it has become "unashamedly middle-aged," typified by the "boring Beaux-Arts Caesar's Palace."[39] Given that Caesar's Palace forms a part of Venturi, Scott Brown, and Izenour's original article of 1968[40]—of which Banham would obviously have been fully aware—this might be interpreted as a lack of sympathy for Venturi, Scott Brown, and Izenour's approach in general and Las Vegas in particular. Indeed, he leaves his *Los Angeles* reader in no doubt that Las Vegas merits little attention compared to

L.A.: "Las Vegas has been as much a marginal gloss on Los Angeles as was Brighton Pavilion on Regency London."[41] Banham had little more to say about Las Vegas in *Los Angeles*, but elsewhere he even finds it has interesting lessons to offer.

In 1975, Banham published the essay "Mediated Environments," which deals with the ways in which images of American building types and cities had been transmitted through the mass media. After discussing New York and Los Angeles, he discusses Las Vegas, a city that only worked in image-form in "the era of Cinemascope and Technicolor."[42] He describes the city as "a classic Pop artefact, as that term had come to be understood by the end of the fifties—an expendable dream that money could just about buy, designed for immediate point-of-sale impact, outside the canons of Fine Art."[43] For his generation, he explained in another essay (1974) that Las Vegas was "a self-sufficient phenomenon needing no discussion; all you had to do was point, as one would have done at the Manhattan skyline two decades earlier. However, it was also obviously the biggest ever exhibition of unalloyed Pop-art, on which visiting aesthetes could exercise fancy stylistic discriminations."[44] Like his response to Los Angeles, the appropriate response to Las Vegas seemed to be to "enjoy" rather than to "learn."

Lesson 2: "Formlessness and Tastelessness"

Banham suggested that a change from enjoying to learning from Las Vegas occurred when Wolfe "upstaged the whole game by pointing out that the designers of the signs were horse-opera characters in string ties who knew nothing of modern art."[45] This change began in the summer of 1965 with the publication of *The Kandy-Kolored Tangerine Flake Streamline Baby*, and Banham thought its impact had its greatest force when it was reprinted soon after with an introduction that returned to "the Vegas theme in order to drive home what had become by then Wolfe's main preoccupation—the irrelevance of established fine-art standards of judgement to what was actually happening in America."[46] What made Las Vegas distinctive, Banham wrote in his 1975 essay, was "its formlessness and tastelessness—by the standards of established culture, that is. The scatter along the strip had no discernible plan; the signs were simply commercial art raised to an intense pitch. . . . Whereas the great image of Manhattan had been of an undesigned but distinct form composed of designed elements of architecture, that of Las Vegas appeared to be an indistinct and undesigned formlessness composed of elements that fell below the threshold of architectural attention."[47]

To have "formlessness and tastelessness" would be a condemnation in conventional critical terms, but it is these very aspects that Banham finds attractive because they "challenge orthodoxies" and provide a "sense of possibilities" that is not based on the predictable or tried-and-tested. Venturi, Scott Brown, and Izenour were also sympathetic to sprawl, describing how the Strip by day "is not enclosed and directed as in traditional cities. Rather, it is open and indeterminate, identified by points in space and patterns on the ground."[48] But they seemed concerned that the Strip in daytime "reads as chaos if you perceive only its forms and exclude its symbolic content."[49] The symbolism may have rescued it from the chaos for Venturi, Scott Brown, and Izenour, but for Banham it was an expression not only of a new, alternative, nonprofessional aesthetic but also a freedom: "for anyone who found anything good in the Vegas environment, established procedures of town planning and standards of aesthetic control had to be wrong. The place did not so much flout those standards—simple opposition would have left the argument with its original polarities—it simply ignored them, which made new polarities necessary."[50] In his 1967 review of Wolfe's book, the nub of his argument was class related: "what Wolfe had discovered in Las Vegas was the mad money of a relaxed proletariat conjuring up a culture and a visual style that had never been seen anywhere else in the world."[51] Las Vegas's "formlessness" represented an alternative to tastefulness, and an acceptance of it showed one was willing to reject "a culture based on aristocratic taste" and embrace the uncertainty and possibilities of "one based in free-form self-fulfilment."[52] The reason for a rejection of Las Vegas's formlessness ultimately might be political rather than aesthetic, an "elitist suppression by a cultural Establishment."[53] Although other interpretations of the political implications of Las Vegas were in currency,[54] Banham held to his opinion that Las Vegas was a city that expressed not only a new aesthetic but also a democratic social order appropriate to the consumer capitalism of the second machine age.[55]

"Formlessness and tastelessness" bring to mind Venturi, Scott Brown, and Izenour's term "ugly and ordinary" in that both terms require inverted commas. The latter requires them to signal that they are making use of conventions that are normally dismissed by professionals as ugly and ordinary as opposed to the more aspirational "heroic and original,"[56] but they are using them in such a way that "they are not merely ordinary but represent ordinariness symbolically and stylistically."[57] Banham's term is also used conventionally to describe Las Vegas, and, like Venturi, Scott Brown, and Izenour, he is turning a term of abuse into a desirable attribute. However, the difference is that Venturi, Scott Brown, and Izenour are using "ugly and ordinary" architecture as a source for a sophisticated, high-culture architecture—in the same way as a pop artist uses sources—whereas Banham is using "formlessness and tastefulness" not as a source for high culture but as an end in itself. The lesson is one of challenging orthodoxies and changing our paradigms of what is visually and politically acceptable and desirable. The application of the lesson of Las Vegas was "Non-Plan," a proposal for the suspension of planning in England to encourage a "plunge into heterogeneity"[58] based on the supposition that "Fremont Street in Las Vegas or Sunset Strip in Beverly Hills represent the living architecture of our age."[59]

Lesson 3: Virtual Architecture

There was one more lesson that Banham had drawn from Las Vegas, and it is a telling one. It was elucidated in *The Architecture of the Well-tempered Environment*, in which he declares,

> What defines the symbolic spaces and places of Las Vegas—the superhotels of The Strip, the casino-belt of Fremont Street—is pure environmental power, manifested as coloured light.... [T]he fact remains that the effectiveness with which space is defined is overwhelming, the creation of virtual volumes without apparent structure is endemic, the variety and ingenuity of the lighting techniques is encyclopaedic.... And in a view of architectural education that embraced the complete art of environmental management, a visit to Las Vegas would be as mandatory as a visit to the Baths of Caracalla or La Sainte Chapelle.

Banham seems to be anticipating some of the "virtual" design in our own time, but as far as he was concerned the "point of studying Las Vegas, ultimately, would be to see an example of how far environmental technology can be driven beyond the confines of architectural practice by designers who (for better or worse) are not inhibited by the traditions of architectonic culture, training and taste."[60]

Banham wittily and perceptively defines Las Vegas as representing a "change from forms assembled in light to light assembled in forms"—another version of "formlessness," if not "tastelessness."[61] His reference to "coloured light" recalls the visionary architecture of Paul Scheerbart and his 1914 book *Glasarchitektur*, with its call for "more coloured light!"[62] Banham links Scheerbart and Las Vegas directly: the nightscape of the city, he suggests, is an example of what Scheerbart was prophesizing and what had "come true in oblique ways he could never have anticipated."[63] Scheerbart had been one of the prophets rediscovered by Banham in *Theory and Design in the First Machine Age*, and his stature remained high in *The Architecture of the Well-tempered Environment*. Alongside the futurist Antonio Sant'Elia, he represents Banham's alternative modernist who challenged orthodoxies and offered a vision of a technologically based architecture underpinned by a keen "mechanical sensibility."[64]

Modernist or Postmodernist?

However reformist or radical his point of view, Banham never loses faith in modernism, and this not only sets him apart from Venturi, Scott Brown, and Izenour but also explains the different lessons he draws from Los Angeles and Las Vegas. His commitment to the "mechanical sensibility" and the "technological century" led Banham to champion architects such as Buckminster Fuller, Price, and

Archigram. He also was a supporter of the megastructure movement and the brutalist "bloody-mindedness" shown by Alison and Peter Smithson and James Stirling.[65] In *Learning from Las Vegas*, Venturi, Scott Brown, and Izenour vehemently attack "the world science futurist metaphysic, the megastructuralist mystique, and the look-Ma-no-buildings environmental suits and pods [that] are a repetition of the mistakes of another generation. Their overdependence on a space-age, futurist, or science-fiction technology parallels the machine aestheticism of the 1920s and approaches its ultimate mannerism. They are, unlike the architecture of the 1920s, artistically a deadend and socially a cop-out."[66] To Banham, Los Angeles and Las Vegas were in the line of descent of his expanded modernism, whereas for Venturi, Scott Brown, and Izenour, Las Vegas could offer that lesson in architectural symbolism and communication that was a break with modernism's heroism and individualism with its (according to them) misguided, inappropriate, and largely implicit symbolism of industrialism.

Banham only ever referred to Venturi, Scott Brown, and Izenour's work and *Learning from Las Vegas* in passing, and he never offered a critical assessment of either their ideas or their buildings. The closest he came was to position their 1968 essay as "against the grain of conventional planning wisdom," remarking that Venturi, Scott Brown, and Izenour "applauded the profusion of shameless illuminated signs, the total independence of those signs from the architecture of the buildings from urban planning as normally understood."[67] Had that been the sum total of Venturi, Scott Brown, and Izenour's project, Banham would have had no difficulty in giving it his full support, but crucially he makes no reference to the reason for their study or the chief lesson they drew from it.

That he did not discuss these lessons can be explained by his consistent opposition to postmodernism—or at least to what he caricatured as postmodernism. The basis of his opposition was that postmodernism "exists chiefly as a series of smart graffiti on the bodies of fairly routine modern buildings. It is all outward show and could be removed, in most cases, without destroying the utility of the rather ordinary buildings behind the jesting facades."[68] He intensely disliked what he saw as the "cleverness" shown by postmodern architects (whom he lists as including Robert Stern, Peter Eisenman, Michael Graves, and Venturi) who are "liable to make heavy weather and great polemical bother about every historical quote they use." He acknowledged that "it looks terrific on the page, but often tawdry on the site, as does much American Post-Modernism. . . . But what's it all got to do with 'real architecture'?"[69]

"Real" architecture, presumably, belonged to the modernist preoccupation with "forms-in-space," which dismissed the Venturi, Scott Brown, and Izenour idea of "symbols-in-space" as the sign of a bad lesson. For Venturi, Scott Brown, and Izenour, "billboards are almost all right."[70] Banham thought they were all right, too, in their place, but he probably preferred cathedrals and bicycle sheds.

Notes

1. Nikolaus Pevsner, *An Outline of European Architecture* (London: Pelican Books, 1960), 7.
2. Ibid.
3. Clement Greenberg, "Modernist Painting [1960]," *Clement Greenberg: The Collected Essays and Criticism*, ed. John O'Brian (Chicago: University of Chicago Press, 1986), 4:86.
4. Clement Greenberg, "Avant-Garde and Kitsch [1939]," *Clement Greenberg: The Collected Essays and Criticism*, ed. John O'Brian (Chicago: University of Chicago Press, 1986), 1:12.
5. Allan Kaprow, "From *Assemblages, Environments and Happenings* [1965]," in *Art in Theory: an Anthology of Changing Ideas*, ed. Charles Harrison and Paul Wood (Oxford: Blackwell, 1993), 708.
6. Jim Burns, *Arthropods: New Urban Futures* (London: Academy, 1972); Gerald Woods, Philip Thompson, and John Williams, *Art Without Boundaries: 1950–70* (London: Thames & Hudson, 1972); and Harold Rosenberg, *The De-Definition of Art* (Chicago: University of Chicago Press, 1972).
7. Rosalind Krauss, "Sculpture in the Expanded Field [1979]," *Postmodern Culture*, ed. Hal Foster (London: Pluto Press, 1985), 31–42. The quotes are from page 31.
8. Ibid., 38.
9. See Nigel Whiteley, *Reyner Banham: Historian of the Immediate Future* (Cambridge, Mass.: MIT Press, 2002), chap. 4.
10. Banham himself did actually comment on Pevsner's distinction between Lincoln Cathedral and a bicycle shed: "Pevsner's remark is a snobbish put-down on a whole class of buildings. They are excluded from the category of architecture, not because they are ill-conceived or ugly, but because they contain bikes!" Reyner Banham, "A real golden oldie," *New Society*, December 13, 1973, 667.
11. Robert Venturi, "Complexity and Contradiction in Architecture," *Perspecta*, 9–10 (1965): 17–56; Robert Venturi, "A Justification for a Pop Architecture," *Arts and Architecture*, April, 22, 1965; Denise Scott Brown, "On Pop Art, Permissiveness and Planning," *Journal of the American Institute of Planners*, May 1969, 184–86; Robert Venturi and Denise Scott Brown, "Significance for A&P Parking Lots, or Learning from Las Vegas," *Architectural Forum*, March 1968, 37–42ff.
12. Tomás Maldonado, *Design, Nature, and Revolution: Toward a Critical Ecology* (New York: Harper & Row, 1972), 60, 64.
13. Adam Raphael (1968), quoted in Reyner Banham, *Los Angeles: The Architecture of Four Ecologies* (London: Pelican Books, 1973), 16.
14. Robert Venturi, Denise Scott Brown, and Steven Izenour, *Learning from Las Vegas* (Cambridge, Mass.: MIT Press, 1977), 53.
15. Ibid., xiii.
16. Ibid., 53.
17. Ibid., 3.
18. Ibid., 155.
19. Banham, *Los Angeles*, 22–23.
20. Ibid., 23.
21. Ibid.
22. Ibid., 236.
23. Ibid., 244.
24. Ibid., 243.
25. Venturi, Scott Brown, and Izenour, *Learning from Las Vegas*, xiii.
26. Ibid., 6.
27. Tom Wolfe quoted in Banham, *Los Angeles*, 133–34; see also Venturi, Scott Brown, and Izenour, *Learning from Las Vegas*, 52.
28. Venturi, Scott Brown, and Izenour, *Learning from Las Vegas*, 161.
29. Ibid,. 3.
30. Banham, *Los Angeles*, 120.
31. Ibid., 119.
32. Ibid., 24.

33. Ibid., 237.
34. Venturi, Scott Brown, and Izenour, *Learning from Las Vegas*, xvii.
35. Ibid., xv.
36. Ibid., 119.
37. Ibid., xvii.
38. Banham, *Los Angeles*, 1.
39. Ibid., 124.
40. Venturi and Scott Brown, "Significance for A&P Parking Lots."
41. Ibid.
42. Reyner Banham, "Mediated Environments or: *You Can't Build That Here*," in *Superculture: American Popular Culture and Europe*, ed. C. W. E. Bigsby (London: Paul Elek, 1975), 78.
43. Ibid., 78.
44. Reyner Banham, "Europe and American Design," in *Lessons from America: An Exploration*, ed. Richard Rose (London: Macmillan, 1974), 88.
45. Ibid.
46. Banham, "Mediated Environments," 79.
47. Ibid., 78.
48. Venturi, Scott Brown, and Izenour, *Learning from Las Vegas*, 116–17.
49. Ibid., 117.
50. Banham, "Mediated Environments," 79.
51. Reyner Banham, "Towards a Million-Volt Light and Sound Culture," *Architectural Review*, May 1967, 332.
52. Ibid., 335.
53. Banham, "Europe and American Design," 88.
54. A diametrically opposite explanation of the social order was offered in 1972 by Tomás Maldonado, who characterized Las Vegas as a city not created "*by* the people, but *for* the people. It is the final product . . . of more than half a century of masked manipulatory violence, directed toward the formation of an apparently free and playful urban environment. . . . But it is an environment in which men are completely devoid of innovative will and of resistance to the effects of . . . pseudocommunicative intoxication." Maldonado, *Desire, Nature, and Revolution*, 65.
55. Banham had even acknowledged this aspect of Las Vegas in his *Los Angeles* book, in which he commented that "Los Angeles sums up a general phenomenon of US life; the convulsions in building style that follow when traditional cultural and social restraints have been overthrown and replaced by the preferences of a mobile, affluent, consumer-oriented society. . . . This process has probably gone further in, say, Las Vegas, yet it is in the context of Los Angeles that everyone seems to feel the strongest compulsion to discuss this fantasticating tendency." Banham. *Los Angeles*, 124.
56. Venturi, Scott Brown, and Izenour, *Learning from Las Vegas*, 93.
57. Ibid., 129.
58. Reyner Banham, Paul Barker, Peter Hall, and Cedric Price, "Non-Plan: an Experiment in Freedom," *New Society*, March 20, 1969, 436.
59. Ibid., 443.
60. Reyner Banham, *The Architecture of the Well-tempered Environment* (London: Architectural Press, 1969), 269–70.
61. Ibid., 270. In his 1975 book *Age of the Masters*, he was making a similar point: "It may sound strange, almost blasphemous, to say so, but it is in Las Vegas that one comes nearest to seeing gross matter transformed into etherial substance by the power of light." Reyner Banham, *Age of the Masters: a Personal View of Modern Architecture* (London: Architectural Press, 1975), 62.
62. Paul Scheerbart, *Glasarchitektur* (1914; repr. London: November Books, 1972), 72.
63. Banham, *The Architecture of the Well-tempered Environment*, 128.
64. See Whiteley, *Reyner Banham*, chap. 1.
65. Ibid., 249–53.
66. Venturi, Scott Brown, and Izenour, *Learning from Las Vegas*, 149.

67. Banham, "Mediated Environments," 80.
68. Reyner Banham, "The Writing on the Walls," *Times Literary Supplement*, November 17, 1978, 1337.
69. Reyner Banham, "The Ism Count," *New Society*, August 27, 1981, 362.
70. Venturi, Scott Brown, and Izenour, *Learning from Las Vegas*, 6.

Contributors

RITU BHATT is assistant professor of architecture at the University of Minnesota.

MICHAEL J. GOLEC is associate professor of design history at The School of the Art Institute of Chicago. He is the author of *Brillo Box Archive: Aesthetics, Design, and Art*.

KARSTEN HARRIES is professor of philosophy at Yale University and the author of five books, including *Infinity and Perspective*, and numerous articles and reviews.

JEAN-CLAUDE LEBENSZTEJN is professor emeritus at Université de Paris I, Panthéon–Sorbonne. He has written many books on artists from Pontormo to Malcolm Morley.

JOHN McMORROUGH is assistant professor of architecture at Ohio State University and a partner of StudioAPT.

KATHERINE SMITH is assistant professor of art at Agnes Scott College, where she teaches modern and contemporary art and architecture.

DELL UPTON is professor of architectural history at the University of California, Los Angeles. He is the author of numerous books, including *Architecture in the United States* and *Holy Things and Profane: Anglican Parish Churches in Colonial Virginia*.

ARON VINEGAR is assistant professor in the Department of History of Art at Ohio State University. He is the author of *I AM A MONUMENT: On Learning from Las Vegas*.

NIGEL WHITELEY is professor of visual arts at the Lancaster Institute for the Contemporary Arts at Lancaster University. He is the author of *Reyner Banham: Historian of the Immediate Future*.

Publication History

An earlier version of chapter 1 was published as "Aesthetic or Anaesthetic: The Competing Symbols of Las Vegas Strip," in "Instruction and Provocation, or Relearning from Las Vegas," special issue, *Visible Language* 37, no. 3 (October 2003):248–65.

An earlier version of chapter 2 appeared as "'Doing It Deadpan': Venturi, Scott Brown, and Izenour's *Learning from Las Vegas*," in "Instruction and Provocation, or Relearning from Las Vegas," special issue, *Visible Language* 37, no. 3 (October 2003): 266–87.

Chapter 3 originally appeared in French as "Hyperréalisme, kitsch et 'Venturi,'" in *Zizag* (Paris: Flammarion, 1981), 311–55. An English translation by Kate Cooper, "Photorealism, Kitsch and Venturi," was published in the journal *SubStance*, vol. 10, no. 2, issue 3 (1981): 75-104.

Chapter 7 previously appeared as "Signs Taken for Wonders," in "Instruction and Provocation, or Relearning from Las Vegas," special issue, *Visible Language* 37, no. 3 (October 2003): 332–51.

Chapter 8 is a version of "Chapter 3: Of Ducks, Decorated Sheds, and Other Minds", from the author's book *I AM A MONUMENT: On Learning from Las Vegas* (Cambridge, Mass.: The MIT Press, 2008), 49-92.

Chapter 9 was previously published as "Learning from Las Vegas . . . and Los Angeles and Reyner Banham," in "Instruction and Provocation, or Relearning from Las Vegas," special issue, *Visible Language* 37, no. 3 (October 2003): 314–31.

Index

Aalto, Alvar, 144
Adams, Bruce, 135, 145
Adenauer, Konrad 75s
Adorno, Theodor 5, 15, 179–80, 191
Agamben, Giorgio, 191
Alford, John, 154, 157
Alloway, Lawrence, 144
Althusser, Louis, 55, 76
Anscombe, G. E. M., 17, 190
Antin, Eleanor, 111–12, 126
Appleyard, Donald, 34–35, 46, 99, 114, 122, 126
Arendt, Hannah, 128
Argan, Giulio, 153
Aristotle, 82, 94
Arnell, Peter, 29, 160
Ashton, Dore, 114, 126
Astaire, Fred, 155
Austin, John, 179–80, 190, 192

Baird, George, 17, 25, 145, 160, 190
Banham, Reyner, 125, 195–96, 198, 200–210
Barthes, Roland, 77
Battcock, Gregory, 75, 77–78, 124
Baudelaire, Charles, 69
Baudrillard, Jean, 15, 182
Bauhaus, 7, 9, 67, 78, 89–90
Bayer, Herbert, 40
Bechtle, Robert, 53, 75–76, 78
Bel Geddes, Norman, 185, 193
Benjamin, Walter, 15, 53, 75, 122, 128, 164, 189
Bergart, Catherine, 29, 160
Bernstein, J. M., 16

Bickford, Ted, 29, 160
Bilbao (Spain), 153–54, 157
Blake, Peter, 127, 148, 166
Blanchot, Maurice, 73
Borden, Iain, 190
Bosanquet, Bernard, 95
Boulez, Pierre, 77
Bourdieu, Pierre, 157, 162
Bourdon, David, 125
Bowman, John G., 155, 162
Brémond, Jean-François, 55
Breton, André, 77
Brooks, Cleanth, 82–83, 95
Brooks, H. Allen, 161
Bryson, Norman, 161
Buren, Daniel, 75
Burns, Jim, 197, 208
Butler, Judith, 1, 15

Caesar's Palace, 61, 63, 103, 105, 133, 151–52, 203
Calakmul Building, 161
California City Cemetery, 65
California City Civic Center, 77
Campbell, Colin, 160
Cannon, Vaughn, 142
Canty, Donald, 46
Carrier, David, 176, 191
Carroll, Noël, 162
Carroll, Paul, 124
Carter, Curtis, 29
Case Study houses, 202
Cavell, Stanley, 3, 5, 15–16, 164, 166, 171–75, 179, 182–93
Chambers, Sir William, 64, 77

Chaplin, Charlie, 186–87
Chase, Linda, 75–76, 78
Clark, T. J., 4, 15, 95
Close, Chuck, 53, 68, 72, 78
Coleman, A. D., 125–26
Colquhoun, Alan, 11, 17, 25, 29, 133, 145, 153, 160, 169, 190
Comay, Rebecca, 15
Conklin, Gary, 125
Cook, John W., 76, 78
Cooper, Muriel, 7–9, 31–33, 39–45, 182, 192
Crawford Manor, 85, 134, 145, 150, 168–71, 190

Dada, 75
Danto, Arthur C., 10–11, 17, 85, 91, 95, 160
D'Arcangelo, Allan, 35, 39, 98, 108, 114, 124, 126, 132, 145
Daston, Lorainne, 32, 44, 46
Davidson, Donald, 157, 162
Deamer, Peggy, 145
DeAndrea, John, 53
Debord, Guy, 5, 15
decorated shed, 148, 158, 165–71, 174–76, 178–80, 184–85, 189, 202
Deleuze, Gilles, 79, 191
de Man, Paul, 4, 15, 160, 171, 190
Derrida, Jacques, 8, 21, 79, 190–91
de Saussure, Fernand, 160
Disney, Walt, 142
Dorfles, Gillo, 58, 61–62
Duchamp, Marcel, 69, 78, 85, 91–93
duck, 148–49, 152, 156, 158, 162, 165–77, 180, 185, 189–90, 202
Dwan Gallery, 102

Eames, Charles and Ray, 202
Eco, Umberto, 33

Eddy, Don, 53, 72
Ehrenzweig, Anton, 11, 17, 34, 46
Eiffel Tower, 60, 152
Eisenman, Peter, 12, 80, 86, 207
Eisenstein, Elizabeth, 6, 16
Eldridge, Richard, 16
Elgin, Catherine, 29
Eliot, T. S., 81, 84, 95
Elkins, James, 160
Ellwood, Craig, 202
Emerson, Ralph Waldo, 11, 14, 17, 192
Empson, William, 16
Engels, Friedrich, 56
Enlightenment, 87
Estes, Richard, 53, 72–73
Evans, Robin, 153, 161
Ewald, François, 191

Ferlinghetti, Lawrence, 6, 16
Flavin, Dan, 158
Foote, Nancy, 75–76, 78
Forster, Kurt, 6, 16
Foster, Hal, 1, 5, 27, 141, 146, 208
Foster, Norman, 155
Foucault, Michel, 79, 178, 191
Frampton, Kenneth, 5, 15, 21, 36–37, 46
Frankfurt (Germany), 74, 129
Fremont Street, 113, 136, 206
Freud, Sigmund, 11, 17, 141, 179–80, 185, 193
Fried, Michael, 104, 115, 124, 126
Fuller, Buckminster, 206
Füssli, Heinrich, 76
Fynsk, Christopher, 191

Gadamer, Hans-Georg, 21
Galison, Peter, 32, 44, 46–47
Gans, Herbert, 37, 46, 100
Gaskell, Ivan, 160

Gebhard, David, 124
Geddes, Jean, 128
Gehry, Frank, 153, 155, 161
Genette, Gérard, 7, 16
Georges, Rip, 124
Gerenmaier, Eugen, 155
Gill, Irving, 199–200
Goings, Ralph, 75, 78
Goldberger, Paul, 139, 145
Golec, Michael J., 17, 29, 31, 147, 160, 192, 211
Gombrich, Ernst, 10, 17, 25, 29, 160, 168, 190
Goodman, Nelson, 19–22, 26, 29
Graham, Dan, 132, 144, 158
Graves, Michael, 86, 207
Greenberg, Clement, 5, 15, 72, 92, 142, 146, 174, 197, 208
Greene, Charles and Henry, 199
Gropius, Walter, 78, 89
Groth, Paul, 147
Guarneri, Andrea Bocco, 95
Guattari, Félix, 191
Guild House, 76, 85–86, 93, 124, 134, 150, 169–71, 185, 190

Haacke, Hans, 75
Habermas, Júrgen, 5, 192
Hackett, Pat, 124
Hacking, Ian, 10, 17
Hall, Peter, 209
Hanson, Duane, 52–53, 72, 78
Harries, Karsten, 79, 95, 149–50, 160, 171, 190, 211
Harris, Steven, 125
Harrison, Charles, 208
Hayes, K. Michael, 190
Hegel, Georg Wilhelm Friedrich, 86–89, 92–93

Heidegger, Martin, 79, 89, 184–85, 193
Heidt, Sarah, 95
Heimann, Jim, 124
Henkin, David, 162
Henry, Gerrit, 78
Heyman, Ken, 101
Hickey, Dave, 125
Hitchcock, Henry-Russell, 145, 193
Holly, Michael Ann, 161
Hopper, Dennis, 102
Huxtable, Ada Louise, 127

Indiana, Robert, 118
Izenour, Steven, 1–2, 7, 10, 12, 14–17, 20, 22–29, 31–33, 38–47, 77–78, 81, 97–99, 101, 103, 105–6, 110–11, 113–15, 118, 121, 124–31, 133–34, 136, 138, 140, 143–46, 148–51, 153, 157–61, 163, 165, 169, 175, 177, 182, 189–90, 193, 195–96, 198–210

James, Henry, 5
Jameson, Fredric, 1–2, 4, 15, 27, 33, 46, 175, 177–78, 189, 191
Jencks, Charles, 1, 17, 25, 27, 29, 33, 91, 95, 145–46, 160–61, 190
Johns, Jasper, 10, 69, 71, 78
Johnson, Mark, 157, 162
Johnson, Philip, 91, 145
Joyce, James, 84

Kahn, Louis, 21, 54
Kant, Immanuel, 5, 93
Kantor, Robert E., 11, 17
Kaprow, Allan, 197, 208
Keaton, Buster, 182–84, 186–88
Keats, John, 85
Kepes, Gyorgy, 126
Kevorkian, Karen, 147

Kezer, Zeynep, 147
Kienholz, Edward, 18–21, 125, 127
Klotz, Heinrich, 76, 78
Koenig, Pierre, 202
Koetter, Fred, 27, 29
Koolhaas, Rem, 146, 163, 175, 189, 191–93
Kramer, Hilton, 91, 95
Krauss, Rosalind, 15, 197, 208
Krebs, Patricia, 128
Kultermann, Udo, 76, 78
Kundera, Milan, 92–93

Lakoff, George, 157, 162
Lampugnani, Vittorio Magnano, 21, 29
Las Vegas (Nevada), 2–3, 6–7, 12, 23, 27, 31–33, 36–45, 61–63, 84, 99–100, 103, 106, 110–11, 115, 122, 126, 129–32, 134–35, 137–46, 148–52, 158, 160–61, 166, 180–81, 185, 195, 198–99, 203–7, 209
Las Vegas Boulevard, 152
Las Vegas Strip, 20, 23–28, 39, 42–43, 98, 103, 108, 110–15, 121–22, 126–28, 143, 148–52, 158, 181, 199, 206
Latour, Bruno, 16
Leach, Neil, 5–6, 16, 27, 29, 192
Le Corbusier, 154
Ledoux, Claude-Nicolas, 77, 91, 171
Lefebvre, Henri, 160
Levittown, 27, 36, 38, 63, 77, 99, 105–6, 108, 116, 121, 125, 131, 144
Levittown studio, 181
Lichtenstein, Roy, 10, 118, 124, 201
Lonchamp, Jacques, 77
Loos, Adolf, 88
Lynch, Kevin, 33–34, 37, 44, 46, 99, 122, 160
Lynch, Michael, 16

Lyotard, Jean-François, 1, 27, 33, 85, 89, 95, 176, 191

Magritte, René, 106, 139
Maldonado, Tomás, 5, 208–9
Malevich, Kasimir, 53, 91
Mallarmé, Stéphane, 77
Malraux, André, 56
Marx, Karl, 56–57
Marxism, 90
Masheck, Joseph, 158
Matta-Clark, Gordon, 127
McBurnett, Ted, 75–76, 78
McEvilley, Thomas, 3, 15
McLean, Richard, 52, 75, 78
McLuhan, Marshall, 91
McManus, Denis, 149
McMorrough, John, 104, 166
McQueen, Steve, 188
Meissonier, Jean-Louis-Ernest, 56
Merleau-Ponty, Maurice, 178
Mertens, Detlef, 15, 170, 190
MIT (Massachusetts Institute of Technology) Press, 7, 31, 41, 44, 84
Moholy-Nagy, Laszlo, 40
Mondrian, Piet, 55, 77
Moore, Charles, 135, 145
Morley, Malcolm, 53, 54, 62, 69, 71–73, 76–78, 211
Morris, Meghan, 16
Moxey, Keith, 161
Mozart, Wolfgang Amadeus, 61
Mulhall, Stephen, 16
Muschamp, Herbert, 161
Myer, John R., 34–35, 46, 99, 122

Nancy, Jean-Luc, 15, 163, 188, 191, 193
Nesbitt, Kate, 89–90, 95
Neutra, Richard, 200
New Jersey Turnpike, 115

Newman, Barnett, 53
New Realism, 76
New Society, 208–9
Niemeyer, Oscar, 153, 158
Nietzsche, Friedrich, 14, 88, 95, 179
Nolli, Giambattista, 36, 126
Notre Dame du Haut, 149, 152

O'Brian, John, 15, 146, 208
Obrist, Hans Ulrich, 146
Oldenburg, Claes, 10, 99, 101–6, 115, 118, 124–25, 127
Opus International 75, 78

Passonneau, Joseph R., 34, 46
Pauly, Danièle, 153, 161
Pawley, Martin, 144
Penner, Barbara, 190
Pevsner, Nikolaus, 93, 153, 161, 168, 189, 196–98, 208
Pincus, Robert L., 120, 127
Plagens, Peter, 124
Poirier, Richard, 83–84, 95
Pollock, Duncan, 61
Pollock, Jackson, 170
pop art, 10–11, 17, 31, 35–38, 44, 46, 52, 68, 84, 98–101, 105–7, 118, 120, 123–25, 132–33, 140–41, 144, 148, 170, 181, 184, 190, 192–93, 198, 201, 204–5, 208
Prefanis, Julian, 95
Pruitt-Igoe housing project, 3

Quine, W. V. O., 11

Rand, Paul, 40
Rapaport, Amos, 11, 17
Raphael, Adam, 62, 64, 208
Rattenbury, Kester, 146
Rausch, John, 70
Rauschenberg, Robert, 10, 91
Reinhardt, Ad, 56, 76
Riley, Bridget, 34
Robbins, David, 127
Rogers, Ernesto, 153
Rogers, Ginger, 155
Ronell, Avital, 5, 16
Rorty, Richard, 2, 9–10, 15, 17
Rose, Barbara, 125
Rose, Richard, 165
Rosen, Charles, 63
Rosenberg, Harold, 92, 197, 208
Rosenquist, James, 118, 124
Rubin, Barbara, 162
Rubin, William, 75
Rublowsky, John, 101, 124
Rudofsky, Bernard, 85, 91, 95
Rudolph, Paul, 64, 85, 134, 145, 150, 158, 169–70
Ruscha, Edward, 35–36, 42, 69, 99, 106–112, 114–16, 118, 121–22, 124–26, 128, 133, 179–81, 183–88, 192–93
Ruskin, John, 196

Saarinen, Eero, 132, 158
Sacks, Oliver, 192
Sacks, Sheldon, 162
Sadler, M. T. H., 77
Sallis, John, 15–16
Sant'Elia, Antonio, 206
Schapiro, Voir Meyer, 76
Scheerbart, Paul, 206, 209
Schindler, Rudolf, 199–200
Schinkel, Karl, 91
Schwangere, Auster, 155
Schwartz, Alexandra, 125, 192
Scott Brown, Denise, 1–5, 7–17, 20, 22–47, 76–78, 80–81, 88, 94–95, 97–118, 120–22, 124–37, 138–52,

Scott Brown, Denise (*continued*)
    158–61, 163–65, 167–75, 177, 179–
    88, 190–93, 195–96, 198–210
Scully, Vincent, 9, 16, 90, 95, 100, 124,
    134, 145–46
Segal, George, 127
Seitz, William C., 75
Serres, Michel, 13, 15, 17
Smith, C. Ray, 138, 145–46
Smith, Tony, 115
Smithson, Pater and Alison, 137, 145,
    161, 207
Smithson, Robert, 126
Southworth, Doug, 126
Sperber, Dan, 157, 162
Stambaugh, Joan, 193
Stauffacher, Barbara, 135
Steele, James, 124, 193
Stein, Benjamin, 128
Stein, Gertrude, 179, 191
Steinberg, Leo, 55, 76, 92
Stella, Frank, 69, 75
Stern, Robert A. M., 145, 207
Stirling, James, 152–53, 161, 207
Summers, David, 152, 156–57, 160–62
Supermannerism, 145
Super Realism, 75, 77–78

Tafuri, Manfredo, 4, 15, 177
Tan Chet-Qua, 77
Taylor, Joshua, 127
Taylor, Mark C., 17
Temko, Allan, 38, 46
Thomas, Morgan, 95
Thompson, Bradbury, 40
Thompson, Philip, 197, 208
Thoreau, Henry David, 179, 191, 193
Treib, Marc, 47, 135, 145
Tschichold, Jan, 40–41
Tschumi, Bernard, 15, 80, 186, 193

Tuchman, Maurice, 127
Tufte, Edward, 32, 41, 46–47
Tuthill, Mary, 127
Twain, Mark, 182
Tzanck, Daniel, 69
Tzonis, Alexander, 161

Upton, Dell, 13, 17, 147, 160, 211
Urmson, J. O., 192

van Bruggen, Coosie, 161
van der Rohe, Mies, 4, 47, 54, 56, 91,
    145–46
Van Doesburg, Theo, 91
Van Eckardt, Wolf, 127
Varnedoe, Kirk, 75, 78
Vasarely, Victor, 113–14, 122, 126
Vattimo, Gianni, 174, 191
Venturi, Robert, 2–5, 7, 9–17, 20–33,
    35, 37–47, 49, 53–57, 59–65, 67–
    68, 70–71, 75–78, 80–84, 87–91,
    94–95, 97–106, 109, 111–16, 120,
    122, 124–46, 148–54, 157–61, 163–
    65, 167–75, 177, 179, 182, 185–87,
    189–90, 193, 195–96, 198–210;
    *Complexity and Contradiction in
    Architecture*, 2, 9, 15–17, 29, 47,
    75–78, 80–82, 90–91, 95, 100, 115,
    124, 126, 129, 137, 145, 148, 151,
    158, 160, 198, 208
Venturi and Scott Brown: *View from the
    Campidoglio, A*, 29, 144, 160–61
Venturi, Scott Brown & Associates,
    110, 113, 117, 124–25, 192
Venturi, Scott Brown, and Izenour:
    Learning from Las Vegas, 2–20, 27–
    29, 31–33, 35, 38, 41, 43–47, 77–78,
    80–81, 83–85, 88–89, 92, 94–95,
    97, 101, 103, 105–7, 109–11,
    113–16, 118, 121–38, 140–49,

151–52, 156–69, 171–72, 174–79, 181–82, 185, 188–93, 195, 197–200, 203, 207–10
Vinegar, Aron, 16–17, 29, 47, 95, 147, 160, 211
Virilio, Paul, 182
von Moos, Stanislaus, 125, 127

Wallraf-Richartz Museum, 76
Wall Street Journal, 53, 128
Warhol, Andy, 10, 52, 55, 68–69, 72, 84–85, 91, 101, 124, 132, 141
Waters, John, 59, 68
Webb, David, 191
Wesselmann, Tom, 124
Whitely, Nigel, 13, 195, 208–9, 211
Whiteread, Rachel, 158
Wigley, Mark, 80, 95
Williams, John, 197, 208
Wills, David, 191
Winch, Peter, 189

Wittgenstein, Ludwig, 11, 17, 94, 172, 179, 189–92
Wolfe, Tom, 12, 17, 38, 47, 91–92, 95, 132, 144, 180, 200, 204–5, 208
Wölfflin, Heinrich, 75
Wood, Paul, 208
Woods, Gerald, 197, 208
Woolgar, Steve, 16
Wrede, Stuart, 124
Wright, Frank Lloyd, 132, 199
Wright, G. H., 189
Wurman, Richard Saul, 34, 46

Yale School of Architecture, 145
Yoshimura, Fumio, 73

Zaero-Polo, Alejandro, 146
Zerner, Henri, 77
Zohn, Harry, 128